# TOP GRADUATE ZHANG XIE

TRANSLATIONS FROM THE ASIAN CLASSICS

# TOP
# GRADUATE
# ZHANG XIE

## THE EARLIEST EXTANT
## CHINESE SOUTHERN PLAY

TRANSLATED AND INTRODUCED BY

REGINA S. LLAMAS

Columbia University Press   *New York*

Columbia University Press wishes to express its appreciation for
assistance given by the Pushkin Fund in the publication of this book.

Columbia University Press
*Publishers Since 1893*
New York    Chichester, West Sussex
cup.columbia.edu
Copyright © 2021 Columbia University Press
All rights reserved

Library of Congress Cataloging-in-Publication Data
Names: Llamas, Regina, translator, writer of introduction.
Title: Top graduate Zhang Xie : the earliest extant Chinese southern
play / translated and introduced by Regina S. Llamas.
Other titles: 880-01 Zhang Xie zhuang yuan. English
Description: New York : Columbia University Press, 2020. |
Series: Translations from the Asian classics | Includes bibliographical
references and index.
Identifiers: LCCN 2020012371 (print) | LCCN 2020012372 (ebook) |
ISBN 9780231197922 (hardback) | ISBN 9780231197939
(trade paperback) | ISBN 9780231552417 (ebook)
Classification: LCC PL2687.Z4385 E5 2020 (print) |
LCC PL2687.Z4385 (ebook) | DDC 895.12/46—dc23
LC record available at https://lccn.loc.gov/2020012371
LC ebook record available at https://lccn.loc.gov/2020012372

Columbia University Press books are printed on permanent and
durable acid-free paper.
Printed in the United States of America

*Cover designer*: Noah Arlow
*Cover image*: Guan Tong, *Plank Road on the Mountains of Sichuan*,
c. mid-tenth century. Courtesy of the National Palace Museum, Taipei

# CONTENTS

# PREFACE

I n 1920, in a secondhand bookstore in London, Mr. Ye Gongchuo 葉恭綽 (1881–1968)[1] discovered one of the remaining volumes of the Ming *Yongle Collectanea* (*Yongle dadian* 永樂大典). This was a massive collection of full-length ancient and modern texts gathered from throughout the empire, compiled by imperial commission in 1403 and completed in 1408. Owing to its size, only two copies of this *Collectanea* were made: one was kept in Beijing; the other, in Nanjing. But fires, war, and pillaging destroyed the Nanjing copy, and of the Beijing copy, only one part was left. Ye brought the volume back to China, made copies of it, and deposited the original in a bank in Tianjin. This volume, in fact, was not an original copy of the *Yongle* text, but rather was a manuscript copy made during the Jiajing era 嘉靖 (1521–1567), possibly to restore a lost one. The volume that Ye deposited in the bank disappeared, but the copies he made from this volume somehow survived and were the basis for editions we now have.

In a fateful turn of events, the Taiwanese scholar and phi-lologist Wang Tiancheng 汪天成, searching for models of book binding in the Rare Book Room of the National Taiwan Library, discovered the library held some volumes of the *Yongle*

*Collectanea* and noticed a volume on drama (volume 13,991 of the *Yongle*, to be precise) included among these specimens. When the volume was delivered to his desk, he realized that this was the same long-lost volume Ye Gongchuo had deposited in the bank in Tianjin.[2] A comparison between this text with the copies Ye had made confirmed that they were, with a few minor discrepancies, accurate copies.

Only gradually did scholars recognize the magnitude of this convoluted and unlikely recovery of a long-lost text. The *Yongle* volume includes three of thirty-three dramatic texts that originally were included in the *Collectanea*. Barring new discoveries, thirty are irrecoverably lost. Among the three extant texts included in the volume Ye found in London, *Top Graduate Zhang Xie* (*Zhang Xie zhuangyuan* 張協狀元) is considered to be the earliest and is perhaps genuinely representative of a southern theatrical tradition. The other two texts, *Little Butcher Sun* (*Xiao Sun tu* 小孫屠) and *A Playboy from a Noble House Opts for the Wrong Career* (*Huanmen zidi cuolishen* 宦門子弟錯立身), are adaptations of northern *zaju* 雜劇 plays.[3] All three of these plays can almost certainly be dated to the late Yuan dynasty and perhaps even earlier, making them among the earliest extant Chinese plays.

Before the discovery of this volume, it was generally accepted, following Ming ideas of the evolution of genres, that theater had its origins in northern Yuan *zaju* plays, and that the first full-length theatrical performances began in this period. The appearance of this volume, and in particular *Top Graduate Zhang Xie*, shook the foundations upon which Chinese dramatic historiography had been established, leading scholars to reassess the history of early Chinese theater and argue for an earlier fully developed southern theater of which *Top Graduate* was proof. In recent years, the debate of the north versus south genesis of Chinese drama has once more been ignited with *Top Graduate Zhang Xie* at the center of the discussion. This shows not only that scholars have not yet reached a consensus on the dating of the text but also that essential questions on the formative process of theater and what constitutes Chinese theater remain part of the discussion.

The plays contained in the *Yongle* edition were not divided into acts, and the distinction in script sizes generally employed from the mid- and late-Ming editions to differentiate singing parts (large) from the spoken ones (small) is not used. Stage directions, however, are written in smaller script and are indicated by leaving a blank space between the characters, and song titles are included in brackets. The modern scholar Qian Nanyang 錢南揚 (1899–1987), in his *Collated and Annotated Three Southern Plays from the Yongle Collectanea*, divided the play into acts, annotated it, and interpreted numerous puns and jokes, clarifying many of the more difficult parts. Wang Jisi 王季思 (1906–1996) included it also in his *Complete Collection of Yuan Plays* published between 1990 and 1999; more recently, Hu Xuegang 胡雪岡, on the basis of Wang's and Qian's texts, but also on numerous modern researcher's elucidations of terms, has published a new edition with many new findings and additional glosses.[4] The translation included in this book is based on Qian's erudite text and is supplemented with references from Wang and Hu.

# ACKNOWLEDGMENTS

An interest in "origins" brought me to *Top Graduate Zhang Xie*, by some accounts the earliest extant Chinese play and reliably dated to the early fifteenth century. When a grant from the Chiang Ching-kuo Foundation brought me to Taiwan, I decided I would start at the beginning and concentrate my efforts on a study of this play. Soon, however, it became clear that, to start with, a complete translation would deliver a much deeper understanding of the play. My advisor, the late Patrick Hanan, had already suggested I translate the play a while back, and in Taiwan, Professor Wang Chiu-kuei 王秋桂 insisted it could be easily accomplished in a year if I translated "two lines a day." At the same time, Professor Chen Fang-ying 陳芳英 agreed to let me sit in on her classes. This combination proved extremely fruitful, and most of that first year in Taiwan was spent translating a little more than two lines a day, attending classes on classical Chinese theater, discussing doubts I had on the translation with Professor Chen and then sending questions to my adviser (who would correct my mistakes), polishing my English, and generally improving the text. This book is greatly indebted to both Professor Hanan and Professor Chen.

Over the years, other scholars near and far have helped the course of my investigations. I am especially grateful to Patricia Sieber for her encouragement and trust, to Wilt Idema for looking at one of the very first iterations of the text and making numerous suggestions, to Steve West for his willingness to give generously of his time, and to all of them for their friendship and for sharing their erudition.

This book has accumulated more than a few personal debts, and it is impossible to list how many students and friends have contributed to it. It has been a pleasure to work with Christine Dunbar and Christian P. Winting at Columbia University Press, and I also greatly appreciate the meticulous work of Ben Kolstad and Kathryn Jorge during the final stages of the book. It has greatly improved the text and the way it appears on the page. I also greatly appreciate the valuable insights and suggestions of the peer reviewers, which has also contributed in no small measure to improve the translation. To all these teachers, friends, and colleagues, I am profoundly grateful.

John, Antonio, and Clara have played no small part in the process of getting this work done, and it is to them that I dedicate this book.

# TOP
# GRADUATE
# ZHANG XIE

# INTRODUCTION

When *Top Graduate Zhang Xie* first appeared in the early fifteenth century, the early southern dramatic tradition (*nanxi* 南戲) already had formed. It has a distinctive musical and narrative structure, its plays are long and organized into multiple acts and scenes, it makes use of the set of roles so distinctive of Chinese theater, and all roles can sing. The terms used to label this tradition—"play-song" (*xiqu* 戲曲), "Wenzhou drama" (Wenzhou *zaju* 溫州雜劇), "drama-text" (*xiwen* 戲文), or "southern plays" (*nanxi* 南戲)—are often articulated in contrast to a northern *zaju* tradition, with a different act structure, singing practice, and musical norms.[1] Furthermore, two of the three plays included in the *Yongle Collectanea* are believed to be adaptations of northern plays, showing that both traditions were already well defined. Finally, *Top Graduate Zhang Xie* (hereafter *Top Graduate*) demonstrates that its author, the collective Nine Mountain Society (*Jiushan shuhui* 九山書會), had a clear understanding of the form. This is evident from its playful use of self-referential allusions to the actor's art—that is, a character telling another not to disclose their artistic secrets to the audience—or through the disruption of established performance conventions, such as the use of a lowly comic role to perform the part of a high-level official.[2] In other words, early southern drama, at the time of the appearance of its first manuscript text, was already a fully conceptualized form.

We know little about early southern drama before this play. From the Southern Song and the Yuan dynasties, we have a smattering of facts contained in documents largely drawn from offhand remarks by scholar aficionados and included in collections of random notes (*biji* 筆記). Among the earliest references, the terms used to designate what we now call southern song-drama vary. The earliest use of the term *xiqu* 戲曲 (literally, "play-song"),[3] now commonly used to designate Chinese theater, is mentioned by the scholar and musician Liu Xun 劉塤 (1240–1319) in a biography of the mid-twelfth-century poet Wu Yongzhang 吳用章. Liu notes that after Wu moved to the southeast, he promoted the music of the capital (Kaifeng) and of the Imperial Music Bureau. While discussing the poet's musical preferences, Liu observes: "During the Xianchun era (1264–1274), *Yongjia* song-drama (*xiqu*) emerged and boorish youth who were much taken with it transformed it. Later, these lewd songs flourished and the correct [central] rhymes declined" (至咸淳, 永嘉戲曲出, 潑少年化之, 而後淫哇盛, 正音歇).[4] *Yongjia* is another term for the area around Wenzhou, considered to be the cradle of southern drama, where it first began as a musical form.

At roughly the same time, the scholar Zhou Mi 周密 (1232–1298) mentions a well-known story of a villainous monk from Wenzhou called Zujie 祖傑. This monk had an illicit love affair with a woman, and when she became pregnant, he forced the son of his disciple to marry her. When the disciple's son could no longer bear the gossip and scorn of his neighbors, he decided to run away, only to be pursued and killed by the monk's thugs. Zujie was influential enough to evade punishment, but "onlookers thinking it unjust and afraid that he would manage

to entirely slip through the net [of the law], composed a drama-
text (*xiwen*) in order to publicize this event" (旁觀不平, 惟恐
其漏網也, 乃撰為戲文, 以廣其事).⁵ Not long after, the well-
known Yuan scholar Zhou Deqing 周德清 (1277–1365), in his
*Rhymes of the Central Plain* (*Zhongyuan yinyun* 中原音韻, 1324),
one of the first rhyme manuals aimed at songwriter aficionados
that discusses the correct tonal pronunciation of words for *ci*
song-lyric (hereafter "song-lyric") composition, explains that "by
the Southern Song capital of Hangzhou, in Wuxing and neigh-
boring areas there were drama-texts (*xiwen*) such as *Lechang
Splits the Mirror in Half* (*Lechang fen jing*) in which song, declamation, and breathing practices all follow Shen Yue's [rhyme
schemes]" (南宋杭都, 吳興與切鄰, 故其戲文如 (樂昌分鏡)
等類, 唱念呼吸皆如約).⁶ The totality of the sources we have
before the appearance of *Top Graduate*—about a dozen or so—
suggest a type of regional musical performance from the area
of Wenzhou (in modern-day Zhejiang), popular among loutish
local youth at the time, that included declaimed or spoken parts,
incorporated some form of narrative storytelling, and required
a certain amount of musical specialization. These performances
seem to have been known by a variety of terms, most prominently *xiqu* and *xiwen* and later *nanxi* but also Wenzhou *zaju*.⁷
Aside from its musical, declaimed, and narrative elements,
however, these early sources tell us nothing concrete about the
structure or mode of the performance. We do not know (1) if
these were long narrative songs or actual plays, (2) if actors (as
opposed to specialized musicians) told or performed a story in
the voices of characters (dialogue), (3) if they used costumes
and makeup, or (4) what the setting and composition of the
audience were like.

Ming scholars were the first to directly question the provenance of this tradition, but by the time they began their records,

they already were removed from the alleged beginnings of southern drama by three centuries, and by more than a century from *Top Graduate*. The first to mention southern theater as an established genre was scholar and aficionado Zhu Yunming 祝允明 (1460–1526), who placed the origins of southern drama at the end of the Northern Song dynasty, during the Xuanhe era in the reign of Huizong (r. 1119–1126). Zhu writes:

> Southern drama appeared after the Xuanhe era, at the time of the exodus to the south. It was also called "Wenzhou *zaju*." I have seen old official documents that noted that at the time an inter-dict was posted by Zhao Hongfu listing some of its titles such as "*Zhao the Chaste Maid and Cai the Second Son*." There were not many of them, but they later increased daily.

> 南戲出於宣和之後, 南度之際, 謂之「溫州雜劇」. 余見舊牒, 其時有趙閎夫榜禁, 頗述名目, 如 (趙貞女蔡二郎) 等, 亦不甚多, 以後日增.⁸

The other often-mentioned attempt to date the beginnings of southern drama appears a little later, in the middle of the sixteenth century in an essay entitled *A Record of Southern Song-Lyrics*⁹ (*Nanci xulu* 南詞敍錄, 1559), attributed to the talented playwright Xu Wei 徐渭 (1521–1593). This is a sustained discussion of southern theater, mostly concerned with drawing attention to and legitimating southern theater as a respectable genre of literary artistic composition. Xu attributed the birth of southern theater to the reign of Emperor Guangzong (r. 1190–1194) in the Southern Song dynasty.¹⁰

> Southern drama (*nanxi*) begins in the reign of Emperor Guang-zong of the Song and were written by people from Yongjia.

The two plays *Zhao the Chaste Maid* and *Wang Kui*, are truly at the head [of the Yongjia productions]. Thus the lines of Liu Houcun: "After we die who knows what is true or false, the whole village listens to the song 'Cai the Second Son' [from *Zhao the Chaste Maid*]." Some say [southern theater] had already risen in the Xuanhe years, and reached its full-fledged form after the move south. It was called "Yongjia *zaju*" or "scamps' songs."

南戲始於宋光宗朝, 永嘉人所作 (趙貞女), (王魁) 二種實首之, 故劉後村有 「死後是非誰管得, 滿村聽唱蔡中郎」 之句. 或云: 「宣和[11] 間已濫觴, 甚盛行則自南度, 號曰「永嘉雜劇」, 又曰「鶻伶聲嗽」.[12]

Zhu Yunming and Xu Wei may not agree on the precise date of when southern drama made its first appearance, but they do agree that this happened at around the beginning of the Southern Song dynasty, in the southeastern area of Wenzhou (also known as Yongjia, in modern-day southern Zhejiang), and that its best-known stories were *Zhao the Chaste Maid and Cai the Second Son* (*Zhao Zhennü Cai Erlang* 趙貞女蔡二郎) and *Wang Kui* 王魁. These were stories that dealt with the theme of brilliant scholars who achieve fame and later abandon the wives and courtesans who had earlier supported them and enabled their success. We know little about the early story of *Zhao the Chaste Maid and Cai the Second Son*. *Zhao the Chaste Maid* is considered to be the forerunner of the canonical work in this tradition: *The Story of the Lute*, attributed to the Yuan playwright Gao Ming (ca. 1305–ca. 1370), but from Xu's disparaging remarks, we know that the two plays were quite different. *Zhao the Chaste Maid* seems to be a conventional story of retribution, in which divine justice is meted out to the ungrateful scholar by killing him with a bolt of lightning, whereas Gao's play is a moral story that highlights the conflicts created between shared loyalties to family and government.[13] Xu Wei in his *Record* observes: "*Zhao the Chaste Maid and Cai the Second Son*. This is the old story of Bojie who abandons his parents, betrays his wife and was killed by a bolt of lightning. It is a coarse and absurd creation. It is, in fact, the first play of early southern theater (*xiwen*)" (趙真女蔡伯喈, 即舊伯喈棄親背婦, 為暴雷震死. 里俗妄作也. 實為戲文之首).[14] These two scholars suggest, although we cannot corroborate it, that scripts could date as far back as the Song. What sources Zhu and Xu had at hand are unknown to us, and these succinct few lines tell us little about either the texts or the stories. For example, Zhu claims that Zhao Hongfu posted some edicts banning these plays, and yet Zhao, who was Emperor Guangzong's cousin on his father's side, was also known for his penchant for dissipation, love of wine, women, and gambling. That such a person would post an interdiction on plays seems somewhat of a contradiction. Furthermore, what were the texts that Zhu saw: Song dynasty texts or early Ming texts. And in Xu's case, how did he know that *Zhao the Chaste Maid* was a coarse work? Did he, like Zhu, have access to a script, or was he writing from hearsay? Did he see it on stage and think it vulgar?

*Top Graduate* and the other two plays included in the *Yongle Collectanea* are chronologically wedged between the earliest incidental comments on a southeastern performance art and Xu Wei's mid-Ming essay on southern drama. But what is really unusual is that nothing in the earlier fragments of information, or between those fragments and the date of Xu Wei's later study, would have allowed us to suppose the existence of a play as consummate and well-constructed as *Top Graduate* or, for that matter, a fully conceptualized theater. *Top Graduate* seems to come out of nowhere—a giant leap in sophistication for early Chinese theater. It is possible that the dearth of information at this time may indicate the continued reluctance of a cultured elite of the day to formally engage with what they may have considered trivial pursuits for moments of leisure, but the inclusion of these texts in an imperial collectanea attests to their popularity and, in addition, has provided us with a unique window into China's culture of entertainment in the early Ming.

## THE DATING OF *TOP GRADUATE ZHANG XIE*

The dating of *Top Graduate* raises questions that go well beyond the time of the composition of the play. Because it is the earliest extant play—all other plays to date, whether northern or southern, are from later dates[15]—and the first manuscript, scholars focus on this play to address the elusive questions of when Chinese theater was formed and what were its sources.[16] It also returns to the matter, ubiquitous among seventeenth-century playwrights and critics, of whether southern theater is a "re-musicalization" of northern songs adapted to southern music, or if it is an independent form that germinated from a mixture of Song dynasty song-lyrics and popular song in the Song dynasty. These two positions on the emergence of southern theater can be observed in two mid-sixteenth-century playwrights and aficionados Wang Shizhen 王世貞 (1526–1590) and Xu Wei. In Wang's view of the formation of southern drama, the genre evolved from a tradition of sung poetry originating in Confucius's compilation of *The Book of Songs*. The ancestry in the foundations of the poetic tradition was intended to legitimate the genre for use by the educated class, establish its repute, and perhaps also justify its value as entertainment. In Wang's description, when a genre became too complex, overused and overwrought, and too demanding to practice, a new form based on the earlier one would appear.[17] Thus, Song dynasty poetry is a divergence from Tang poetry, and Yuan dynasty song is a departure from the Song *ci*-lyric. Wang created a common ancestry to all dramatic song in the song tradition of the previous dynasty, the *ci*-lyric, but argued that musical appreciation and preferences by northerners—including Mongols—differed, so songs were adapted to suit musical regional tastes: "The song-lyric (*ci*) did not please northern ears, and so northern song-drama appeared, and because the music of these songs did not harmonize with southern ears, southern song-drama appeared" (詞不快北耳而後有北曲,北曲不諧南耳而後有南曲).[18] While Wang's contemporary Xu Wei did not entirely disagree with this approach, he did give southern drama a composite form: "Its arias are but Song dynasty *ci*-lyrics with added popular songs from the alleyways that do not harmonize with the *gong* and *diao* keys and modes, thus gentlemen rarely pay attention to them" (其曲 則 宋人詞而益以里巷歌謠,不叶宮調,故士夫罕有留意者).[19] Unlike Wang's earlier mutations of genres, southern drama was not just one additional step in this transformation of genres, but rather was something that also emerged popularly from the alleyways: "It was made up of small songs from the villages; it did not make use of modes and had almost no regular pattern (*jiezou* 節奏). The [songs] were merely gathered from what the peasants in the fields or the girls in the market could sing offhand, that is all" (徒取其畸農, 市女順口可歌而已).[20] Placing the source of these songs in the idealized simple milieu of the town market gave them the possibility of an "original source," that is, of the beginnings of a tradition, much like the canonical *Book of Songs*, originating in the songs of the peasantry. It underlined the uncorrupted and genuine nature of these songs and their tradition, while also equating the simple and natural with the popular and uneducated. The popular nature of southern dramatic songs was evidence of its genuine or uncorrupted beginnings, and the naturalness of the form was expressed in a manner that made it free from the prosodic and stylistic complications of the educated elite. This was later also applied to the question of modal harmony or prosody, as I will explain.

Until recently, modern scholars have similarly been divided into two camps: one group establishes the date of *Top Graduate* some time in the Song, although the precise time varies from the late-northern Song, to the early and mid-Southern Song; and another group argues that it cannot be earlier than the Yuan dynasty, although, similarly, this can be early, mid, or late Yuan.[21]

Scholars who claim a Song dynasty composition of the play partially do so on the basis of the dates established in the Ming by Zhu Yunming and Xu Wei in their discussions of the origins of *nanxi*, and other small fragments of information. The scholar Wang Guowei 王國維 (1877–1927), whose seminal work on drama *A Study of Song and Yuan Drama* (*Song Yuan xiqu kao* 宋元戲曲考, 1913–1914) appeared before *Top Graduate* had been discovered, stated that Zhu Yunming's claim for a Song origin of *nanxi*—based on one single instance—could not be substantiated. Wang noted, however, that *nanxi* already existed in the Yuan, but that it was probably an evolution of the earlier southern *xiwen*, a regional and independent art form the area around Wenzhou, unrelated to *zaju* that he believed preceded *nanxi*.[22] The postulation that there was a former *xiwen* and a later *nanxi* did not take hold, because the use of these terms seems arbitrary in our extant sources. But the idea that a form of theater called *xiwen* or *nanxi* appeared as early as the Song prevailed and was influential in the later dating of *Top Graduate*.

The first to establish a Song date for *Top Graduate* was Qian Nanyang, and many modern scholars have followed his lead or have tinkered with the period to settle for an approximation.[23] In addition to citing Zhu Yunming and Xu Wei's claims, Qian also draws on internal evidence in the text. For example, references in the prologue to the Crimson and Green, a well-known association of comedians active during the Southern Song in Hangzhou, and to the Imperial Music Academy, an institution that provided the court with entertainment, but that was considered too expensive and dismantled in 1164, are used to establish limits in time.[24] These references have provided the *terminus ante quem* for the composition of the play. If the play makes reference to an obsolete institution—the Imperial Music Academy—then it has to have been composed some time before the Academy was dismantled in 1164. This assumes, of course, that the reference could not be an anachronism.

The other piece of evidence often quoted by scholars suggesting a Song date, and the source of much dispute, are two lines of verse in act 23 attributed to the Song dynasty poet Cao Bin 曹彬 (1170–1250): "North and South of the village, the sounds of the pawlonia-leaf flutes; behind and in front of the mountain, white cabbage flowers" (村南村北梧桐角, 山前山後白菜花). Two lackluster and unremarkable lines that could have been composed by anyone, and whose authorship is difficult to ascribe. And yet, two dates are proposed for the composition of the poem, one in the mid (1186) and the other in the late (1235) Southern Song. These dates, in turn, establish the *terminus post quem* for the composition of *Top Graduate*. In other words, this play can only have been written after these lines had been composed.[25]

Indeed, other internal elements have been used to identify an approximate date for the play, including, for instance: the character Wang Deyong 王德用 (987–1065), who acts as prime minister in the play and who was at one time head of the Northern Song Bureau of Military Affairs (*Shumiyuan* 樞密院); the insertion of the All Keys *chantefable* (*Zhugongdiao* 諸宮調) in the introduction, a unique Song and Jin dynasties sung and recited form of storytelling (discussed later); the idiosyncratic and fundamentally comic nature or the play, which is unseen in later plays; the changes in the representation of the ungrateful scholar motif, from the contemptible heartless scholar to a still-despicable but filial and responsive one; and the ending of the play in a happy reunion, a required feature of later plays.[26] All of these elements have been used to determine the Song date hypothesis and have prevailed until quite recently. But more to the point, because *Top Graduate* is our first extant text, the play has become the archetype of early southern drama, including the region it represents (Wenzhou), the language of performance (Wenzhou language/dialect or one of the Wu languages/dialects), the dramatic structure and roles it displays, and the musical arrangement and song composition it exhibits.[27] This means that although some scholars may acknowledge that our text may be a later edited edition of an earlier version, it nonetheless is discussed as a close enough approximation to the earlier Southern Song theater. Whether or not it is verifiable, *Top Graduate* has become *the* earliest model for early southern drama.

This methodology, however, raises serious problems. The dates, and the features used to establish these dates, set the boundaries for a historical time frame in which the play may have been composed (either before the Music Academy was dismantled, or after Cao Bin's poem was composed) but they do not consider the process of creation, or the inherent protean nature of the theater and the mutability of its dramatic texts. Rarely is a play set at the time of its initial composition; it undergoes countless revisions, changing each time it is performed. Although some scholars do acknowledge an editorial process and believe *Top Graduate* to be the last instance of this process, the earlier versions of this play also are drawn from elements within the play, or more specifically, from the introduction of the text. For example, Yu Weimin argues that four different versions of the text exist: one is the earlier explanation of the inclusion of the All Keys in the introduction; the second is mentioned in the second poem of the introduction ("Others have performed the *Biography of Top Graduate Zhang Xie*"); the third is the performance of the play; and the fourth and final is the editing of the play by the officials who included it in the encyclopedia.[28] While these four versions can be considered part of the dramatic analysis of the play, how are we to know this was not the intended creation of the composers of the play? Can we really use these two poems and the All Keys as evidence? Similarly, how can we be sure that the landmarks mentioned previously—Wang Deyong, the Music Academy, or the Crimson and Green—were not the result of a creative act by informed playwrights inserting accurate references from the past into a contemporary play? Why could *Top Graduate* not be a fabrication by a group of aficionados well versed in that time period? And if we were to consider the All Keys a genuine piece from an earlier period, how do we know evidence did not come from this ballad?

In contrast, proponents of a Yuan date have based their research mostly on the discussion of tune titles and possible dates of composition. Aoki Masaru 青木正兒 (1887–1964), looking at songs in *Top Graduate* included in Ming song collections, was the first to suggest a Yuan date. But only recently have scholars begun to analyze this possibility in depth.[29] This analysis has been prompted by the fact that the title of the play is mentioned in a variety of places, including one of the other two *Yongle* texts, and arias of the play are collected with little or no changes in late-Ming and Qing formularies.

In fact, the first reference we have to *Top Graduate* as a play appears in one of the manuscripts from the *Yongle Collectanea—A Playboy from a Noble House Opts for the Wrong Career*. In the fifth act of this play, the main actress, Wang Jinbang 王金榜 has surreptitiously been invited by Wangyan Shouma—the patrician playboy of the title—to perform for him at his house. As she arrives, complaining of the potential dangers she will confront should his father find her there, she hands him a collection of playbooks and sings the names of the works for him. While he browses the texts, she mentions a *chuanqi* called *Zhang Xie Slays Poorlass* (*Zhang Xie zhan Pinnü* 張協斬貧女), which is presumably a version of the same *Top Graduate* play we now have.[30] Arias from the play also appear in Ming collections of dramatic songs (or song formularies). These formularies were designed both as guiding manuals in song composition for drama aficionados and as a means of organizing and preserving dramatic songs.[31]

As the popularity and appreciation of drama as a form of literati entertainment—and as a medium to showcase one's literary talent—increased, more extensive and elaborate formularies were composed. The earlier ones included mostly the names of the keys and modes under which songs were categorized as well as the song titles and song models.[32] But beginning with playwright and connoisseur Shen Jing's 沈璟 (1553–1610) *Augmented, Collated, and Rectified Southern Nine Keys and Thirteen Modes Formulary*, these song collections begin a process of augmentation and refinement, expanding the number of arias included in the formularies by drawing them from early and contemporary plays, specifying their origin, noting the filler words (*chenzi* 襯字), including the tones of characters, indicating the rhyme, and pointing out the beat. This polishing trend continued well into the Qing dynasty, but in the Ming, it reached its supreme model in the *Compilation of Yuan Formulary of the Correct Original Nine Southern Modes* by Xu Qingqing 徐慶卿 (1574–1636) and Niu Shaoya 鈕少雅 (ca.1563–1661).[33] Xu and Niu's collection was carefully crafted and researched and is perhaps the most reliable source of song information for this period. In addition to including the modes, tune titles, and song forms—the number of lines to a song, words to a line, the tones and rhymes, and the singing particularities of each song—it also records the original textual occurrence of the song, the period, its author when available, and other instances of this song.[34]

Tunes from *Top Graduate* appear in six southern formularies, from the Ming to the Qing, beginning with Shen Jing's in which we find four songs. In Xu and Niu's *Compilation*, the play is dated to the Yuan dynasty; it is called a *chuanqi*, a common term in the Qing for southern drama, and thirteen songs from *Top Graduate* are included.[35] A comparison of the arias in Shen's and Xu and Niu's collections shows almost no differences, and when these two collections are compared with the current *Yongle* text we have of *Top Graduate*, the differences are again, not critical. In other words, it is possible—given the excellence and accountability of Xu and Niu's formulary—that this is a Yuan play, and that the text included in these later formularies was drawn from the imperial *Yongle Collectanea*.[36]

Scholars who propose a Yuan date have also looked carefully at song titles and have noted that aside from the common pool of songs and song titles from which northern and southern theater drew—including the Tang *Extended Melodies* (*Daqu* 大曲), Tang and Song dynasty song-lyrics, and the All Keys *chantefable*—a number of songs are shared in northern and southern dramas. Because these songs are found only in drama texts, they are believed to have been composed sometime in the

Yuan dynasty.[37] The question scholars pose is whether these songs belong to a northern or a southern tradition, where are they first encountered, and which tradition makes common use of them. This renewed look at song titles was sparked by Korean scholar Yang Hoi-seok 梁會錫 in an article questioning the established dates of the play and raising doubts about the methodology of earlier scholars. Yang essentially approached this problem by partially applying the erstwhile method of tracing the source of a song (or poem) and comparing its structures, including number of lines, characters to a line, tones, and rhymes, as well as its use in northern and southern texts. For instance, in one of his examples under examination—*Yingxianke* 迎仙客—he contends that this tune can be traced back only so far (to the Jin dynasty) and that it is widely used in northern drama and rarely appears in southern plays.[38] So, this play is probably a Yuan composition. While his thesis has been refuted by other scholars, it nonetheless sparked an intense debate on the dating of *Top Graduate*, with most scholars following this line of research.[39] Yang Dong 楊棟 uses the historicity of song to determine *Top Graduate*'s date, illustrating his argument with examples such as the tune title "Great Shadow Play" (*Dayingxi* 大影戲), which appears in act 16 of *Top Graduate*. He contends that this song must have been composed after this type of shadow puppet performance appeared, possibly after it is first mentioned in Wu Zimu's and Zhou Mi's city memoirs. Similarly, he affirms that the song entitled "Repossession of Xiangyang" (*Fu Xiangyang* 復襄陽) should have been composed either after 1133 when General Yue Fei 岳飛 (1103–1142) recovered Xiangyang and the surrounding six provinces from the Jurchen army (Jin 金), or during the time of General Meng Gong 孟珙 (1195–1246) when Xiangyang was recovered from the Mongols in 1239.[40] This dating method applies the same before-and-after limits to the text,

establishing a date by using tunes as specific objects to determine time. But this method can be misleading. For example, in
the case of the tune "Great Shadow Play," we know from the
dearth of information we have on the theater before the appearance of *Top Graduate* that popular performance art forms could
be extremely widespread before the form is mentioned in any
text or appears in print. In *Top Graduate*'s case, as probably in
this one too, by the time the form captured the interest of the
educated elite, it already had been conceptualized and had been
well established in the entertainment culture for some time.
Similarly, the "Repossession of Xiangyang" may provide a *terminus post quem* for when the historical event happened, but what
does it tell us about the date of a play? It could have been composed at two moments in time—1133 or 1239—or it could have
been added at a much later date.[41]

Even if we could agree on a date for this text, we would have
to take into account an established tradition of revision, adaptation, and expansion of earlier stories to new genres, as well
as the inherent instability of dramatic texts prone to the practice of rewriting and revision. If the textual history of northern
drama can be used to illustrate the process of textual transformation, then determining what form of text—if indeed a prior
text existed—the editors of the *Yongle Collectanea* worked with,
and how extensive their revisions might have been, is highly
conjectural. Scholars working on Yuan drama have noted that
in the early Ming, court drama texts were constantly being
adapted and revised—the palace offices in charge of imperial
entertainment and performance would submit texts to a court
censor for approval for performance, so as a result, a certain uniformity would be implemented in these texts.[42] These scholars
also argue that earlier palace performance may have prized song
over dialogue, but palace versions changed over time, in a trend
that appears to have drastically reduced the arias of the central

roles and expanded the spoken parts of the other roles.[43] Outside the palace, but perhaps influenced by the imperial adjustments to plays, literati aficionados and critics interested in the theater carried out a similar, but more elaborate, editorial process that ultimately qualified Yuan plays to be used as reading material for literary consumption. This transported the plays to the residences of the educated elite and wrested them away from the entertainment milieu of stages and actors, but not from its genre as performance. In this editorial process, which culminated in the canonical work by Zang Maoxun 藏懋循 (1550–1620) *Selections of Yuan Plays* (*Yuanqu xuan* 元曲選, 1615–1616), scholars singled out the finest plays, homogenized their language, corrected their prosody, harmonized the music, streamlined the dialogue, and regulated the roles. They also took major liberties, removing, rewriting, or adding scenes; changing the content of the plays; and adapting their original values to those held by the cultured elite.[44] By the end, these plays may have had little in common with the original manuscripts, but let me insist, they did retain a concern for the essential performance nature of the genre.

*Top Graduate* must have undergone some editorial process to homogenize the language and format to include it in an imperial encyclopedia, but the changes may not have been so comprehensive, because the aim was to include an example of a widespread performance art.[45] Because the dating of *Top Graduate* is largely built on incidental and conjectural evidence, it must remain an unsolvable problem until we find a repository of texts that genuinely predates the early Ming dynasty. Similarly, the questions of when Chinese drama first was formed, what its sources were, and the primacy of north over south, for the moment, remain difficult to solve; indeed, this already may have been the case in the Ming. But for now, our earlier extant manuscripts are the three *Yongle* texts, including *Top Graduate*.[46]

# A NOTE ON AUTHORSHIP

*Top Graduate* is the work of a collective author, the Nine Mountain Society, a writing society first mentioned in a thirteenth-century memoir of the city of Lin'an (modern-day Hangzhou). Writing societies were urban writing clubs composed of educated members of society, clerks, entry-level licentiates, or perhaps simply men with artistic ambitions, time on their hands, and an interest in popular entertainment. The members of these societies were known as men of talent (*cairen* 才人), or more generally "poets," and were presumed to work closely with performers.[47] The dearth of information on these clubs in the histories and local gazetteers has prompted scholars to rely on what little information can be found in plays and Song dynasty city memoirs. For instance, in the late-thirteenth and early-fourteenth centuries, the anonymous deliverance play *Zhongli of the Han Leads Lan Caihe to Enlightenment* (*Han Zhongli dutuo Lan Caihe* 漢鍾離度脫藍采和), the Daoist immortal Zhongli Quan comes down to earth to observe the troupe leader and actor Lan Caihe because he believes he has the potential to become an immortal. Zhongli has arrived in a cloud and is sitting in the theater waiting for the actor to arrive. When Lan enters, Zhongli asks for a performance. Lan suggests that his repertoire is large, thus prompting Zhongli to berate Lan for bragging. Lan defends himself:

[*Zheng Gong* mode. To the tune *You hulu*]
*The mo [role] Lan Caihe sings:*
How can we, roving performers, act on our own?
These are newly drafted plays by the talented men of a writers' association.

*Zhongli Quan speaks*: "Since it is composed by men of talent let me hear them."

(正宮. 油葫蘆) 末, 藍采和唱:
俺路岐們怎敢自專, 這是才人書會嶄新編的.
鍾離權白: 既是才人編的, 你說我聽.)[48]

The troupe's reliance on the generosity of men of talent for their plays suggests a higher literary and artistic value placed by the urban audience on the texts coming from these societies. Because the greatest historical value accorded to this play is as a record of theatrical practice—a window into the activities of a family troupe in an urban center, and its social exchange with local society—the information contained is often taken at face value. Aside from noting that the troupe relied on the help of a literary society, the detail it provides on these societies is almost nil. We cannot be sure if literary societies really wrote for these troupes, if this troupe is simply trying to elevate its status, if the literary societies produced plays only for themselves to be staged in amateur competitions like the claim made in the introduction to *Top Graduate*, or if the authors of these societies—the men of talent—composed the plays collectively or as a single author. In *Top Graduate*, for instance, the Nine Mountain Society indicates a group.

In addition to being written by a writing society, *Top Graduate* adopts a self-referential angle in act 26, which also has been interpreted as indicating the name of the member of the writing society responsible for the play. In this scene, our heroine Poorlass enters the stage disconsolate that scholar Zhang Xie has long been gone and there has been no news from him. She is followed shortly after by Li Xiao'er, the middle-aged clownish son of the Lis, a village couple. Li is singing the song "Wu xiaosi"

(吳小四), which hints at Zhang Xie and Poorlass's relationship. Poorlass immediately recognizes the allusion and asks him about the provenance of the song:

> POORLASS: Xiao'er brother, what are you singing?
> XIAO'ER: I was not singing.
> POORLASS: I do have ears, you know. Keep on singing and let me listen.
> XIAO'ER: You (*laughs*) have ears too? I'll sing, but don't think I made it up. Someone composed ten stanzas, but I can remember only two.
> . . .
> XIAO'ER SPEAKS: I didn't make it up. Two elder members (*Shuang laoren* 雙老人) of our writing group (*shuyuan* 書院) composed it. There is still another stanza.

An idiosyncratic interpretation of this passage suggests that *shuang* (literally, "a pair" or "a couple") here translated as *two* could be, in fact, the surname of the member of the writing society that composed the play: Shuang Second Elder, member of the Nine Mountain Society.[49] It is not impossible, given the metatheatrical dimension of this play, that this is a genuine reference to the writing club member who wrote the play. But whether or not *shuang* does refer to the surname of the playwright remains a mystery.

*Top Graduate* is by no means the only play whose collective author included "men of talent." Of the other two plays included in the *Yongle*, *A Playboy from a Noble House* was written by a Talented Man from Hangzhou (*Hangzhou cairen* 杭州才人) and *Little Butcher Sun* was written by a Hangzhou Writer's Society (*Guhang shuhui* 古杭書會). *Top Graduate*'s collective author is the Nine Mountain Society, believed to be a Southern Song association of writers from Wenzhou. This is based in part on internal evidence in the text (specifically the two lines in the introduction: "We have complete command over the grand events of Wenzhou, and in a *chantefable* we'll sing their origins for you"), and in part, on the geographic association of the name "nine mountain" with Wenzhou.[50] Conversely, in the table of contents of the formulary by late-Ming scholar Zhang Dafu 張大復 (1554–1630), the *Cold Mountain Studio Formulary* (*Hanshantang qupu* 寒山堂曲譜), we find a Yuan play called *Dong Xiuying by the Flowers and Under the Moon: The Story of the Eastern Wall* (*Dong Xiuying huayue dongqiang ji* 董秀英花月東牆記) attributed to a certain "quick-witted" *Shi Jiu Jingxian* of the Nine Mountain Society 九山書會捷機史九敬先.[51] This date is claimed by champions of a Yuan *Top Graduate* as evidence of a later time period. They argue that the society was a Hangzhou—not Wenzhou—feature, as those in favor of the Southern Song date propose. More important, this is the only instance in which a name is attached to a specific composition. Because we do not know who this person was (an actor? a writer? the head of the society?), we cannot establish what importance the society accorded its individual writers. What this example does illustrate is that, at this stage, authorial attitudes toward plays were not proprietorial, and no single individual member, at least in the text, stands out.

## HOW THE PLAY INTRODUCES ITSELF

### *The Prologue*

*Top Graduate* begins with what we now consider a conventional opening for any southern play: two spoken or declaimed song-lyrics expressing the author's outlook on life and

summarizing the play.[52] Before these two songs, there is a quatrain outlining the main events of the story called the title (*timu*
題目), although it is not read by any role. It is possible that this
originally was a banner displayed at the entrance to the theater,
informing the public of the subject of the play, and was kept
when the play was included in the encyclopedia.[53] The title, as
well as the two opening lyrics, are now commonly called the
*Fumo kaichang*, literally, the *Fumo Role Opens the Performance*
or simply *Opening the Performance*.[54] *Top Graduate*'s two-poem
prologue represents our first instance of this convention, and it
is also the most remarkable and original of them all. The prologue is composed of two Song *ci*-lyrics of two stanzas each and
is followed—although this is unusual, and not part of the conventions of later drama—by an All Keys *chantefable*. The first
poem *Shuidiao getou* begins with a reminder to the audience of
the ineluctable passage of time and the need to enjoy moments
of leisure and pleasure without remorse. The second stanza
introduces and promotes the troupe of actors in charge of providing the entertainment. The actors introduce themselves in
the first person, directly to the audience as a group of amateur
actors, and emphasize their musical prowess, innovative comic
repartee, and generous makeup, possibly a synecdoche for costume. Thus, we are introduced to a group of aficionados promoting their acting skills and underscoring their resources, all
of which promises to result in an entertaining spectacle. The
second poem, *Manting fang*, reinforces the troupe's abilities by
matching their comic and musical prowess with two celebrated
institutions—the Crimson and Green troupe of comedians and
the Imperial Music Bureau—and it also informs us that they
are playing in competition with other amateur troupes, which
probably is the reason for the emphasis on innovation and pro-
fessionalism. In the last stanza, the troupe claims an innovative

rendition of what already is a familiar and well-known piece, *The Story of Zhang Xie*, and concludes with the *fumo* role quieting the audience who keenly anticipates this new and consummate version of the play, with its beautiful music, proficient musicians, new and inspired comic banter, and spectacular costumes. As the role of the *fumo*—who introduces the play—begins to hush the crowd in preparation for the inception of the play, it insinuates a raucous audience gathered for the performance and full of expectation. *Top Graduate*'s prologue describes a troupe in an urban competition, promoting an original spectacle to audience members who await the beginning of a performance that promises, above all else, to make them laugh and keep them entertained.

The introduction is composed *as if* it were a marketing ploy for a performance of amateurs in a public competition with other troupes at a moment in time. Although the locality is not explicitly stated, their claim in the introduction is that they are conversant with the affairs of Wenzhou: "We distinguish among the grand events of Wenzhou, and in a[n] All Keys we'll sing their origins for you," suggesting their audience is either from the place or has an interest in it. Indicating their amateur pedigree would imply the troupe had a higher social status and education, which would indeed add a greater literary caché to the play. And flaunting their musical and comic skills as well as their costumes would advertise their proficiency, innovation, and resources. Drawing attention to the circumstances of the performance, the introduction to the play makes all of these promises to attract an audience to a *newer* and *better* performance of *Top Graduate*.

From its introduction, *Top Graduate* draws attention to its nature as theater. The ingenious publicity stunt at the beginning of the play is made clearer when we observe how these two opening lyrics make evident, through the use of time, the illusion and artifice of theater. Because everything is inscribed into and fixed in this moment of performance, the opening claims to innovation and competition erase the time lapse between the first performance and all subsequent ones. It fixes the illusion of the first time in a past, where an audience would recognize the institutions that establish the paragons by which the troupe measures its proficiency: the Crimson and Green or the Imperial Music Bureau. From the moment of its inception, then, any time the play is performed again—and theater is founded on repetition—the same claim to innovation would be made, the same comparison drawn to the same institutions, and the assumption that an audience composed of members with similar interests also would be made. For example, a twenty-first-century performance would make—warping time—the same claim to innovation and proficiency, but it would do so by declaring that its cutting-edge standards of performance were established more than five hundred years ago and noting that it was putting on a performance in competition with troupes that existed centuries ago. It also would have to persuade the audience that its professed originality was as fresh now as it was some centuries past. Naturally, we cannot know whether this imaginative use of time was a creative composition that intentionally emulated a theatrical competition in a past time, thus deliberately using landmarks that would situate the play in a period removed from its date of composition, or whether this introduction is an "authentic" representation of a first performance that repeatedly has been performed through time, as it is often read. In both cases, however, although one may be a conscious act of creation and the other the product of the progress of time, the result is a bold declaration on the nature of theater and repetition: that where the action is always present, the subject is always past.

## *The All Keys of* Top Graduate Zhang Xie

Following the introduction, and seemingly composed by the Nine Mountain Society is an All Keys on the story of *Top Graduate Zhang Xie*, alternating prose and song passages.[55] This form is first mentioned in Wang Zhuo's 王灼 treatise on the Song dynasty song-lyric *Random Notes from Green Rooster Studio* (*Biji manzhi* 碧鷄漫志, preface 1149), which credits a certain Kong Sanzhuan 孔三傳 (ca. 1070) as its first creator and notes the admiration for the form among the local gentry (*shidafu* 士大夫) who widely memorized and imitated it.[56]

In an All Keys, the sung passages are written to different tunes. Each unit, consisting of two or more songs, generally is ascribed to a different key or mode (*gongdiao*), thus often changing the key of the music.[57] The All Keys suites tend to be quite short, mostly including two or three songs, but rarely exceeding eight songs in one suite. Thus, if keys were intended to change every song or two or three songs, the desired aesthetic musical effect of this form would be pitch variation. This musical organization—the consecutive use of songs in suites and the specification of the key at the beginning of each song—is one of the elements that prompted drama historians to identify the All Keys as one of the foundational sources of northern *zaju* drama, and more recently, also of southern drama.[58]

Although modern musicologists have tried to make sense of the musical system of the All Keys, it remains unclear what the frequent change in keys accomplished. Rulan Chao Pian, for example, argues that one plausible reason could be that modes were instrumental for musicians of both string and wind instruments to tune string instruments and to establish and clarify the pitch for musicians and singers alike. For now, however, we can only conjecture that if modes did have a musical value, constant change or its equivalent (i.e., notation jumps) would have been possible but extremely challenging.[59] How such a complex musical organization came to form part of an essentially comic composition puzzles scholars to this day. The relation of the All Keys to southern drama is explained in the section "Music: Introduction."

The All Keys in *Top Graduate* is considered to be a "southern" All Keys, precisely because it makes use of an All Keys (or so it is called in the prologue) but with no indication of the actual keys or modes. Because the musical element in the All Keys was essential for its performance, what happens when one of its main features disappears? Is it still an All Keys? Is it possible to have a southern All Keys? In this All Keys there are only five songs, each with one single stanza. These songs are expressive, and describe either the scene or Zhang Xie's emotions; not one of these five songs reappears in the play. The shortness of the songs and the length of the narrated sections all point either to an adaptation of a preexistent All Keys or to a new exclusive composition for this play. The play sequencing certainly indicates deliberation: the introductory poem announces the summary of the story as an All Keys, and the conclusion of the All Keys announces the theatrical performance of the play. Compared with earlier complete All Keys like Master Dong's *Story of the Western Wing* (*Dong Jieyuan Xixiang ji* 董解元西廂記), the songs are shorter and the spoken parts are longer, but we have no means to identify its origin. Either way, it is clear that the All Keys in the late Yuan was a known genre and that it still had some aesthetic value.


## A Second Prologue

After the end of the All Keys, which coincides, in Qian's arrangement, with the end of the first act, a second, perhaps

more conventional, introduction generally repeats the attributes and standards of the first one with some variation. The
main male role (*sheng* 生), not yet in character, enters the stage
thanking the troupe of musicians and declaims a song-lyric
to the tune of *Wang Jiangnan*. When he finishes the poem, he
assumes the character of Zhang Xie, which he will play for the
rest of the performance, and he proceeds to sing a song-lyric
entitled "The Red Sway of the Candle's Shadow," the same tune
the troupe was playing upon his entrance, but not a common
prologue tune. Both song-lyrics establish the same benchmark
of the first prologue: their comic acumen, the excellence of their
makeup and costume, and the proficiency of their music, with
standards on a par with the music bureau—in the first prologue,
they mention the Jiaofang 教方, or Imperial Music Bureau,
and in the second, they compare themselves to the elite Imperial Conservatory of Music (Liyuan 梨園) of the Tang dynasty.
But the second prologue adds, with regard to music, the following: "This version is wondrously new and singularly distinct: we
have changed the source of our *ci* lyrics and shifted our keys and
modes" (此段新奇差異, 更詞源移宮換羽). Because southern
theater did not make use of keys and modes, we need to ask what
is this line doing here? Was this also an adaptation of an earlier northern play? Or are we confused about the nonapplicabil-
ity of keys and modes to early southern drama? Both prologues
also mention authorship: one mentions an unnamed writing
association, and the second directly names the Nine Mountain
Society. And both stress the plot of the story as well as the originality and versatility of this new version. The two versions are
extremely similar, perhaps too similar to be included in the same
play, and of course, the question is why. What was the need to
inform the audience twice of their skills? Furthermore, given
the space restraints and cost of the *Yongle Collectanea*, why not

reduce anything extraneous? Although many questions cannot be answered regarding this second prologue, we can safely infer that the editors kept the text as is because of the creative nature of the introduction and its aesthetic value. Whether the prologue was genuinely intended as a marketing ploy for a competition, or whether it was a conscious act of creation, its originality can be appreciated to this day.

## TOP GRADUATE ZHANG XIE IN CONTEXT

### *The Ungrateful Scholar Play*

*Top Graduate* belongs to a group of early drama stories that relate the story of a young scholar who leaves his family and wife to take the imperial examinations and does not return home.[60] The motif of the ungrateful scholar, as it is generally known, was subsumed under the large category of marriage, which takes up about one-third of the totality of extant *nanxi* plays, but the theme of the ungrateful scholar play prevails in popularity.[61]

These stories attempt to exploit the tensions that accompany duty, ambition, and success, and that can lead to duplicity, betrayal, and revenge. They place a premium on female virtue and endurance, while questioning the social disruption that ensues from male ambitions for status and power. The aims of education, the examination system, the misuse of position and power, and the consequent destabilization of harmonious social relations are all bound up with the young scholar's quest for success and prestige. In most of the plays, the tension created between male aspirations to power and female virtue generates a social conflict that culminates in divine retribution or female revenge. In the process, the plays disclose the conflicting demands placed on the scholars by state and family, revealing that their filial principles remained flawless, but their social values were woefully deficient. These plays are a judgment on the ethical values of the scholars and, by extension, the failure of the state's administrative system, its pedagogical approach, and the process by which it selected its administrators. The plays are not specific critiques of individual figures, but rather they use the characters as synecdochic figures—in which scholars stand for a failed education system, and female characters stand for orthodox moral values.

The subject matter of the ungrateful scholar, which may have already existed in the late Song, had by the early Ming era become very popular. Shen Jing 沈璟, the Ming connoisseur and playwright, listed the famous ungrateful scholar stories of his day together in a poem on the fickleness of love:

| | |
|---|---|
| [正宮] 刷子序 | [*Zhenggong mode*] *To the tune Shuazi xu* |
| 書生負心 | The ungrateful scholar |
| 叔文玩月 | *Shuwen* sported with the moon |
| 謀害蘭英. | and plotted to hurt Lanying. |
| 張葉生榮 | *Zhang Xie* rose to prominence, |
| 將貧女頓忘初恩. | and immediately forgot Poorlass's former kindness. |
| 無情, | Heartless, |
| 李勉把韓妻鞭死, | *Li Mian* flogged his wife, maiden Han, to death, |
| 王魁負倡女亡生. | and when *Wang Kui* betrayed the courtesan, she died. |
| 嘆古今, | Alas, in ancient and modern times, |
| 歡喜冤家, | the *joy of happiness turns to deceit*, |
| 繼著鶯燕爭春. | and follow the *squabbles of orioles and swallows in spring.*[62] |

To understand how *Top Graduate* differs from these other plays, and its literary and historical value, let me explain briefly how the subject matter of the ungrateful scholar is treated in *nanxi*. The six stories alluded to in this poem—*Chen Shuwen, Top Graduate Zhang Xie, Li Mian, Wang Kui, Joyful Love Turns to Deceit*, and *The Tricked Girl*[63]—all deal with the general theme of the poor but talented scholar whose single aim is to take the imperial examinations. He takes leave of his newly wedded wife and aging parents and goes to the capital where he passes the examination with high honors and is named top graduate. Once he acquires fame and a position, the scholar discards his earlier provincial wife for a daughter of the nobility.[64] Thereupon, his former wife goes to the capital in search of her husband and finds him, only to be disavowed. The denouement of the stories generally seeks justice for the forsaken woman. In the case of the very early stories, the virtuous wife is avenged by Heaven.

The stories begin at the moment of parting, as the hopeful scholar leaves to take the examination, generating tensions of different orders, which reflect both the dichotomy between public interests (knowledge and morality) and private interests (status and lineage). From their inception, the plays forewarn us of an imbalance between the demands that government placed upon candidates for civil service and the values they were expected to uphold. The plays focus on the scholar who is called on to administer that state, on one hand, and to maintain and improve the family position, on the other. Typically, as in *Top Graduate*, the scholar is preparing to leave home after having expressed his great ambition for rank and office, and the desire to serve the emperor. It is the occasion for parents to impart words of caution and advice and to warn the son about the dangers of the road, as well as the lure of the city's excitement and female beauties.

Zhang Xie's moment of parting is slightly different because, as he leaves for the capital, he is still a bachelor. In the play, the parting scene is wrapped in comedy: the mother is concerned for her son, who is also the principal administrator of the family's money lending business. In the All Keys, Zhang Xie reacts with exasperation as he announces to his parents his wish to leave for the capital to take the exams and repay his parents kindness by improving their family status (*huan menlü* 還門閭):

> *Mo speaks:* Their son said: "After ten years of mastering the civil and military arts, this year I [finally] get to sell them to the imperial house. I want to change your status in life and requite your kindness, so why must you weep?"

> 孩兒道: 十載學成文武藝, 今年貨與王帝家.欲改還門閭, 報答雙親,何須下淚?[65]

The imperial examinations are presented in *Top Graduate* and the other ungrateful scholar plays as the unquestionable legitimate means of access to power. But at the same time, these texts impugn the motivation of scholars, reflecting one aspect of the neo-Confucian view on learning in which true worth was defined by one's success in realizing one's moral nature.[66] According to this view, all things had an inherent natural principle (*li*), a living force that endowed them with their existence and that could be understood by intelligent minds through the investigation of things. If scholars applied themselves to study, including the study of the classics, they would be able to comprehend that principle. Because the natural principle of things could never be entirely unraveled, study became a lifelong process. Learning referred both to the "moral" principle inherent in all things and to empirical cumulative knowledge of particulars. Neo-Confucians viewed learning primarily as a means to improve one's mind for the sake of individual growth, not for social advancement. These plays, however, clearly stress the opposite. It is true that the young scholars express a desire to apply their knowledge and serve the emperor, but this is immediately qualified by the material aspect of their desires—that is, "to sell" one's abilities to acquire rank and profit and to improve the family's status. The plays describe scholars striving for material prosperity rather than working to realize themselves as idealistic moral exemplars of officialdom.

The gap between knowledge and the moral man is highlighted by the contrast between the ambitious young scholar and his virtuous female companion. In *Top Graduate*, the indebted scholar marries Poorlass, the orphan girl who has nurtured him back to health after he is beaten and robbed by a bandit. When she returns late after spending a day collecting money for his trip to the capital, he insults and beats her, at which point she protests:

Husband, you are a man in search of success and prestige, don't act like this.

(旦) 丈夫, 汝是圖功名底人, 莫便恁地做作.

While the implication is, of course, that education was an instrument of moral reinforcement, it also shows that the scholar's material quest for fame and power was a single-minded aim acquired at the expense of virtuous conduct. Education was not fulfilling its goal, showing that the formative process of this elite group was defective because of the gap between the moral and ritual codes of behavior and their implementation. In other words, whereas the moral code could perhaps be learned, study did not instill in the scholar an ethical conscience. The plays, however, do not critique the desire for material comfort, which, in any case is displayed in its pronounced commercialism—with its demands for a product (scholar), investments (parents), and benefits (imperial salary)—but it is rather a lament for the absence of a morally strong scholar who could see beyond the immediate familial needs to the greater needs of society.

Although these candidates possessed values (filial piety) and understood the demands society and family placed on them, their position of power allowed them to choose between the normative and the instrumental, between the social longing for altruism and their own private desires. That such men who aspired only to fulfill their own private desires should reach the top rung of the examination ladder exposed a flawed educational and examination system, embodied in a figure that was glorified as the icon of talent: the rare scholar of humble origins who came to be lauded as the top graduate. The hypocrisy and moral failings of the scholar brought him into conflict with the virtuous female roles, contrasting figures that allowed the play to move forward in a balance between virtue and vice, sacrifice and injustice, melodrama, and absurdity. At first, the only way to solve these problems was through revenge and retribution; in *Top Graduate* and later plays, that tension was resolved through happy endings and gratification for all.

## The Other Source of Tension: Familial Duties and Female Roles

The other source of tension in the play relates to status and lineage. While scholars' ambitions and desire for success were understood to be "every man's aim" and familial hopes to change their social status were contingent upon the son's accomplishments, the plays also reveal ambivalence within the family, which is represented as a gender-specific conflict in which female considerations of lineage are set against masculine ambitions for office. Although Zhang Xie adheres to the same issues of trust, abandonment, and reconciliation, the plot structure has been constructed to reach the same ends through very different paths. Thus, let me first briefly explain the general nature of familial duties and female roles.

In almost every extant ungrateful scholar play, the matter of lineage and filial responsibility are foremost among the family's considerations. In general terms, mother and daughter-in-law seek to hold the family together and continue the family line, whereas father and son express a clear desire for status, further emphasizing the dichotomies of gender. For example, in the play *The Golden Hairpin*, the son has just married and is about to depart. Parents and wife repeatedly warn the scholar not to squander money in the courtesan's quarters or vie for the daughters of the nobility. Although the father agrees with the son's wishes, he also warns him on behalf of the family:

Son, what you say is reasonable, so go and prepare your luggage. I only hope that your studies will bring you recognition and profit; that they will change your status and fulfill our wishes. Son, I hope that this time when you pass the imperial examination, you will promptly return home in honor and glory. But I am worried at your departure. You have been married for only three days but must already separate. Do not forget your parents in the front hall or the spiritual debt of husband to wife. Do not hanker after the daughters of the nobility! And do not force your parents to wait by the door longing for you!

孩兒說得有理, 就安排打疊行李, 只望你讀書求名利, 改門閭, 稱我心意. 孩兒, 願此去龍門及第, 身榮貴早回鄉里. 孩兒, 出去我挂心機, 你夫妻三日便分離, 記得堂前爹共媽, 也須念夫妻恩義, 休貪戀丞相人家女兒, 休教爹媽倚門望你.[67]

A little later in the same text, the gender demands are inge-
niously argued, wittily drawing on quotations from the classics.
Mother and daughter-in-law seek to hold the family together
and continue the family line, but father and son express a clear
desire for status. From the feminine point of view, they should
protect what they already have and account for the family's lineage; from the masculine viewpoint, men should bring honor to
the family for posterity. The wife (*dan*) and mother try to dissuade
the scholar with the Confucian *Analects*, while father and son
(*sheng*), relying on the *Classic of Filial Piety*, justify men's duties:

> *Female role speaks*: In vain you have studied the books of Confucius
>    the Sage and know nothing of propriety and righteousness.
> *Male role speaks*: What do the books say?
> *Female role speaks*: Have you not seen in the *Analects* when Confucius
>    says, "When one's parents are alive, one should not travel far?"
> *Male role speaks*: Wife, you remember the words from the *Analects*,
>    but do you remember what the *Classic of Filial Piety* says?
> *Female role speaks*: What does the *Classic of Filial Piety* say?
> *Male role speaks*: You have to establish yourself and leave a name for
>    later generations in order to make your parents famous; this is
>    the loyalty of the filial [son]. Although I find it hard to set aside
>    my feelings, when it comes to fame and honor . . .[68]

(旦白) 官人枉讀孔聖之書, 不曉書中禮義. (生白)書中怎麼
說? (旦白) 不見論語中孔子曰, 父母在不遠遊.(生白) 娘子, 你
記論語中說,可記孝經篇說? (旦白) 孝經篇[怎]麼說? (生白)
立身揚名於後世,已顯父母,孝之忠也.情雖難舍,功名之事 ...

The worries expressed by the families are generally of two
different orders. On one hand, the need for caution reveals the
dangers and insecurity scholars were prone to on the road to
the capital, which could jeopardize both the son's aspirations and

the family's hopes for improving their status, as well as the con-
tinuity of lineage and the family's livelihood. On the other, in
many of these plays, the scholar is exhorted not to be led astray
by the lure of the capital's bustling life and lively women.[69] In the
All Keys in *Top Graduate*, for example, the parents advise their
son: "Before dark you must first find lodgings for the night; only
after the cock crows should you cross the pass; when you come
to a bridge, you must dismount and when you come to a ford do
not attempt to go first"(未晚先投宿, 雞鳴始過關. 逢橋須下馬,
有渡莫爭先). Zhang Xie alludes to these caring injunctions later
in the play, when he reaches the capital city.[70]

Yet, although the dangers of the road pose a real threat to
their son's livelihood, the lack of faith expressed by their words
of caution highlight their mistrust and doubt of the scholar's
moral stamina. The greatest tension created within the family is
reflected in the benefits brought by the daughters of ministers
and the scholar's thirst for status and power. The noble daughters,
usually the only offspring of the prime minister, play the second
female role (*tie* 貼), and are described in positive terms, with
talent and a beauty that reflects their innocence. Their strategic
position as coveted daughters of a top official of marriageable
age was the natural counterpart to the Top Graduate. And the
Top Graduate, attracted by their feminine glamour, their social
status, and political benefits seemed only too glad to exchange
vows with them. Thus, the initial fear voiced by the female roles
is justified as the talented scholars abandon their former wives
for these elegant daughters of officials, satisfying their yearning
for status and power. Ironically, the talented scholar and minister's refined, cultured daughter are an imperfect match and are
the final cause of disruption in these plays.

The most conspicuous female character, however, is the "husk
wife"(*zaokang fu* 糟糠婦), so called because, as first wife, she has

endured the hardships and poverty of the scholar's earlier strug-
gle. She is also called the "three-day wife" because she is separated from her husband shortly after they have been married.
The first wife is described in absolute terms as a paragon of virtuous conduct. Her impeccable filial piety toward her parents-in-
law, and her refusal to remarry after her husband abandons the
family are the most highly praised virtues, but her capacity for
onerous hardship without complaint is in fact the most admired
quality, and one that calls attention in these plays to a particular
fascination with feminine endurance. Endurance is one of the
pillars on which female virtue is built and, like determination
in chastity, is a measure of her character.[71] Once the scholar succeeds, contrasting action moves the plot ahead, where the harsh
and rigorous travails of the husk wife are compared with the
material well-being of the scholar-official, and her determination to uphold virtue set against his weakness of will and dis-
loyalty to the family who nurtured him. It is this contraposition
between feminine resolve and the male's impotence to act firmly
that elevates the female role to her prominent position.

Overall, however, what the plays describe is the family's fear
of loss of not just their emblem of hope, but of their life's investment, which is set against the scholar's acknowledgment of
indebtedness to his parents. The initial premonition expressed in
the family advice (and mistrust) as well as the realization of the
scholar's failings turn into the leitmotif of the play. Hereafter, the
play moves ahead through antithesis, setting the scholar's ambition against the virtue of the wife; his flaws are juxtaposed to her
absolute virtue, showing also that virtue could be inborn, and, in
fact, not only acquired through book learning. The problem of
inborn versus acquired virtue lurks in the background of these
plays, in the necessary contrast between the exemplary women
and unethical scholars.

*Top Graduate's* plot includes all the same topics of the ungrateful scholar play—parting, the perils of the road, the mistrust of the scholar, gender dichotomies, the glorification of endurance, and the abuse of power—yet these are woven through different developing lines. When the scholar leaves, the perils of the road are framed comically within a dream and its interpretation, which foretells what will happen on the road. On the way to the capital, Zhang Xie is robbed and beaten, but a mountain god comes to his rescue, and with divine assistance, he reaches the temple where the destitute Poorlass lives. Poorlass is the single orphaned daughter of a local formerly wealthy family whose straitened circumstances confined her to live in the temple. She works for people in the village weaving hemp and silk and picking tea, and is protected by two villagers who establish themselves as her benefactors: Grandma and Grandpa Li. When Zhang Xie reaches the temple, Poorlass takes care of him and nurtures him back to health. In a moment of gratefulness, Zhang Xie marries her. Soon after he leaves the temple for the capital to take the exams, the same expression of mistrust is uttered by Poorlass and the Lis, her benefactors, during the parting scene. As might be expected, when Zhang Xie passes the imperial examinations as Top Graduate, the prime minister wants him for his son-in-law. Here, however, the plot diverges from the norm, and Zhang Xie turns down the marriage offer from the prime minister. But he declines not on account of his earlier marriage to Poorlass, but rather by declaring that he is not inclined to this union, that he will not submit to the pressures of the powerful, and that his filial duties require he first inform his parents. Zhang's rebuttal is considered a humiliation by the prime minister's family: his daughter Shenghua dies of shame, and the prime minister swears to quash Zhang Xie's career and avenge his daughter's death. This circuitous presentation of events, however, in no way lessens the criticism toward the inability of the education system to form scholars of moral rectitude, but instead expands its political assessment to include the obvious abuse of power these scholars underwent when they did not comply with the personal demands of their seniors in power.

Possibly owing to audience dictates, the plays, at least from *Top Graduate* onward, required a just and happy ending (*tuanyuan* 團圓). If in the terse references we have to foundational plays, the immoral scholar is chastised and retribution ensues, meted out by divine law, the denouement in *Top Graduate* (and later plays) is resolved with the virtuous "husk wife" compensated in real life by a return to a harmonious married family life plus status and wealth.

Was this shift from the ungrateful and immoral man toward the cooperative husband to counter the wife's misfortunes brought about by a discomfort with the raw violence of the earlier texts? Did it reflect in any way contemporary socioeconomical changes? Was it based on popular demand by an audience's desire to renegotiate the spiritual and material fate of their heroines' aspirations? We cannot accurately answer these questions, but we can surmise that the demands of the audience changed toward what was considered one of the essential principles of social exchange: reciprocity.

## Repayment

Social relations were governed by a delicate and well-balanced web of reciprocal exchange with the coin of exchange tacitly understood. In these transactions, which run up the ladder of Chinese society, it was made clear that anyone who had made a social investment would eventually be compensated. One of the basic principles of social relations in Chinese society is *bao*, or reciprocity of action. *Bao* is applied to almost all forms of human relations and expands within the public sphere, in the hierarchy governing the five principles of correct human relations (*wulun* 五倫), and in the private sphere, through relations between equals, whether family or friends.[72] In the early formative stages of southern Chinese drama, one of the main concerns of the parting moment, when the scholar leaves to take the exams, is the long-awaited moment of reciprocation, when he will repay the efforts of his parents and the kindness of his wife. Promises of repayment of a moral and material nature are strongly voiced by the scholar in reply to expressions of doubt. He assures his family of his unwavering filial piety and gratitude, and of his intent to raise the family status. But in the end, perplexed by his own success, the scholar forfeits his integrity, showing a lack of ethical understanding and moral fortitude.

Such doubts foreground the outcome of the plays, in which the male role does indeed fail to reciprocate kindness with gratitude. For example, the calculated option of Zhang Xie—who decides to eliminate from the root his obligations to indebtedness by killing his virtuous wife Poorlass—demonstrates the wisdom of the female character's doubts at the moment of parting, warning us repeatedly of the fragile balance between moral debt and repayment. But while *Top Graduate*'s attempt to kill Poorlass seems to be setting up a straightforward theme of the ungrateful scholar who must be punished for his unconscionable treatment of a faithful woman, the play complicates the problem by developing conflicting ethical obligations both of a private and public nature. So, the cause-effect pattern, in which good or evil actions are repaid evenly, is never that clear. In *Top Graduate*, *bao* as a social obligation is more complex and crosses more social spheres than in any other play. This obligation is firmly established in

Zhang Xie's filial conduct toward his parents. It exists between Poorlass and Zhang Xie when he marries her and is understood between Zhang Xie and the prime minister but is rejected as a form of abuse when he refuses to marry his daughter.

When Zhang Xie marries Poorlass, who nurses him back to health after he has been attacked by a bandit, he does so to compensate her for her kindness, to express his gratitude, and perhaps to clear her good name (because he has been living in the temple with her). This shows, on Zhang Xie's part, a more complex reasoning on matters of integrity, gratitude, and filiality. Zhang Xie's initial gratitude, however, turns rapidly into regret after he leaves Poorlass. On his way to the capital (act 18), he confirms that his moral obligations have forced him into this trap: "Recently, I was forced to marry Poorlass, but it was not part of my life plan as a scholar and once more it sets constrains on myself" (近日須諧貧女, 未是吾儒活計, 依舊困其身). And later (act 20): "Poorlass, that low-bred! I'll beat her more dead than alive. If it wasn't for the terrible plight I was in, I would have never gone near her" (貧女那賤人, 十人打底九人沒下! 自家不因災禍, 誰恨肯近傍你每). Zhang Xie understands the rules of correct social behavior and reciprocation, but makes it seem to us that circumstance provided him with no alternative: to requite her kindness and maintain her respectability, he had no choice but to marry her. But from the moment Zhang Xie holds office, the blame is shifted to Poorlass for "coercing" him into marriage, and later humiliating him by arriving in the capital looking like a beggar. *Bao* now ensues from Zhang Xie who feeling reviled, seeks reciprocation by demanding revenge on Poorlass. Similarly, when he refuses the prime minister's offer, he does so on account of his filial nature—he wants first to inform his parents of the outcome of his exams—and because he refuses to be coerced by the powerful. Both show principled behavior, an understanding of personal obligation, as well as a conscious rejection of other tacit social norms. Rejecting the prime minister's daughter was an imposition he could and should reject. All the tensions created between the normative and the instrumental, or between what is morally correct and what he does in practice, are finally resolved when he ascends the social ladder and can break the norms with impunity. Zhang Xie faces no final punishment, but the main female role receives compensation.

Unlike her male counterparts, the main female role in these plays, despite being profoundly humiliated, is not vengeful. When Poorlass is thrown out of the *yamen* after seeking out Zhang Xie in the capital (act 35), she departs with sarcasm: "I shall buy a stick of good incense and pray to Heaven: 'I want your deceitful heart to be forever honored" (買炷好香祝蒼天, 願你虧心, 長長榮貴).[73] And after Zhang Xie attempts to kill her, she hides Zhang Xie's uncouthness from her benefactors, and simply complains of her ill fate. But alone in the temple, Poorlass unceasingly reminds us of Zhang Xie's unrequited kindness toward her, and her resentment at having been denied what he justly owes her. Poorlass is virtuous and helpless to the end, and it is clear that her destiny entirely relies on her good fortune. Fortune, we understand, is allotted by Heaven, who takes pity on her sufferings. Because her well-being is contingent on the survival of the main male role, the expected revenge of earlier stories, where divine providence kills the male role, cannot come upon Zhang Xie. Requital in *Top Graduate* arrives in the form of material compensation for the female role, and not only does Poorlass survive but also her earlier social status is restored, her beauty praised and appreciated, and her position in life elevated. Revenge in *Top Graduate* becomes female compensation rather than retaliation toward the scholar.

# STRUCTURE: SCENES, ROLES, COMEDY, AND MUSIC

## *1. Scenes*

*Top Graduate*, as it appears in the *Yongle Collectanea*, was not divided into acts, perhaps owing to the *Collectanea*'s restrictions of space.[74] The modern editor of the play, Qian Nanyang, divided the play into acts according to the entrance and exit of roles, the plot of the story, and the musical organization of the play. He pointed out that one of the fundamental criteria for the composers of the play was a balance between the comic and more raucous acts, generally played by the comic roles, and the quieter ones mostly sung by the main male and female roles.[75] In addition to a consistency between the more earnest scenes of the main roles (and some secondary roles) and the rowdiness of the comics, this balance is also determined and closely tied to the plot of the story and role participation.

The structure of act composition is juxtaposed rather than integrated, and the plot follows this same pattern, dividing the story into two main but parallel threads enacted in the stories of Zhang Xie and Poorlass, and a subthread following the vicissitudes of Shenghua, her mother Lady Wang, and the military commissioner, Wang Deyong. Act sequence thus alternates between the actions and emotions of Zhang Xie and Poorlass— his moment of parting from home is juxtaposed with Poorlass's orphaned loneliness at the temple and so forth—following the larger pattern of the plot concerned with the pervasive, conventional theme of the grief of parting and longing, the agonies of uncertainty, and the happiness of reunion. Acts specifically devoted to the Lady Wang and her daughter are also inserted at moments in the story. Thus, each act is an autonomous unit of space and time (Zhang Xie about to depart; Poorlass orphaned in the temple), determined by role and character, and loosely tied by the development of the plot. Short acts with a single role are few and far apart, and these are generally expressive, disclosing the unique emotional state of one of the two main characters.

The scene, rather than the act, is the smallest structural unit in dramatic composition. One act can be composed of a single scene or multiple scenes that generally are marked by the entrance and exit of roles, the number of songs a role sings, and the events within the act. An act opens when a role (or roles) enters the stage singing, or declaiming a popular saying,[76] and it concludes with a declaimed quatrain, uttered by one or simultaneously by various roles. When a scene concludes in the middle of an act as one or more roles exit the stage, it does so in the same manner. Thus, each act as an independent unit can be composed of additional independent units framed by the entrance and exit of roles. Although scenes within acts are bound by the sequence of occurring events, in some cases, especially of comic scenes, scenes are quasi-independent units unrelated to the main storyline. For example, act 2 is divided into three scenes: (a) Zhang Xie's introduction to the play, (b) Zhang Xie and friends, and (c) Zhang Xie and his father. The first scene is indispensable, because it introduces the play (for a second time) and ushers in our main character, Zhang Xie. But the second scene, enacted by Zhang Xie and the two comic roles (mo and jing), could be removed without affecting the inner coherence of the act or the overall plot of the story. Such scenes between comic roles are a recurring constitutive peculiarity of this play: the structure of scene 2 of act 2 is repeated (without Zhang Xie) in scene 2 of act 8, and the second part of act 4, in which the diviner discloses the servant's (mo) future also could be removed without sacrificing the plot. The independence of these units has led scholars to insinuate that such scenes are evidence of the continuation of the early short comic skits between a wit and the fool.[77]

Because this play *is* a comedy, the proportion of comic parts integrated with the more serious parts is also large, showing, as Qian Nanyang noted, an endeavor to balance woeful moments with humorous ones.[78] This reluctance to sanction any form of misfortune to taint the play is particularly clear in act 32 in which the death of Shenghua is offset by the absurdity of her father, Wang Deyong. One reason for this overwhelming emphasis on the comic could be the commercial context *Top Graduate* claims to reflect in its introduction: as a performance in an urban competition that caters to the preferences of the audience for new music and fresh jokes. Whether the prefaces reflect a reproduction of a real setting, or a creative emulation of a "curtain-raiser," *Top Graduate* delivers on its promise to amuse the audience with an abundance of music and comedy, showing that theater was already conceived as an art of entertainment for which the primacy of the experience focused on the production of pleasure.

Although the pattern to act sequencing is based on the plot, individual act composition has a demonstrable symmetry and consonance. The deftly crafted act 16 consists of two large mirroring scenes divided by a song suite with alternating songs sung between the two main roles. These two scenes, which relate two different themes—a wedding and a feast—are also matched by the roles. The first wedding scene includes the temple god (a *jing* comic role), Grandpa Li (a *mo* second male role), his son Xiao'er (a *chou* clown role), and the two main roles, Zhang Xie and Poorlass. The second banquet scene includes the same number of roles and characters, but because only one actor can play the comic role (*jing*), Grandma Li (also a *jing*) has to remain out of the first scene and return in the second. This shows the limitations of the role system, but it also provides the playwright—through the allusions of other roles to the double function of the comic as god and Grandma Li—with a means to parody the play within the play. The farce of the first scene is a mixture of the gluttony of the two comic roles (who eat and drink surreptitiously) and the seriousness of the marriage ritual mediated by the omniscient *mo* role in the character of Grandpa Li. The second scene, with the same division and function of roles, concentrates on mime (physical farce). Scene balance can be seen, for example, in scene nine during which Zhang Xie is mugged by the local mountain bandit (*sheng/chou*), and in the next scene, is saved by the local god (*sheng/jing*). Such balance is evident in act 10 in which scene patterns are also repeated, in scene 1—three comics and Zhang Xie—and scene 2—three comics and Poorlass, as well as in independent acts, such as act 24 or 28, in which the *jing* persecutes the *chou* on money matters, and so forth.

## 2. Roles

***Origins and Role Formation*** Roles are an integral part of the structure of a play and are instrumental in generally segmenting the play through their comings and goings. The basic number of roles—seven roles[79]—first appears in this play. Their basic function as mediators between the actors and the characters already can be perceived in this play. But the dearth of particulars about performance in *Top Graduate* and the fact that we cannot see the performance of these roles—for example, that we do not know if and how the main male and female roles utilized a specific manner of singing, employed a set group of gestures, or were costumed and made up in a codified manner that would be widely understood by the audience—necessarily limits the technical aspect of our discussion of roles. The two comics and the *mo* or second male role, by virtue of the number of characters they play, allow for a closer look at the nature of the function of early roles, but their task is intimately tied to comedy, which is discussed in the following section. Let me first turn to the origins and theories of role formation.

Wang Guowei, the first modern scholar to analyze roles in Chinese theater, noted that actor characterization begins in the early Sui and Tang dynasties, roughly at the same time as a type of comic skit called the "Adjutant play" (*Canjun xi* 參軍戲).[80] The Adjutant play originated in the early Tang dynasty, and began as a form of punishment for a corrupt official (the *canjun*) who was negligent in his duties. The official was accused of accepting bribes, but because the emperor thought highly of his talent and valued his services, he exempted him from severe punishment. Instead, the emperor ordered his court players to ridicule the disgraced official in public:

> In the Kaiyuan era, [the performers] Huang Fangchuo and Zhang Yegu *played* the Adjutant (*Canjun*). This began with Shi Dan of the Han, magistrate of Guantao. [Shi] Dan had committed the crime of accepting a bribe, but because Emperor He cherished his talent, he spared him from punishment. Every time there was a banquet, [the emperor] ordered him [Shi Dan] to put on white clothes and don a jacket, and commanded his performers to humiliate him. After some years, the emperor pardoned him. That he later [invested him] with the rank of adjutant is incorrect.

> 開元中, 黃幡綽, 張野孤弄參軍. 始自漢館陶令石耽. 耽有贓犯, 和帝惜其才, 免罪. 每宴樂, 即令衣白夾衫, 命俳優弄辱之, 經年乃放. 後為參軍, 誤也.[81]

Scholars of Chinese theater see this short satirical skit as crucial in the evolution of Chinese dramatic history, because it hints at early theatrical practice. For the first time, we see in this description an independent, actor-based comic skit that was produced on command and could be repeatedly acted by performers who moved freely on stage, rather than as a choreographed group. It put a premium on language, satirized a past event and was enacted by actors playing historical characters. For Wang Guowei, the *Canjun* skits were close to true theater, but they were still short of what he considered theater proper. Nonetheless, these short performances demonstrated clear concepts of staged, practiced, and repeated imitation, with a simple idea of staged characterization built through two or three conflicting characters, which made use of costumes and painted faces. In other words, we see here the formation of a type of individualized performance based on actors' expressive skills, and not just their physical capacities.[82]

Although the Adjutant play provided the basis for characterization, roles do not begin to germinate until the Song dynasty, in the description of a Song dynasty imperial entertainment called *zaju*. These performances are explained in one of the earliest memoirs on the city of Hangzhou written around 1235, *A Record of the Splendors of the Eastern Capital* (*Ducheng jisheng* 都城紀勝) by a certain Nai Deweng 耐得翁. The *Record* notes that a *zaju* integrates five performers, each with a different function:

> In the *zaju*, the *moni* is the leader. Every performance is constituted by four or five persons. Initially, in the first section they perform the well-known routine called the *yanduan*. Then they play the real comedy (*zaju*); together these are called the "two sections." The *moni* type (*se*) acts as the leader, the *yinxi* type gives orders, the *fujing* type acts stupid and the *fumo* type cracks jokes. At times they add another person called the costumed official (*zhuanggu*).

雜劇中, 末泥為長, 每四人或五人為一場, 先做尋常熟事一段,
名曰艷段；次做正雜劇, 通名為兩段. 末泥色主張, 引戲色分
付, 副淨色發喬, 副末色打諢, 又或添一人裝孤.[83]

According to this text, a *zaju* was performed by a troupe
leader, someone who gives orders, a comic (or wit) and a clown
and, at times, a costumed official. The two important types for
later role genealogies are the fool and the wit—the *fujing* and
the *fumo*—considered to be the central performers of the Song
*zaju*. The *Record* further explains that a *zaju* was a fully constituted story, a succession of events, with a beginning, a development and a conclusion told in a humorous manner: "The whole
thing generally concerns an event from the past, or a historical
happening and is treated in a comic vein. Basically, it is to warn
by example, or it may hide indirect criticism and remonstrance.
Therefore when they reveal it little by little, they are called the
'faultless insects'" (大抵全以故事, 世務為滑稽, 本是鑒戒, 或
隱為諫, 故從便跌露, 謂之 "無過蟲").[84] We cannot know what
these stories were like, how they were presented, if they were
performed as theater in the voice of characters, or how detailed
they were. The Yuan official and poet Hu Zhiyu 胡祗遹
(1227–1295), in an often-mentioned preface to a poem, explained
the interest of the court for *zaju* and noted that it was called
*za* (or miscellaneous) because these performances treated
themes across the whole spectrum of Chinese society: from
the vicissitudes of court politics, to the ups and downs of village
life and human relations, to medicine, religion, and commerce,
as well as the differences in customs and languages. Hu Zhiyu
concluded that *zaju* "in every instance captures the feeling, and
fully expresses the manner of things" (無一物不得其情, 不窮
其態).[85] The *zaju*, according to the *Record*, presented a story in
a humorous vein, clearly intended to entertain, but it also had

to include a heuristic component and serve a moral purpose.[86] It is unclear whether the leader of the troupe and the one who gives orders had any function in the performance other than a seeming administrative one, or what was the nature of the costumed official. In contrast, the two comics performed a routine, which is explained in terms closer to a farce (act stupid, make jokes) than to the remonstrative ideal expressed in the description of the *zaju*. Whether this edifying quality was added simply because it was a palace performance, or because comedy's value as *pure* entertainment troubled the educated and duty-bound literati, is an open question. The *fujing* and the *fumo* seem to have carried the weight of the performance, but because we do not know the nature of the performances, or how the story was enacted, we cannot be sure whether these roles enacted characters, what genre they performed in, or what their temperament was, all basic elements in determining a role. Our information relates only to their expertise as comedians—two stock types performing a comic routine. One reason, then, why these two comics are presented as the forerunners of the role system is for their continuing typecasting as the *jing* and *mo*, and their lasting function as wit and fool,[87] that is, the well-known and complicit pairing of the figure of authority and lucid wit, and its antagonist, the seemingly dimwitted fool and racket maker.[88]

A little over a century later, the remonstrative element in comedy appears to have been transfigured into a physical and more hostile form of farce with the types essential to a comic (butt/fool) routine—the *fujing-fumo* duo and the *canjun*—blended into one definition. In the late Yuan, the scholar Tao Zongyi (1316–1403) notes that a comedy features "five people," two of which are the comics: "One is called the *fujing*. In ancient times it was called the adjutant (*canjun* 參軍). One is called the *fumo*. In ancient times it was called the Grey Hawk (*canggu* 蒼鶻).

The hawk can strike wild birds just as the *mo* can hit the *fujing*—hence its name" (院本則五人]. 一曰副淨, 古謂之參軍. 一曰副末, 古謂之蒼鶻鶻, 能擊禽鳥, 末可打副淨, 故云).[89] Tao adds that "the *fujing* makes idle talk (*sanshuo* 散說), recites lines (*dao-nian* 道念), does somersaults (*jindou* 筋鬥), and makes gestures (*kefan* 科汎)," disclosing the essential dual farcical (verbal and physical) nature of the *jing* role at the time.[90] Tao, who may have drawn his information from the *Records*, does not explain how he links these two types, the *fujing* and *fumo*, with the Adjutant and the Grey Hawk. No cogent explanation is given for the connection between the Adjutant–Grey Hawk duo and the *fujing–fumo* duo, but he may have established this attachment on the basis of a tenuous understanding of the similarities of comedy and its earlier performance types. By creating this association to slapstick farce (the *mo* can hit the *fujing*), both the element of ridicule and its remonstrative intent are dissolved in favor of a more violent type of comedy.

One last text that may give us clues on the origins of roles is the mid-fourteenth-century *Green Bower Collection* (*Qinglou ji* 青樓集, ca. 1360), a selection of biographical notices of actresses described according to their skills and specialization. A foreword added later to this text, a "Foreword to the *Green Bower Collection*" (*Qinglou ji zhi* 青樓集誌, 1368), notes the same five players of a *zaju*, but adds that these five types also were known as

the Five Costumed *Cuan* Players. Some say Emperor Huizong of the Song (1082–1135) saw [some players] from the country of *Cuan* come to court with their [regional] dress, footwear, headdress, and face make up and particular gestures. [Huizong] had his performers imitate them. They called these performances "*Cuan* plays."

又謂之 (五花爨弄). 或曰, 宋徽宗見爨國來朝, 衣裝鞋履巾裹, 傳粉墨, 舉動如此, 使優人效之以為戲, 因名曰「爨弄」.[91]

*Cuan* is identified as a kingdom in the southwest, in modern-day Yunnan province. Here again, we have isolated intelligence linking the *Cuan* to an earlier performance form. Of greater import is that this explanation of the *Cuan* adds to the idea of imitation—first articulated in association to the remonstrative Tang Adjutant play—an aesthetic dimension.[92] The aim of the *Cuan* was purely artistic: to reproduce the exotic beauty and uniqueness of the fashion and customs of people from other parts.

The main text of the *Green Bower Collection* also mentions female performers who specialized (*gong* 工) in certain types of performances, such as the *soft moni* (*ruan moni* 軟末泥) or were good at performing the painted *dan* comedies (*huadan zaju* 花旦雜劇), or could perform *dan* (female) and *mo* (male) *zaju* comedies. According to the text, although these comedies were divided into male and female parts,[93] both men and women could perform *zaju*, and both men and women could perform the *moni* types, showing some form of specialization, in which case both male and female performers could carry out similar tasks. Nothing indicates, however, that they adhered to techniques of acting or character representation. They are performers acting out types that reveal their gender (male or female), and function in the troupe (comic, leader and so forth)—and because no story we know of would provide the framework for a character to develop, they also are not characters.[94]

It would take another two hundred years before literati paid attention to roles in their written works.[95] By the time playwrights and aficionados of the theater began to probe the origin of roles in the Ming dynasty, theater was well established among literati circles and had been popular both in cities and in the countryside for some time. The first inquiries into roles address mostly their etymology and, rarely, their function, but it is clear that by then the origins of these roles had long been lost.

For example, Hu Yinglin 胡應麟 (1551–1602) believed that the role names refer to the opposite of what they mean; thus, the feminine principle, which generally is represented by the night, is given the name *dan* (main female role), meaning dawn or light. Similarly, the first to come on stage is the *mo*; hence, his role name means "last."[96] Another Ming scholar, Zhou Qi 周祈, in his work *Mingyi kao* 名義考 traces the names of roles to mythical animals. For example, the "*chou* 丑 comes from *niu* 狃, which is a dog with an unruly nature; and the *jing* 淨 is fierce looking. In the *Guangyun* dictionary it is said that it resembles a leopard with one horn and five tails as well as a fox with wings."[97] A more sober argument is made by Zhu Yunming in his *Weitan* 猥談, in which he suggests that because of the popular origins of names, it is impossible to know their etymology. Zhu states:

> [Some say that] the names *sheng, dan, jing,* and *mo* are contrary of what they are, and some attribute [their origins] to Zhuangzong of the Tang. Both [opinions] are wrong. [The names] originally came from the local language of the marketplace of the Jin and Yuan eras. That which is called "scamps' songs" is what today is called the language of the marketplace. The *sheng* is the male role, the *dan* is dissembling as a female role, the *jing* is called the *jing'er*, the *mo* is called the *moni*, and the *gu* is an official. They are in local language, and have no particular meaning.

> 生淨旦末等名有謂反其事而稱，又或託之唐莊宗皆繆云也．此本金元闌闠談吐，所謂鶻伶聲嗽，今所謂市語也．生即男子，旦曰粧旦色，淨曰淨兒，末曰末尼，孤乃官人，即其土音，何義理之有．[98]

Zhu Yunming's description mixes designations of character types of Song dynasty performances with early Ming role categories. He mentions the *mo* as the *moni*, possibly indicating a category of secondary male roles. Two *mo* categories are also mentioned in *Top Graduate*: one is the *moni* who is called in by the *mo* role, and the other is the *fumo* (assistant). But the function of this role in *Top Graduate* is the same as the *mo*, showing that all these terms were not yet fixed. The *fumo* became the conventional opening role in southern drama from *The Lute* onward to the point of calling the introduction to the play "the *fumo* introduces the play" (*fumo kaichang*), as mentioned previously.

**The Seven Roles in Zhang Xie** *Top Graduate* makes use of a total of seven roles: the main male role (*sheng*), the main female role (*dan*); three roles that participate in most comic sections: the second male role (*mo*), who fluctuates between being the wit and a serious role, and two humorous ones, the comic (*jing*) and the clown or (*chou*). The two secondary roles of importance are the added-on female role (*tie*) and the extra role (*wai*).[99]

The earliest collective description we have of these southern roles comes from the mid-Ming playwright Xu Wei. Xu's descriptions of the roles are short, focus on their function or etymology, and assume prior knowledge of the role system, so they are not informative. For example, as Xu notes: "The *sheng* is the term used for the male [role]" (生, 即男子之稱).[100] Because *sheng* is a term commonly employed to designate Confucian scholars since, at least, the Han dynasty (i.e., *rusheng* 儒生), but has many other uses always in relation to a male occupation—such as master (*xiansheng* 先生), disciple (*mensheng* 門生), and student (*shusheng* 書生)—it is perhaps too familiar in its association with scholars to find a unique original source.[101] The *sheng* as the main male role appears for the first time in this play. After this play, the character it represented of the talented, educated, and ambitious youth of, in theory, high moral stature was established for the ungrateful scholar play. The main female role or *dan*, the counterpart of the scholar and match, is a young woman of moral stature—she is filial, sacrificing, and chaste. Here, too, Xu Wei assumes prior knowledge of this role, and without mentioning its category, directly informs the reader of the etymology of the term: "In the Song dynasty, female performers placed their instruments in a basket to carry them onstage. This was called the 'flower pannier'" (宋伎上場, 皆以樂器之類置籃中, 擔之以出, 號曰「花擔」).[102] Xu explains that the term *dan* or pannier, was simplified to *dan* 旦. Because this role is also part of the northern tradition, the term has been extensively researched, but the source of the term remains obscure. One possible, and reasonable, explanation for its etymology is that it is a simplification of the character *jie* 姐 used to designate a female performer. This same etymological explanation is given for the term designating the second female role, *tie* 貼 (i.e., deputy, secondary), which is often simplified as *tie* 占.[103] Because the *sheng* and *dan* are serious roles, even when in dialogue with the comic roles, they are performed seriously—they do not joke, are not teased by other roles, and are not affected by the comedy. They also perform most of the short single-role scenes, and much of the songs and long declaimed verses are performed by these roles. The only straightforward definition of a role is the *wai* or extra, which Xu Wei glosses as an "additional *sheng* role" (生之外又一生也).[104]

Xu Wei traces the *jing* and the *mo* roles to the earlier *canjun* and *canggu* types, respectively. He notes that the term *jing* came from a contraction of the term *canjun*, but quotes his contemporary Hu Yingling on the theory of opposites, commenting that because the *jing* has a painted (smudged) face, he is called "clean." He also notes that the *mo* role (meaning "last") is played by younger actors so they appear last in the plays, which is clearly not true.[105] Xu adds that the *jing* is "the most respected of roles among actors" (優中最尊).[106] For the clown role (*chou*), believed to be exclusively a feature of southern theater, Xu writes: "it paints its face with powder, its appearance very ugly" (以墨粉塗面, 其形甚醜), and concludes that the term commonly used in theater for this role (*chou* 丑) is a simplification of the character for ugly.[107] In short, like his contemporary Hu Yingling, Xu no longer knew where role names came from, but both Hu and Xu's postulations as connoisseurs were possibly intended to be used to compete with earlier and current definitions of already recondite terms, as a means to establish some form of authority as discerning and learned critics.

In *Top Graduate*, roles can play one or multiple characters, and these roles are not *all* gender specific. The two main roles are fixed: and the main male and female roles can play only themselves and their respective genders are established. Zhang Xie is a main male role (*sheng*), and the role plays only this one single character, while Poorlass is the main female role (*dan*) and plays only this female character. All other roles can play more than one character and switch between gender roles. For example, the second female role (*tie*) plays two female characters and is gender specific, whereas the *wai* plays both Zhang Xie's father, a male character, as well as Lady Wang, the mother of Shenghua, the prime minister's daughter. But the *mo* and the two comic roles (*jing* and *chou*) are by far the most conspicuous in terms of the number of characters the roles play: the second male role (*mo*) plays fifteen different—all male—characters (or sixteen, if we count the *fumo* servant as a variant of this role), and the two comics (*jing* and *chou)* play a variety of characters that can be male or female. The comic *jing* plays thirteen, four of which are female characters, and the clown plays nine with only one female character. The *chou* plays nine characters, many of which are menial and similar in function to those played by the *jing*, but also plays two major ones, the robber and the prime minister. Although the comic roles participate in long comic exchanges, many are generic character-types without a proper name, showing perhaps that character types were conceived in terms of role. Characters are always introduced by their role type—the friend *mo*, or the merchant *jing*, and so forth—indicating the primacy of role, and showing that the actor's performance was already a synthesis of norms and conventions. When an actor entered the stage, an audience familiar with stage conventions may have recognized the function of the role, regardless of the character it played.

The nature of the character and the role does not influence the gender of the actor, and actors can play both male and female roles. In southern theater, although the main male role and the character it plays need to be matched—that is, the *sheng* always plays a male character, whereas the *dan* always plays a female character—role and actor do not have to match. Hence, the gender of the actor playing the main roles would not have to comply with the gender of their characters. In *Top Graduate*, the gender of the actor playing the main female role is the object of some self-referential banter, which raises doubts about the gender of the actor. When Poorlass learns that Zhang Xie has passed the exams, she goes to the capital to look for him. As she reaches the *yamen*, the gatekeepers have been ordered to block all women from entering the premises, so she announces that she is Zhang Xie's wife, at which point the guards, looking at her unbound feet, make jokes that could suggest she is being performed by a male actor. But we do not know if this is true—it also could be interpreted as a reflection of her peasant status. Furthermore, the play *A Playboy from a Noble House* included in the same volume as *Top Graduate* describes the life of a small troupe where the main attraction is the young female actress. The status of the two main roles (*sheng-dan*) informs us only that they are the main male and female roles in the troupe acting the main male and female characters. Because we do not know by what means they performed their characters, we cannot know what skills these roles required.

The creation of roles may have been conditioned to an extent by the demands of the stage, and in particular, for the actor's need for economy and efficiency of effort. Once theater begins to adapt longer narratives to the stage and increase the number of character types, troupes had to find ways to cope with the changes with a limited number of actors; thus, actors had to play more than one role. Presumably, actors were compelled to standardize and perfect their acting techniques, synthesizing into a symbolic form the gestures, speech, and facial design of their character groups. This synthesis of acting techniques transformed by actors into a series of norms and conventions became a role—a kind of shorthand people in the theater would understand as a means to facilitate performance and perhaps also, composition.

*Defining Roles* In its simplest definition, a role is a method of performance that mediates between the actor and the character on stage. One working definition of the term was advanced by Zeng Yongyi as follows:

> A role is just a sign that can only be expressed through the body of the actor costumed as a character. The role symbolizes the type and temperament that the character possesses. The role informs the actor of the artistic attainments he should have and his position in the troupe.

> 腳色:「只是一種符號, 必須通過演員對於劇中人物的扮飾才能顯現出來. 它對於劇中人物來說, 是象徵其所具備的類型和性質; 對於演員來說, 是說明其鎖應具備的藝術造詣和劇團中的地位.」 108

This definition is based both on roles as they appear in late Ming and Qing dynasty dramatic texts as well as on what we can now observe on-stage, and reflects a more elaborate description of roles than what we have in *Top Graduate*. The term we use for roles (*juese* 腳色 or *jiaose* 角色) first appears in *Top Graduate*. At the end of act 1, when the All Keys reaches its conclusion, the *mo* role, about to exit, states: "You performers (or 'roles' *juese*) backstage, boldly strike the drums to urge us on while the *moni* role gives us a dance" (後行腳色, 力齊鼓兒, 饒個擪掇, 末泥色饒個踏場). Here, the *sheng* main male role enters but not yet in character. The term *juese* originally referred to a short biographical sketch used by officials in the Song dynasty when they entered government service, at which point they noted their place of origin, ancestors for three generations, and their current place of residence. It is not clear how, however, it came to designate all the "roles" or performing members of a troupe, as it is hereafter understood.[109]

Roles mediate between the actor and the character the actor plays, and include three levels of performance: the actors, the roles, and the character. The relationships among these three levels of performance vary as the role system develops, but the dual actor-role, role-character, and character-actor already are evident in this play. In the above definition, the relationship between the actor and the role is one of skill: it refers to the sets of competences an actor needs to represent a certain character (or groups of characters with the same traits) on stage. The relationship between the role and the character, in contrast, is determined by how the role makes use of this set of acquired skills to represent the character (or type's) temperament. The skills learned by the role need to indicate whether it is a comic or serious role, its status in the troupe, and its relation to other roles and characters. Because the role represents the character in a symbolic manner, through its gestures, sounds, and words, it will inform the actor of the level of artistic achievement it needs to possess to perform the character. Character, in turn, is exemplified by human fact: it depicts gender (male or female), age (young or old), status (rich or poor), and disposition (good or bad). Because the role, with its synopses of techniques, acts as an intermediary between the actor and the character, the relationship of role to character is not the same as that of role to actor: the role has to play the character according to the techniques of the role. Because much of the role *is* technique, the relation between role and actor is not restrictive: a middle-age actor can perform the role of a young man, or a middle-age actress, that of an ingénue. The role skills, however, cannot be taken as absolute norms. Although they indicate how an actor has to play a character—its gait, dress, mask, singing manner, gestures, and so forth—the actor still needs to understand the character he is playing to represent it coherently. In *Top Graduate*, we see only the beginnings of this system and, at least with minor roles (the comics), it is clear that it is the role that informs the character.

Since the depiction of character in Chinese drama is not concerned with psychological depth, characters reflect exemplary models of human conduct, and display the most outstanding traits in a category of individuals. These traits are projected into a single individual (or a group) as absolute moral and social qualities. One good example in this play is the second male role (*mo*) who plays a large variety of characters. The main routine of this role is to play the wit alongside the two comic roles (*jing* and *chou*) who set up jokes while the *mo* caps them. This role maintains a distance (perhaps typical of the wit) with the comics, and it is also engaged in reflecting on and examining the actions of other characters in the play. Although the role has a double function as a wit and as an arbiter of morals, it is this last function, which serves to restrain and stabilize other roles and characters, that determines his performance. It is also how the role is perceived by the audience, and an occupation that the role will preserve well into later drama.[110] In other words, the relation of the actor to the *mo* role is one of form, and the relation of the *mo* role to the character, is one of content.[111]

Our assessment of the function of roles is necessarily limited because the information we can draw on this subject comes from the text itself, not from performance. We can only understand roles in *Top Graduate* through literary markers—their language and songs—and, with the exception of the two main roles, their continuous character change in the play. For instance, the wit the *mo* expresses, the repetition of his routine, and the omniscience of his remarks are all exemplified in each of the many characters he plays. We come to understand aspects of his performance technique through the uniformity of language and action he displays across the characters he plays. We are also given terse stage directions that add information about gestures (mime, acrobatics, and so on), and in moments of dramatic self-referentiality, allusions are made to the actor behind the role, or to the actor playing various roles. All these elements inform us of the nature of the role, but they do not inform us of how the roles were performed, what gestures or singing techniques they used, or the nature of their dress and face masks. In short, it is impossible to know whether these early performances were as stylized as those we see now on stage.

### *3. Comedy and the Comic Roles*

It is often stated that in the early Chinese literary and philosophical tradition, Confucian puritanism with its emphasis on the general seriousness of literature and its aversion to any form of frivolous pleasure, left little space for any form of humor. One reason for this is that earlier manifestations of comedy— whatever is laughable (*guji* 滑稽), can be jeered at or teased (*xue* 謔浪), or is made fun of—could subvert social formality, break down social order, and undermine the five cardinal human relations (*wulun* 五倫).[112] Because so much comedy is believed to be derisive, the immanent respect inherent in and expected from human relations (between lord and subject, or father and son, husband and wife, and so on) would be violated, allowing for a degree of familiarity considered inappropriate. Humor had the potential to destabilize the regulation of human emotions built-in in Confucian orthodoxy, which prescribed self-control and restraint as a means to guide emotions toward righteousness. In other words, ideally, proper decorum had to be maintained at all times.

Humor was also believed to be a sign of intellectual shallowness, and given that much popular literature includes a degree of farce, irony, and other aspects of comedy, agreement was widespread that the use of humor in novels and drama—genres considered to be inferior to poetry—reinforced their subordinate status. This attitude served only to increase the disdain by certain strata of the educated elite toward these art forms and dismissed these literary genres as unworthy of a scholar's attention. But these assumptions are only partially accurate. On one hand, the subtleties of each culture articulate different humorous expressions and respond to humor differently, some of which may be more universally understood. On the other, most of the so-called popular written genres in China were also the product of the educated elite.[113] Humor abounds both in the novel and drama, and was a requisite of southern plays and inherent to its structure, showing that these "inferior" genres were in fact an expansive and critical outlet for the elite.

*Top Graduate*, the first southern play, broadly shows the structural function of comedy as a means to balance the mood of the play. It is employed as a compensating tool between the moments of extreme pathos and the absurdly funny, to prevent the play from completely sliding into either an affective sphere and to become an overly somber piece or a long farce. Although comic scenes in *Top Graduate* abound, are often lengthy, and at times seem like bizarre insertions unrelated to the theme of the story, their comic power and dynamism manage to downplay, even trivialize, the ungrateful scholar theme. These scenes underplay the criticism directed at the scholar and the education system, and served, in practice, to diffuse potential political censorship; but comedy as an end in itself, also served to draw the audience's attention toward the representation of an otherwise-sensitive theme: a critique of the administrators employed by the state.

*Farce and Role Routine*   Comedy's aesthetic intent is both internal, to entertain the audience, providing respite from the more emotional and moralizing parts of the play, and external, to ease tensions in society at large. Comedy in *Top Graduate* is farcical, both verbal and physical, and has an unusually dominant role. Typically, the verbal repertoire makes use of the ambiguity of language, puns, homophones, quips on the formation of characters, and the formality of rhyme, riddles, onomatopoeia, and incongruity, both in the form of absurd remarks and discordant replies. It also makes use of scatological and gross humor and indulges the voracity of the sensual desires of the eternally insatiable comics. Its physical aspects include demonstration of skills with its abundance of boastfulness and consequent incompetence when putting ones claimed talent into practice, but also mime, and self-referential remarks to role-acting and costume. The verbal and physical aspects of farce both have an undeniable element of hostility and intimidation hidden from view by the immediacy and speed of comedy. Farce is also tangentially political, targeting the status quo of figures in power, as well as the intersecting realms of the divine and the human, where pleasure-seeking gods demand to satisfy their mundane desires in exchange for divine protection to the community.

Comic scenes are generally conducted by three roles: the clown *chou*, the comic *jing*, and the additional male role or *mo* who acts as intermediary. A specific dialogic routine is carried out between the *mo* role and one of the two comics (*jing* or *chou*) in which the *mo* is constantly responding or capping the jokes of one of the two other roles or, as is also often the case, restating the obvious. This routine is always the same and is repeated in scenes where the *mo* and one of the comics appear—for example, in all scenes between Grandma (*jing*) and Grandpa Li (*mo*), or the prime minister (*chou*) and his assistant (*mo*), as well as in the scenes in which the three comics appear together. The *mo* typically begins his response with "one can say that, . . ." (*youdao* 又道). From the exchanges between these two roles and the brevity of the sentences in the dialogue, the performance must have created a rhythmic effect, adding intensity to the comic dialogue, similar to modern day crosstalk (*xiangsheng* 相聲) comedy. Any time these roles appear together, their dialogues are based both on the nature of roles and the pattern of language. For example, in act 8, two merchants are climbing a mountain on their way to the capital to sell their wares. The *mo* merchant runs into the *jing* merchant who boasts of his fighting skills:

> *The robber runs onto the stage shouting:* Hey you! Stay where you are! *Mo traveler:* Yuchi blocks Shan Xiongxin![114] *Jing traveler:* Hey, you're the robber. *Mo traveler:* Don't give the game away! *The robber shouts:* You fifty men in the forest, no need to

come out, I'll handle them. *Mo traveler:* What a fine pair these two make! *Jing traveler:* And just who are you going to handle? *Robber:* I'll handle you. Come on, try to resist me! *Jing traveler:* So, you've come to rob our things! *Mo traveler:* Even *I* know that!

These exchanges do not include a punchline to the joke, at which point the audience conventionally would experience the disappointment of unrealized expectations. Rather, the *mo* conducts a contiguous commentary, not in dialogue with the comic, but directed away, to the audience or reader, making a reference to commonly known stories ("Yuchi blocks Shan Xiongxin!"), or restating the obvious ("Don't give the game away!" "What a fine pair these two make!" "Even *I* know that!").[115] This same routine between a comic and the *mo* role, applied throughout the play, divides the language of the roles in comic scenes into sequences of small segments without a collective semantic meaning. When these exchanges include a main male and female role, these serious roles are often alienated figures with little participation in the exchange.[116]

Although most of the comedy is verbal, much slapstick also is carried out by these same roles but more prominently, by the *jing* and the *chou* roles. For example, in two corresponding acts (24 and 28) the *jing-chou* duo, in a more aggressive performance, chase each other around the stage—the *jing* innkeeper asking the *chou* student to pay her the rent. In a mirroring scene underlining the mechanical nature of physical farce, the *jing* bookseller demands that the *chou* Xiao'er pay him for the examination result booklet he has just purchased. Reproducing the same routine shows the formulaic nature of the structure of comedy, but the proximity of the scenes, the use of the same roles, and similar language suggests that the authors toyed with the similarities of act structure and composition to make them resonate with each other. These scenes also expose the hierarchy between the two comic roles. Although, on the surface, these two roles seem evenly paired—they undertake similar characters and exhibit a similar array of self-indulgent tendencies—the uniformity of characters of the *jing* role contrasts with the unusual importance attributed to the characters played by the *chou* role. This indicates not only that a hierarchy existed between these roles—the *chou* being the lowliest—but also that the stability of the *jing* role was due to a seniority that may have originated in the earlier *jing–mo* pair. These two roles are the genuine taboo breakers and the ones that hold a social mirror to the basest human inclinations and desires—gluttony, sex, greed, vulgarity, indolence, and aggressiveness—and also embody them. On the surface, the roles poke fun at social inhibitions and conventions, invert social status, and generally allow for moments of release, but they also present the audience with the uncomfortable reality of human passion: that base human inclinations are inherent in our very nature.[117] Thus, one medium by which the audience understands the import of curbing improper human passions is the restraining function exerted by the role of the *mo*, who continuously reminds the crowd of the comic roles' ill-judged and foolish actions.

The *mo* has a standard routine he carries out with the other comic as a temperate wit. This role is not always paired with a *jing* or a *chou* and can remain a neutral or mediating role, commenting on the idiocy of the comics ("You never reflect on your own faults"), revealing his judgment on the actions of other roles, including the main ones (when Zhang Xie rejects the prime minister's daughter), and settling disputes between the serious roles (when Zhang Xie beats Poorlass). A kind of rational detachment—a voice of reason—gives this role an authority over other roles and over the play in general. By capping or commenting on the jokes and antics of the comics, he shows his superior wit and keeps the farce within permissible limits. By commenting on the baseness of other characters' actions, he informs the audience of the alternative correct ethical behavior. And by alluding to the internal workings of the theater, he reminds the audience of the theater's illusory nature. The *mo*'s comments, directed at the audience, place the role at the threshold between the theater and its viewers; between drama's intended act of deception and the real world of the spectators; and, most important, between containment and release. His continuous commentary on the antics of the comics incorporates the audience into the role's viewpoint and compels it into assimilating his position. Thus, although the audience laughs with complicity at the tomfoolery of the comic's representation of human imperfection—our collective imperfection—the *mo* at the threshold reminds the spectators that these actions are socially proscribed. The *mo* is the most orthodox of roles, the one that reins in the comedy, and establishes and insures reasonable moral standards in the theater.

*Metatheater and the Absurd*    In addition to this formulaic farcical nature of the play, theatrical self-referentiality, although used sparingly by comparison, is also part of the comic spirit of the play. Metatheater is employed throughout the play both as humor—perhaps intended as a parody of the object under consideration—and also to underscore the fictional nature of the theater. The most conspicuous instance of this gimmick is an ingenious break away from what seems to be theatrical convention: the play makes use of the lowliest role, the *chou*, to perform the character with the highest status, the Military Commissioner Wang Deyong. This upending of role and status is effective both as an irreverent parody of power and as a mechanism of comedy. This is possible without giving offense because Wang is portrayed as a positive character, even though his principal comic trait is the "absurd."

Both the inversion of role and character and the nature of the comic routine this role plays are entirely absurd. To every situation Wang responds by reversing logic, overturning expectations, displaying irreverence, and parading the absurdity of life: he sits on top of his assistant when he cannot find a chair; he condemns his daughter for killing the fleas in his jacket as an act contrary to Buddhist dictates; when Zhang Xie introduces himself for the first time, Wang ignores his attempts at politeness and answers with gibberish; and when his daughter has just died, he makes absurd remarks to his assistant. In sum, Wang's distinctive comedy pushes at the limits of rational thinking and common sense, and although the inversion of role and character clearly display a calculated irreverence toward the structures of power, it is not a political critique, and it does not seem intended to be a social corrective because Wang is a moral figure. The apolitical interpretation is also sheltered by the very nature of the theater—by the inherent qualities of the role that is expected to act thus, and by the repeated allusions to the deceptive and fictional nature of the theater. This is also the case in the representation of the divine world, a parody not of religious ideas and practices, but of the gods themselves, whose cravings for the pleasures of the mundane world fit perfectly into the disposition of the comic roles.

Multiple references to the inner workings of the theater appear across the play, including the division between the actor and role (act 35) or the limitations of roles that play multiple characters (act 16), or of theatrical composition when Commissioner Wang asks his assistant to call his wife and child, and the assistant describes his journey to the inner quarters in words, without moving an inch (act 21). Thus, on the surface, comedy in *Top Graduate* may subvert social formality, but underneath, it works in consensus with established values and does not break the social order.

## 4. Music

*Introduction*    In the introduction to *Top Graduate*, the *mo* role entices an audience to watch a play performed by a troupe of aficionados that promises to creatively entertain them. Because the story was familiar to the audience, the incentive the prologue proposes to attract the public is a rescripted comic routine and an improved musical program set to standards comparable to the Imperial Music Bureau. Musical proficiency is clearly one of the measures the troupe has to demonstrate to attract a crowd.[118] But the music of theater is plagued by the same problems of ephemerality and transmission—since music was transmitted orally, from master to student, and playwrights and musicians did not have an adequate means of notation, all we have left from this medium are the song forms as they appear in the plays, anthologies, and song formularies. One look at *Top Graduate* or any later southern dramatic text will immediately inform us of the importance of music and of its structural organization: texts are largely a collection of single songs and song suites interspersed with (mostly comic in our case) dialogue and declamatory pieces written in parallel prose. Still, these texts reveal nothing of the aural nature of the song, rendering a reconstruction of what the music actually sounded like with any precision impossible. Thus, the following discussion derives from the few scattered materials that discuss the southern musical culture of the times.

The earliest sources we have on any aspect of dramatic performance deal mostly with the performance of song. One of the earliest treatises is the *Discussion on Singing* written by the obscure Yuan musicologist Yannan Zhi'an. Although this text is mostly an informative inventory of terms and has little practical value for singing instruction, it was appended to almost every major commentary on drama beginning with the well-known work by Zhou Deqing, who included it in his *Rhymes of the Central Plain*. The *Discussion* is a short collection of twenty-six entries that mainly catalog terms related to aspects of song and singing. The core of the entries addresses types of voice modulation, breathing, rhythm in song, parts of a melody, types of singers, types of song alternation, types of mistakes made when singing, and so forth. It also identifies song by region, quantifies categories of singers, enumerates occasions and topics for singing, and spells out some taboos and rules of etiquette, such as the following:[119]

Taboo in singing: Amateurs do not sing the songs of professionals, or dandies sing popular ditties; men do not sing love songs, nor women sing heroic/manly tunes; southerners do not sing northern songs (*qu*) or northerners southern ones (*ge*).

凡歌之所忌: 子弟不唱作家歌, 浪子不唱及時曲; 男不唱艷詞, 女不唱雄曲; 南人不曲, 北人不歌.[120]

The *Discussion* is not directly relevant to the practice and execution of song—it does not teach singing—but its categories display a concern with the phonological aspects of song performance and its articulation: enunciation, tones, the relation of tone to melody, the length of words, and the combinations of sounds. It also names breathing techniques, and some elements of linguistic prosody, such as pitch, intonation, rhythm, and pause. All these elements became foremost in the study of what we refer to as the "music" of drama.[121] This concern for song performance is reflected, too, in a second source mentioned earlier: song formularies compiled later to assist theater aficionados in song writing. These formularies designed as guiding manuals for song composition included much of the information on the music of song. The best collections incorporated the mode, the title of the song, and the song structure, and provided prosodic and phonological models for playwrights as well as guidelines for composition and rhetoric. The earliest of these southern song formularies, the so-called *Nine Mode Formulary* (*Jiugong pu* 九宮譜) and the *Thirteen Mode Formulary* (*Shisandiao pu* 十三調譜) appeared in the fourteenth century, at roughly the same time as the better known northern counterpart Zhou Deqing's, *Rhymes of the Central Plain*. Although the earlier *Nine* and *Thirteen* are no longer extant, they formed the basis of the *Old Edition of the Southern Nine Mode Formulary* (*Jiubian nan-jiugong pu* 舊編南九宮譜) composed by the Suzhou scholar Jiang Xiao 蔣孝 (Jinshi 1544), who was committed to explaining the fundamental importance of harmonizing tones and music, to correct the phonological and prosodic mistakes in the composition of southern song, and to match the music to string and wind instruments.[122] As noted, the very best of its kind is the meticulous product of the Qing scholars Niu Shaoya and Xu Qingqing's *Yuan Formulary of the Correct Original Nine Southern Modes*, which included not just the modes and tune titles, but every part of the song, including the number of lines to a song, words to a line, the tones and rhymes, and the singing particularities of each song. In addition, the original provenance of the song and its authorship were all spelled out with extreme detail.[123] Still, despite all the information these formularies provide, although we can understand much of the phonological and prosodic elements of song composition, we cannot reconstruct the music and do not know how they sounded.

One final source of information on music comes from random bits of information included in scholarly notebook collections (*biji* 筆記). These notes, often critical and judgmental, provide information even if cryptic, on the nature of the music, its variants, and its impact in society. So, let me begin with two examples drawn from these collections.

*Random Notes on Music*   Among the earliest pieces of information on southern dramatic music, we have a comment by the Jiangsu official Lu Rong 陸容 (1436–1494) who states, in one of the few entries on music culture in his *Records from the Bean Garden* (*Shuyuan zaji* 菽園雜記), the following:

> [The people of] Haiyan[124] in Jiaxing, Yuyao in Shaoxing, Cixi in Ningbo, Huangyan in Taizhou and Yongjia in Wenzhou, all have the habit of practicing to become actors, and are called "The Brotherhood of Xiwen [Southern Drama]." Although these are scions of good families, they are not ashamed of performing it.

> 嘉興之海鹽, 紹興之餘姚, 寧波之慈谿, 臺州之黃岩, 溫州之永嘉, 皆有習為優者, 名曰: 「戲文子弟」, 雖良家子不恥為之.[125]

Lu's note is the closest in time we have on the musical tendencies occurring in the southeast a few years after *Top Graduate* was published. He is also the first to note that Wenzhou was one region where they practiced this type of drama (*xiwen*) and to assert that it was performed by amateur troupes. This same claim is made in the second song to the introduction (act 1) of *Top Graduate* by the *mo* role: "Although we are sons of good families, we can do it all." Whether this was the norm, or a sporadic hobby of the scions of the elite, or whether *xiwen* were performed only by the sons of the elite or also employed actors, we do not know.

A little later, we find a snappish comment by the mid-Ming Jiangsu scholar Zhu Yunming, already removed from *Top Graduate* by about seventy years. In a section on song writing, Zhu complained of the changes wrought on southern music, suggesting that certain musical and singing conventions were being disregarded in favor of a new musical fashion.

[Works of southern drama] are now found everywhere, but they have changed and are no longer the same as before. Moreover, their singing has become increasingly absurd and I find that watching or listening to them is extremely annoying. They have already lost all notes, pitches, manner of singing, and the modes. Idiotic people and stupid musicians change the music as they like, absurdly styling it the musical airs of Yuyao, or Haiyan, or Yiyang or Kunshan and so on. They change the vocal manner [of the singers] and hurriedly pursue changes in modulations, inventing in all manner of ways. Indeed what utter nonsense! If they set it to wind and string instruments, one must laugh in spite of oneself. Yet ignorant gentlemen secretly delight in it, but they are mutually deceiving themselves.

今遍滿四方, 轉轉改益, 又不如舊. 而哥唱愈繆, 極厭觀聽, 蓋已略無音, 律, 腔, 調 (*yin, lü, qiang, diao*). 愚人蠢工, 狥意更變, 妄名餘姚腔, 海鹽腔, 弋陽腔, 崑山腔之類, 變易喉舌, 趨逐抑揚, 杜撰百端, 真胡說耳. 若以被之管弦, 必至失笑, 而昧士傾喜之, 互為自謾爾.[126]

Although Zhu's grievances tell us as much about the changes that were happening in southern dramatic song as they reveal about his avowed northern musical preferences, his note raises three issues that are still relevant to dramatic historiography: (1) it shows that new modes of southern theater were disrupting preexisting musical conventions (including a vocalizing manner); (2) it notes the vigor of local trends in musical theater and the visceral musical and cultural differences and affiliations between north and south; and (3) it implies that southern drama was an *a cappella* style of singing, with no instrumental accompaniment. Although these questions are pertinent in creating a coherent narrative of early southern drama, our dearth of information does not make it feasible to conduct detailed examination. Yet even these paltry findings can give an idea of the dominant tension in musical culture at the time: the friction between those who sided with the more formal and regulated northern dramatic music and the bourgeoning unconventional southern dramatic music not subject to the same prosodic and musical conventions.

Zhu was a scholar and well-known calligrapher from Suzhou who tried repeatedly to pass the imperial exams without success. The objection and exasperation he expressed in his note is aimed at the changes wrought by the contemporary performances of works of southern drama on conventions that seem to have been established on the northern popular musical standards of the Jin and Yuan dynasties. In a footnote inserted following the terms *yin, lü, qiang*, and *diao*, Zhu explains each of the four terms:

> The notes are the seven notes, the tones are the twelve tones. The vocalization (*qiang*, literally the oral cavity) refers to the number of words (*zi*) in a song structure, the length of each word, the pitch and speed [at which the words are delivered], and the modulation of sound; each has its order. The modes [*diao*] refer to the old eighty-four modes and the latter seventy-seven modes. Today only eleven remain. The *zhenggong* cannot be placed in the same category as the *zhonglü*. Of these four, not one can be incomplete.

音者七音, 律者十二律呂. 腔者, 章句字數, 長短, 高下, 疾徐, 抑揚之節, 各有部位. 調者, 舊八十四調, 後七十七宮調. 今十一調, 正宮不可為中呂之類. 此四者無一不具.[127]

We cannot know how well-versed Zhu was in musical theory, but his terminology in this note is more appropriate of music officials in the Imperial Music Bureau than of someone making cursory comments on contemporary music. The seven notes and the twelve tones (sometimes called pitches) refer to the five basic notes of the pentatonic scale, which later added two semi-tones; and the twelve tones refer to the twelve fundamental notes originally created from twelve bamboo reeds cut to different lengths and thicknesses. The combination of the seven notes and the twelve pitches created the modes (*gongdiao* 宮調), which Zhu calls the "old eighty-four keys/modes."[128] The notes and tones refer, respectively, to the notes on a scale and the harmonization of song. What the modes precisely refer to at this stage is unclear, but it was clearly a distinctive element of northern music. In a preface to an edition of Zhou Deqing's *Rhymes of the Central Plain*, Zhu reinforces his dislike for southern dramatic singing styles by admitting the pleasure he takes in (northern) music, confessing the difficulties of northern song composition, and restating his disapproval of contemporary musical trends emerging from the southeast: "Unfortunately, there are also the tunes of the Wenzhou and Zhejiang southern drama (*xiwen*) of the Southern Song—only sounds of chirruping birds. Where indeed is their melody?" (不幸又有南宋溫折戲文之調, 殆禽噪耳, 其調果在何處?)[129] Zhu's gloss on musical terms seems incongruously theoretical, as if drawn from a music handbook to validate his allegiance to a northern style of music. But it also underlines the lingering preference for northern song we find in other southern playwrights a few years later.

*North and South* The dichotomy between northern and southern music expressed in Zhu Yunming's statement, almost a century after the fall of the Yuan, is still present in the mid-sixteenth century and can be partially if superficially understood through Xu Wei's *Record of Southern Song-Lyrics*. In his *Record*, Xu pointed out the cultured elite's particular attachment to northern drama and compared it with the high prestige the office in charge of foreign music in the Tang dynasty had enjoyed. He also noted the preference by the court music institutions at the time, for music manuals from Kucha (Qiuci 龜茲 in modern-day Xinjiang) over the more traditional Han music, and concluded by comparing it to the present moment, noting that "today's northern song-drama still ranks higher than southern music."[130] Xu blamed this widespread enduring fashion for northern music on the ignorance of those intent on accommodating the pleasures of the political and intellectual elite's preference for northern musical culture.[131] The nature of the music, or at least how different music affected listeners is described in the concluding paragraph to Xu's essay:

> Listening to northern tunes (song-drama) makes one feel imposing and powerful and causes one's hair to stand on end. It's enough to build one's determination to proceed with courage. Truly, "barbarians" excelled at rousing anger. What is called: "Its sounds are pressing and inhibited in order to manifest their resentment" exemplifies it. Southern tunes (song-drama) are slow paced and leisurely, flowing and meandering, elating people who thoughtlessly abandon their composure. Truly, this is the gentle charm of the south. What is called "The sounds of the fallen state induce thoughts of sorrow," exemplifies it.

> 聽北曲使人神氣鷹揚, 毛髮洒淅, 足以作人勇往之志, 信胡人之善於鼓怒也, 所謂「其聲嘺殺以立怨」是已. 南曲則纡徐綿, 流麗婉轉, 使人飄飄然喪其所守而不自覺, 信南方的柔媚也, 所謂「亡國之音哀以思」是也.[132]

Xu's contrast of the fierce barbarian with the sorrowful sounds of a state in decadence contains political undertones that seem to condemn both the martial nature of northern musical culture, as well as an excessive self-indulgence of the southern one. His comparison of northern and southern musical trends can be read as a reflection of historical fact—as a metaphorical denunciation of the moral degradation of society whose political and military neglect had resulted, in the past, in the intrusion of the northern cultures to the annihilation of the genuine Han culture. This tone of resentment is also a call for literati to engage in what he considered to be the legitimate inheritor of Han culture, southern culture, and southern music. It was Xu's means of validating southern music and appeal to the southern literary elite to use this dramatic form as a viable instrument of their creativity.

Conversely, Zhu Yunming's seems like a genuine rejection of popular southern dramatic traditions, not the antiquarian's pose intended to display political allegiances. His rejection applied not just to musical melody, but to the manner of singing— vocalization or *qiang*—and, by extension, the language. The term *qiang* is generally used to refer to the correct enunciation of a word (*zi*), as well as to the tonal effect of the word, the speed of delivery and the modulation of voice.[133] But when the term is associated with a specific locality, *qiang* refers to the distinctive style and flavor of singing—the merging of the tone and enunciation of local language with the music—of the particular place it is associated with. Thus, a *qiang* or vocalization manner, its language, prosody (tone and rhyme), and phonology are all closely associated with the language and identity of a place. Zhu's complaint was not just directed toward the musical changes but also toward the emerging southeastern local singing styles—styles he considered unorthodox, perhaps even improper—and that soon were to become one of the distinguishing features of dramatic differentiation. These styles were closely tied to the culture of the place.[134] Clearly, regional singing dramatic styles in local languages were eclipsing an earlier, possibly more structured and northern-based singing style, and this was not to Zhu's taste.[135]

*The Four Regional Musical Styles*   The musical airs of Yuyao, Haiyan, Yiyang, and Kunshan were distinctive local musical and vocalizing styles. These are now known collectively as the "Four Vocalizing Styles of Southern Theater" (*Nanxi sida shengqiang* 南戲四大聲腔), a term coined in the 1980s as part of a larger attempt to understand the complexities of regional theaters in China. But what we know about these vocalizing styles, with the exception of the Kun singing, which has been better documented, is very little.[136] As a matter of fact, we are still not even sure in what language these songs were sung. For example, the late-Ming scholar Gu Qiyuan 顧起元 (1565–1628) pointed out that the Haiyan style was popular in Zhejiang and was performed in—or at least included much of—official mandarin language or a local modification thereof: "Haiyan makes use of an abundance of official language and it is used [in performance] by people in in both capitals"(海鹽多官語, 兩京人用之).[137] Because the official language was the means of communication of the educated elite and the imperial administration, performances carried out in this language would be understood by officials and educated men from other parts of the empire serving in the region. This remained the preferred mode of performance for official banquets until the Kun style outclassed it. Yiyang, in contrast, was sung in local language, and was popular among the local gentry and the people. Gu seemed not too pleased with the use of local language when he noted: "Yiyang wrongly employs local language and the gentry in all quarters takes pleasure in it" (弋陽則錯用鄉語, 四方士客喜閱之).[138] Over time, aficionados

have confirmed the use of local language in southeastern theater. For example, Zhou Deqing in the Yuan already pointed
out that in the area around Hangzhou, performances of drama-
texts (*xiwen*), such as *Lechang Splits the Mirror in Half*, followed
southern rhyme schemes.[139] This was reiterated by the imperial
prince and drama aficionado Zhu Quan 朱權 (1378–1448) when
in the preface to his 1398 *Qionglin yayun* 瓊林雅韻序, a rhyme
dictionary for northern song-drama, he stated the difficulty of
understanding southern dialects: "In the north there are no dialects, but the widespread southern drama of Wu (Jiangsu) and
Yue (Zhejiang) . . . all make use of local dialects and these are
called Yi languages. They are also called 'shrike tongues' [i.e.,
unintelligible languages]. If they are not translated, they cannot
be understood" (北方無鄉談而在南戲流傳的吳, 越 . . . 之地
皆有鄉談, 謂之彝語, 謂之鳩舌, 非譯不通).[140] And this was
corroborated again when scholars would translate the plays for
their own entertainment, as in the case of the late Ming, Zhejiang scholar Chen Maoren 陳懋仁 (after 1606), who noted that
wealthy families from Quanzhou kept their own troupes and
trained them: "But because they use local language and I cannot
understand what they are saying, I tried to translate [their plays]
for fun but I did not keep them"(然皆土腔,不曉所謂,余嘗戲譯
之而不存也).[141] Local-language theater never fades, but in this
region, or at least among the cultured elite, a hybrid form mixing northern and southern musical features began to take shape
and eventually became the dominant musical form. The bulk of
our dramatic literature from the seventeenth century onward is
mostly in this form.[142] Kun drama is the result of its long history
and practice in the region—it adapted its music to string instruments and its singing and speaking were both heavily influenced
by Wu phonology but with mandarin vocabulary.[143] In short, this
arrangement, for which the southerners could stand by musical

northern ideals but sing with southern softness, became the preferred dramatic style of the elite all the way to the nineteenth
century.

Although southern theater is native to the southeast, and
*Top Graduate* its earliest extant play, *Top Graduate* is not written in local dialect and makes little use of local dialect even in
the spoken and comic parts in which it is later conventionally
used.[144] One reason for this relative lack of dialect could be that
our version of the play was edited to be included in an imperial
encyclopedia, but it is also possible that this type of theater was
produced in larger cities and intended for a literate and semi-
literate group versed in a form of standardized vernacular. The
register of language both in the spoken and sung parts is very
close to a spoken vernacular and, occasionally, sprinkled with
local dialect. *Top Graduate* also makes extensive use of proverbs
and idiomatic expressions—nuggets of folk wisdom voiced by all
characters at different times (but which predominate in the lines
uttered by the *mo* role) that often carry a value judgment to some
past or future action. These judicious axioms add color and spice
to the dialogue of the play and give it a distinctive sense of a
shared cultural background, but not specifically local or regional.
On the contrary, these popular sayings encourage prudence and
would have been understood by all.[145]

*Music Accompaniment*   Finally, the matter of whether or not
early southern theater was accompanied by musical instrumentation remains, to this day, a matter of debate. In *Top Graduate*,
when the main male role enters the stage, he requests the
troupe to play an overture. But, it seems, not all southern theater included instrumental accompaniment—Zhu Yunming
deplored attempts of regional music to set their songs to string
or wind instruments, suggesting like other early aficionados,

that southern theaters were sung *a cappella*. Southern music is often described as sung only to the beat of a clapper or a fan. For example, as Yang Shen 楊慎 (1488–1559) writes, "Southern sung poems are not accompanied by wind or string instruments and do not have musical norms (i.e., musical modes), just like the *Yiyang* musical style. This has been so since the Tang and Song dynasties."[146] (南方歌詞, 不入管弦, 亦無腔調,[147] 如今弋楊腔也. 蓋自唐, 宋已如此.) And his contemporary Lu Cai 陸采 (1497–1537) observed the popularity of southern song and its singular *a cappella* nature:

> At the beginning of our (Ming) dynasty, there was a certain Liu, head of a [music] section in the Imperial Music Bureau. Because our founding emperor liked southern music, Liu created new music that could be sung. Because the new music adhered a little more to the various keys/modes than the music from Zhejiang, it was popular in the southern capital (Nanjing) until today. But recently the songs of Zhejiang have been gaining popularity, and female singers have abandoned the northern style for the southern. Still, no string music can be attached [to their songs].
>
> 國初教坊有劉色長者, 以太祖好南曲, 別制新腔歌之, 比浙音稍合宮調, 故南都至今傳之. 近始尚浙音, 伎女輩或棄北而南, 然終不可入弦索也.[148]

These occasional lines of information, however, do not provide what form of southern theater they are referring to. The terms *xiwen* and *nanxi* were used very generally for the southeastern region from the Yuan onward, yet the music and language of Wenzhou is very different from the language of Fujian. The confusion becomes greater when we realize that *Top Graduate*'s introduction emphasizes both instrumentation and the switching of *Keys and Modes*.[149] Thus, despite the information we have on the language of performance or the music of theater, all we have left is the music structure as it appears in the play.

*The Musical Structure of* **Top Graduate**   All drama in China is regional and local from its inception, and its earliest mode of differentiation has been "musical": it is based on its vocalization mode, and this includes both the local language, the melody used in the song and the manner of singing.[150] Because at the heart of the song is the natural musicality inherent in local language, phonology (enunciation, tones and the relation of tone to melody, length of words, and the combinations of sounds) together with some elements of linguistic prosody, such as pitch, intonation, rhythm, and pause, are all part of what we call the "music" of song.[151] As a matter of fact, most early treatises on the "music" of Chinese drama are largely concerned with the performance of song, that is, the manner of singing, its enunciation and rhythm.

Given the importance of pronunciation and cadences of language, an original Wenzhou musical style based on local language and musical preferences must have existed.[152] Furthermore, because Wenzhou (and Yongjia) is considered to be the cradle of southern drama—both its earliest play *Top Graduate*, as well as its canonical play *The Lute*, were composed here—its form, which makes use of songs and song suites to tell the story, also has become the model for early southern drama.[153]

*Origins of Song Titles*   Scholars have looked into the composition of *Top Graduate* and traced the titles and at times the structures of the songs to verify Xu Wei's claim—that southern drama was a mixture of Song dynasty song-lyrics and popular song. But beginning with Qian Nanyang, they have repeatedly come to the conclusion that although many of the songs do indeed originate in the Song dynasty song-lyric (*ci*-poems), as well as other traditions, the so-called songs from the alleyways account for very few. Of course, the song arrangement could have been revised by imperial editors, but this would have meant adapting and rewriting a great deal of the play. Of the 168 songs included in this play[154] the majority of the song titles can be traced back to the Song dynasty song-lyrics (sixty), but also are found in the Song and Jin dynasties All Keys (twenty-seven), and Tang and Song Music Bureau songs (seventeen). The rest can be traced to the Extended Melodies (*daqu*) of the Tang and Song (nine), Tang dynasty songs (seven), songs also found in Song dynasty *changzhuan* medleys (three), and some coexist with northern plays (five).[155] There are, by some accounts, twelve, and by others twenty, popular songs, or rather, songs that cannot be found elsewhere.[156] In *Top Graduate*, not much attention is paid to the tones showing that, perhaps, the lyrics were intended to fit the music.

*No Keys and Modes*   Our earliest information on the specifics of the structure of southern drama appears quite late, but we know from Xu Wei's *Records* that southern drama did not make use of key/modes (*buxie gongdiao* 不協宮調): "I do not know who conceived the nine keys. I expect it must have been someone from the Music Bureau at the beginning of this dynasty; they are most nonsensical and ridiculous" (今南九宮不知出 於何人, 意亦國初教坊人所為, 最為無稽可笑).[157] A criticism he repeated often in his short text, specifying that modal classification was an alien artificial construction added by literati to southern musical forms.

His disapproval is often paired with what he considered to be the origins of southern drama: "Its arias are but Song dynasty *ci*-lyrics with added popular songs from the alleyways that do not harmonize with the *gong* and *diao* keys and modes, thus gentlemen rarely pay attention to them" (其曲, 則宋人詞而益以里巷歌謠, 不叶宮調, 故士夫罕有留意者).¹⁵⁸ And later: "When Yongjia *zaju* flourished, it was created from the small songs of the villages. Originally they had no [fixed] keys and modes, rarely a [fixed] rhythm and were simply taken from the casual songs sung by farmers and market girls. What is popularly called 'melodies that follow one's heart,' is it [not] the same skill?" (永嘉雜劇 興, 則又即村坊小曲而為之, 本無宮調, 亦罕節奏, 徒取其畸農, 市女順口可歌而已, 諺所為 "隨心令," 即其技歟?).¹⁵⁹

Having keys and modes was clearly part of the prestige of music, and songs that adhered to musical norms were superior to those (southern ones) that did not. But southern theater is said to make no use of keys and modes, and these are never indicated. Because we do not really know what value the modes had at the time—although perhaps by this time not musical—we cannot understand fully what Xu was reacting to. It is possible that "keys and modes" were used as some inherited form of official musical or phonological arrangement, to formalize or homogenize music, or maybe as a means to standardize rhyme and tonal schemes, something comparable to what the Yuan scholar Zhou Deqing claimed in his *Rhymes* when he stated that one reason for composing his manual was to teach the correct (central) tonal patterns of song composition (*zhengsheng* 正聲) to amateur songwriters "to cleanse the base customs of the southeast" (一洗東南習俗之陋).¹⁶⁰ They did, however, imply some form of "musical" categorization for song classification, as I mentioned earlier.

Xu's essay was written with the intention of establishing southern drama as an independent musical genre and detaching it from the notion that southern drama derived from an earlier northern tradition, so the lack of keys and modes also meant a freedom from the normative strictures these keys and modes seem to have involved. Xu embraced the simplicity of southern drama and aimed to establish a popular origin for this tradition. Thus, whatever their function, keys and modes were not inherent to southern drama and not part of the authentic nature of the genre.

*Music Units* The smallest unit of music in *Top Graduate* is a song, and like later southern drama, a play is an organized collection of songs, interspersed with dialogue and sporadic poetic recitation. Each song is called a *qupai* 曲牌 (literally, "titled song"), which refers to the title as well as the relatively fixed song structure of that song, and includes a specific number of lines, words ($zi$) to a line, and preestablished prosodic norms of tone and rhyme.[161] The *qupai* as song is a literary and musical unit that often originated elsewhere first. The standard explanation of the origin of these song-titles is that they came from earlier songs or poems of other dynasties. And there are a variety of explanations for the adaptation of music to song or song to music. On the basis of the preexisting nature of song patterns, we consider two options for music composition: either music is composed and adapted to the song, or a song is composed to a preexistent musical pattern. Most scholars believe this was the case in *Top Graduate*, and yet this does not explain the provenance of many of the song structures. The fact is that both processes—setting a song to new music or fitting a song to an existing tune—are difficult when adapting music to established song patterns, and composers took many liberties: the formal pattern of the song—the number of lines, the words to a line as well as the tones and the rhyme—were sometimes respected, but other times, the difficulty of setting fixed patterns to new music resulted in the use of additional filler words inserted (*chenzi* 襯字): the words helped the flow of the melody and could make the meaning clearer, but the pattern changed.[162] In some cases, the title of the song and its structure match with, for example, the original composition of a song-lyric; more often, however, the adaptation could entail changes so great to the pattern of the song that the only recognizable part of the earlier song was the title.

The songs are arranged in sequences of songs typically divided into three parts: a prelude (*yinzi* 引子), one or more middle songs (*guoqu* 過曲), and a coda (*weisheng* 尾聲). This is the form most southern drama takes and is commonly known as *qupai ti* (literally, "titled-song structure").[163] But the variations to this organization are many: a series of different tunes; one tune used repeatedly; one tune used repeatedly but changing the first two lines (*huantou* 換頭); a repetition of suite patterns; or mixing tunes with suites among other variations. Although no clear norm or limitations to the organization of song suites is apparent, Xu Wei claims that a certain harmony was to be observed:

> The arrangement of tunes in a suite must be carried out according to a proximity of sound. Among them they should all belong to the same class and these cannot be mixed up. For example *Huangyin'er* is followed by *Cuyu lin*, and *Zhoumei xu* is followed by *Diliu zi*; they have a natural fixed order. Composers can observe [this order] in older tunes and just have to respect it.

> 然曲隻之次第, 須用聲相鄰以為一套. 其間亦自有類輩, 不可亂也, 如 (黃鶯兒) 則繼之以 (簇御林), (畫眉序) 則繼之以 (滴溜子) 之類, 自有一定之序, 作者觀於舊曲而遵之可也.[164]

What is the proximity of sound? And what does it mean to belong to the same class? Are they the same key and mode even when southern drama did not have keys and modes? Some form of organization based on the musical features? Or based on the rhyme? Or were they simply following the organization of former times? Fifty years in the life of a musical performance, especially in the midst of changing fashions, is a very long time. By the time Xu Wei wrote his defense of southern drama, the music used by southern dramatic forms was not quite yet the literary Kun style that would become the dominant form, but also it no longer was the music that made this play popular enough to be included in an imperial collectanea.

Thus, music was not the only element changing in these plays—song arrangement, prosody, and rhyme were, in Xu Wei's time, all in the midst of a radical alteration to a new mode of singing that eventually would be adopted by the elite and would change dramatic history for ever. *Top Graduate* provides a rare glimpse into a moment in the formation of Chinese drama. The overarching structure determined by the plot of the story, the division in acts and scenes, the roles and the general music structure was gradually refined, but generally prevailed.

## CONCLUSION

In sum, the translation of *Top Graduate* that follows is based on the text transcribed in the early fifteenth century. It is a snapshot of a play that already had no doubt undergone many decades of change. The nature of theater, in which a play is constantly adapted by writers, musicians, and actors in response to different audiences, makes attempting to date the text with precision a fool's errand. That said, for our first full extant play in the tradition, the text is remarkably coherent and sophisticated, suggesting just how much must have come before it, however fragmentary the evidence. *Top Graduate* reflects a stage in the long tradition of balancing scenes of different tone and intention, of the development of the story of the ungrateful scholar, of the creation of a distinctive set of roles used to play a plethora of characters, of experiments in language register, and in the formation of standards of music. As such, despite the difficulties of fleshing out any of these key theatrical components, *Top Graduate*, since its discovery in a London bookstore a hundred years ago, has rightly earned its place as a central text in our understanding of the foundations of Chinese theater.

# TOP GRADUATE ZHANG XIE

*By the Nine Mountain Society*

## THEME

Scholar Zhang leaves for Chang'an to sit for the imperial exams.
Poorlass Wang suffers from hunger and cold in the old temple.
The foolish Xiao'er makes a crude display of wind and moon.[1]
A fierce robber wreaks havoc on Wuji Mountain.

## ACT 1

*The* MO[2] *enters and declaims:*
(*Shuidiao getou*)
The passing of youth hastens the onset of white hair,
and time dims our rosy cheeks.
Our lives float by,
like duckweed stems drifting east and west.
On the path, reds and purples contend;
outside the window, orioles chirp and swallows warble,
while fallen flowers fill the empty hall.
But such is the way of the world,
so, what is the use of toil and fret?

Although we are sons of good families,
we can do it all:
we are equally versed in the plucking of strings and the blowing
    of pipes,
and even sing of the moon and jest with the wind.[3]
We are especially good at inserting comic skits and cracking jokes,
and we are not stingy with the white powder and lime,
so, our songs fill the hall with laughter.
Yes, exactly like the Yangzi with its thousand-foot rolling waves,
we have our own particular style of performance.

*Declaims again*:
(*Manting fang*)
Let this hubbub rest for a while,
hold your laughing banter,
and fix your attention on this distinctive tradition.
We play in the style of the Music Bureau,[4]
and are really comparable to the Crimson and Green.[5]
We promise to entertain you with our endless flow of songs and
    jokes;
all of you will marvel at our disquisitions.
We are in no way the same
as those upstarts who follow us,
and who vaunt their unearned fame.
Your people have performed the *Biography of Top Graduate*
    *Zhang Xie*,
and performed it successfully.
But this writing group
aspires to snatch the first prize.
We have complete command over the grand events of Wenzhou,
and in a *chantefable*[6] we'll sing their origins for you.
At the sound of the gong,

gentlemen please settle down,
and listen attentively to our story.

*Sings*:
(*Fengshi chun*)
Zhang Xie is well versed in the classics,
but weary of his hometown and not yet a success,
he wants to reach the Spring Hall and pass the examinations,
so he takes leave of his parents,
and departs alone from home.

*Speaks*:
Audience:
All things in the world he regards as inferior,
and esteems only study.

But what about Zhang Xie? His family lived in Sichuan, in the prefecture of Chengdu. And who did not know this man or respect him! For truly, from morning 'till night he was at work on the classics and histories: he read them at dawn and practiced them at dusk, his mouth ever chanting, his hand ever turning the pages. Yes, indeed!

Just as in the alchemist's furnace
the fire never ceases,
Under his study window
the candle's flame flickers low.

Suddenly one day he announced to his parents: "This is the year of the great examination and your son wants to go to the imperial city to sit for it. I seek a little travel money to use on the road." Had his parents not heard a word of this, nothing would have happened, but once they heard these words, two streams of tears rolled down their cheeks. Their son said: "After ten years of mastering the civil and military arts, this year I [finally] get to sell them to the imperial house. I want to change your status in life and requite your kindness, so why must you weep?"

> *Sings*:
> (*Xiao chongshan*)
> A while ago I had an unhappy dream,
> that left me deep in thought:
> never in my life have I traveled in government service,
> and I really worry about how I'll handle it.

*Speaks*: The son said to his parents, "Since ancient times it is said that at the first watch you muse, at the second watch you imagine, and at the third watch you dream. Generally speaking, emotions cannot be controlled and dreams are illusory. For the most part, life and death are determined by fate and wealth and status allotted by Heaven. Why worry? The parents, seeing their son so anxious to go, gave him several taels of gold and silver to serve as traveling expenses. They heaped endless advice on him saying: "Before dark you must first find lodgings for the night; only after the cock crows should you cross the pass; when you come to a bridge, you must dismount and when you come to a ford do not attempt to go first." Their son assented to his parents' loving entreaties and left right away.

> *Sings*:
> (*Langtao sha*)
> Up the winding road he went, leaving his village behind,
> and turning his head to look toward home,[7]
> beneath the white clouds, he discreetly brushed away his tears.
> As far as his eyes could see lay an expanse of wilderness, with no
>     inn in sight;
> he could hear only the rushing flow of water.

*Speaks*: But let's stop this digression. That day, as he journeyed on, his heart felt heavy and somber. At home he had never tilled the land in spring or gathered harvest in the fall. Truly, he had been thoroughly spoiled! Every day he took the classics and histories as his companions, and writing brush and inkstone as the tools of his trade.

When the road was level, everything was fine, but how could he not fear that very high mountain called Wuji! How tall was the mountain? It seemed to pierce the sky, soaring into the blue heaven; wild geese and swans could not fly over it, and gibbons and apes were afraid to climb it. Layer upon layer of towering peaks, how on earth can a man tread such dangerous paths! Full of barbs and thorns are the branches of hanging rattan.⁸ People mostly walk on level land, but he alone has to pierce the clouds.⁹ Even though he had never attended a feast at the Jasper Pool,¹⁰ one would think he was an immortal on earth. In the distance, he could hear echoes of the crying and moaning of wild apes calling their young; close by he could see the rustling and fluttering of the falling leaves breaking away from their stems. No inn lays ahead and no human lodging behind.

*Sings*:
(*Fansi yuan*)
The northern wind scours the land, tossing specks of willow floss.¹¹
In the high mountain stands no inn,
only a bare and desolate scene.
Huddling up, where will I spend the night?
As I contemplate these thoughts,
the road stretches far before me.

*Speaks*: Before he had finished, a strange wind began to whistle and the leaves of reeds swayed to and fro. Wild birds gave out startled cries and mountain gibbons tried to out-scream the other. He saw only a wild beast, its golden eyes glittering like two copper bells, its patterned body resplendent, like half a roll of bright-colored silk. He bared a set of teeth like rows of sharp blades, with ten pairs of claws closely aligned like steel hooks. The beast leapt out from the thick forest onto the grassy path, and Zhang Xie was so frightened that his earthly souls left him, and his heavenly spirits began to flee his body. He fell to the ground in a fainting spell. An instant later, he could only hear the tread of shoes and the sound of steps. When Zhang Xie lifted his head to look, he saw not a wild beast but a person. And how was he clothed? He was wearing a tiger skin scarf around his head and a tiger skin cloak; he had a pair of incandescent eyes and a violent temperament: "Leave all your gold and pearls and I'll spare your life. If you refuse, I'll have no mercy on you."

*The* MO *makes a gesture.*

*Sings:*
(*Raochi you*)
Zhang Xie spoke with deference:
"Consider that I am a student,
on my way to Chang'an to take the imperial exams.
I have just a few trifling possessions,
to be used on the road for my traveling expenses;
I am begging for your mercy. Do not rob me."

*Speaks:* The robber paid no heed to Zhang Xie's pleas. As anger rose from his heart, wickedness grew from his gall. With his left hand he held Zhang Xie by the hair and with his right hand he held a glistening, threatening rat-tail-shaped sword. With the back of the sword he struck him right and left about the body, and as Zhang Xie, mute, dropped in pain, stole his bundle and his gold.

And what of Zhang Xie's fate? Like the loving crow and the happy magpie perched on the same branch,[12] twists of fortune and misfortune cannot be foretold. And now, rather than sing and narrate this *chantefable* why don't we perform the story? You performers[13] backstage, boldly strike the drums to urge us on while the *moni*[14] role gives us a dance.

*The* MO *exits.*

# ACT 2

*The* SHENG[1] *enters and speaks:* Greetings

*The troupe answers.*

SHENG: I've imposed upon your hospitality and your kind gift of an overture.

TROUPE: It is we who are troubling you, brother.

SHENG: Gentlemen, give us a "The Red Sway of the Candles' Shadow" to send us off.

*The musicians start playing their instruments and the* SHENG *dances to several melodies on the stage.*

*The* SHENG *declaims:*
(*Wang Jiangnan*)
'Tis a pleasant story,
its plot superb.
Clapping and poking fun at others isn't much fun,
and playing football or stick ball are a sheer waste of time.
But we will give our all at playing pipes and flutes.

Although we're most experienced at cracking funny jokes,
we'll entertain you by mingling in songs.
When we enter or leave the stage we'll change the exeunt verse,
and in between we will have you shaking with laughter,
and brimming with joy.
Just now, I heard a riff
but I don't know what tune it is?

TROUPE: "The Red Sway of the Candles' Shadow."

SHENG: Master Musician, strike up a tune.

TROUPE: Very well.

SHENG: That's enough! I shall assume the likeness of top graduate
Zhang Xie.

TROUPE: Much obliged.

ZHANG XIE:[2]

The silent painted halls are best suited to feasting and pleasure;
the embroidered curtains screen the spring wind.
Ripples shimmer in the passing cup, filled with unstrained wine—
deep into the night rolls the red sway of the candles' shadow.

*The troupe cheers on and* ZHANG XIE *sings*:
(*The Red Sway of the Candles' Shadow*)
"The Red Sway of the Candles' Shadow"
is most fitting to our carefree roving, and so very amusing.
Things wonderfully exotic and strange are well worth a look,
and beautifully woven into the script.
We truly sing in the fashion of the Music Academy,[3]
and who can compete with our comic repartee?
The Nine Mountain Society
has changed nowadays,
and has a unique style of performance.
There is one that smears lime and white powder on his face:
stepping to a beat, appearing and disappearing,
all delight in him.
If you, illustrious gentlemen who crowd our halls,
have seen this play performed in another form,
know that this version is wondrously new and singularly distinct;
we've changed our song-lyrics, and switched our keys and modes.
All of you please quiet down.
A man's eyes are hard to deceive:
we await your lucid evaluation.

*Declaims:*

For generations Zhang Xie's ancestors lived in Sichuan.

Year after year, he pored over volumes of books by the studio
window,

for he wished to go to the imperial palace to assist the enlightened
emperor,

but fortune had not come his way and this sank him into
melancholy!

The tip of his brush, steeped in ancient and modern lore,

would at times fly across the walls in his cloud-mist calligraphy.[4]

Fame and rank, wealth and status are all human desires,

but we fully understand that all things are determined by Heaven.

When night came, Zhang Xie had an inauspicious dream,

so he thought he'd better go and look for some friends, hoping to
get their advice.

*The* MO FRIEND *and the* JING[5] FRIEND *enter the stage singing and
dancing.*

JING FRIEND *makes a gesture and speaks:* Welcome.

MO FRIEND: As soon as you come out you've got to open your big
mouth. But please noble brother, you go first.

ZHANG XIE: No, no, most righteous brother, you go ahead. Eldest
brother, it is you who must go first.

ZHANG XIE *and* MO FRIEND: Let's go by order of age.

ZHANG XIE:

*Ai!* Don't be surprised that I am still unsuccessful;

a day will come when the bound dragon reaches the sky.[6]

For ten years, under the window, I've been unknown to all,

but once I succeed the whole world will know me.

But I am talking nonsense.

MO FRIEND: *Ai!*

JING FRIEND: I love you, too!

MO FRIEND: Clearly, everyone desires me. *Ai*! But this *ai* has nothing to do with the *ai* for coveting. *Ai*![7]

JING FRIEND: There you go again. Another *ai*!

MO FRIEND: Ok, that's enough:

> The classics need not thwart your aspirations,
>
> and your erudition will lead you to snap the cassia twig.[8]
>
> Once you succeed, your name will appear at the head of the list of
>
> dragons and tigers,[9]
>
> and in another ten years you'll stand by the phoenix pool.[10]

But I am talking nonsense.

JING FRIEND: Brother, you started talking.

MO FRIEND: Nonsense.

JING FRIEND: You too brother, spoke up.

ZHANG XIE: Sheer nonsense.

JING FRIEND: I'll also speak! Also speak!

MO FRIEND: At this point, we beat the drums.[11]

JING FRIEND: Blurp!

MO FRIEND: How much can you eat before you're stuffed!

JING FRIEND: Last night I was reading in front of the lamp.

MO FRIEND: Strange!

JING FRIEND: I studied until the cock crowed.

MO FRIEND: You didn't sleep the whole night!

JING FRIEND: It was too noisy outside.

MO FRIEND: Perhaps they were celebrating your success?

JING FRIEND: No, there was such a racket outside that I opened the door to check.

MO FRIEND: What did you see?

JING FRIEND: A rat dragging a big old cat along.

MO FRIEND: You mean a cat dragging a rat.

JING FRIEND: A rat dragging a cat.

*The three repeat the sentence in unison. The* MO FRIEND *questions it, and the* JING FRIEND *laughs.*

JING FRIEND: Never mind, it is a hard word to rhyme with. I did the best I could.

MO FRIEND: One could say you are a modern day Du Fu!¹²

ZHANG XIE: What are your literary achievements?

JING FRIEND: I can compose poems.

MO FRIEND: And I've memorized the whole *Treatise on Rhymes*.¹³

JING FRIEND: The *Treatise on Rhymes*? What's so hard about that? One toes, two foes.¹⁴

MO FRIEND: What about three and four?

JING FRIEND: Three cash of sauce, four of tomatoes.¹⁵

MO FRIEND: Why bring up the market bill?

ZHANG XIE: Last night I had a dream.

JING FRIEND: I am very skilled in describing dreams and also interpreting them.

MO FRIEND: What did you dream about?

ZHANG XIE: Last night I dreamt that between two mountains I suddenly ran into a tiger. It injured my arm and leg. It looked like a tiger and yet also like a person, like a person and yet also like a tiger.

JING FRIEND: Alas, what a pity you were alone in the dream!

MO FRIEND: Why?

JING FRIEND: Had you been traveling with Zilu, it would have been just a matter of a punch and a kick.

*The* JING FRIEND *makes the gesture of hitting the* MO FRIEND.

MO FRIEND: Hey, I'm not a tiger any more than you're Zilu.¹⁶

JING FRIEND: That's a dream I cannot describe.

MO FRIEND: That's one pill I cannot prescribe.¹⁷

JING FRIEND: I have heard that in front of the *yamen* there is a dream interpreter. We should invite him over and thoroughly inquire.

ZHANG XIE: That is an excellent idea.

JING FRIEND: Tomorrow morning we'll ask this diviner Li to come over.[18]

ZHANG XIE: The Maker of Things has never obstructed a scholar's career.

MO FRIEND: The world's events do not follow human calculations.

*Together*: In the last analysis all is arranged by fate.

*The* MO FRIEND *and the* JING FRIEND *exit.*

ZHANG XIE *sings*:
(*Fendie'er*)
Strolling among the flower covered paths,
I have to go home,
to ask my parent's opinion.

*The* WAI *role acting as* ZHANG XIE'S FATHER *enters and continues the song*:
In the thatched hall,
I can hear the sound of boots;
my son has returned.
If you don't work at your studies,
you'll be a good-for-nothing all your life.[19]

ZHANG XIE *speaks*: Greetings, father.

FATHER:

He's pored over a myriad volumes,
and writes with divine inspiration.
If fate is on your side, you can rectify and benefit the world,
but if fate is adverse, you will be of no service to others.[20]

Only if morning and night you're at the classics and histories, reading them by day and practicing by night, can you begin to speak of the idea of fate. If the time is not yet ripe, pearls with a crooked thread cannot be threaded with bound ants,[21] but if your fate is met, you can hope to catch the fish with a straightened hook.[22]

ZHANG XIE *sings*:
(*Qianqiu sui*)
When it comes to the classics,
reading them carefully and chanting them quietly,
is a course of real pleasure.

FATHER:
When the results of the imperial exams are announced,
I hope you will bring honor and status to our house.

ZHANG XIE:
Father, I want to inform you,
That now I want to leave.
But, I've yet to receive
your kindly instructions.

*Together*:
All we desire is that you to be in good health,
so that next year, when the time comes,
your return as top graduate can be proclaimed.

FATHER:
(*Same tune*)
I heard you
had a dream last night;
describe it to me in detail.

ZHANG XIE:

Between two mountains,

I was pounced upon and beaten by a phony tiger.[23]


FATHER:

Peoples' dreams

are not to be trusted;

so let's just go and pack your luggage.


*Together:*

What we desire is honor and wealth,

I am sure the Peach Blossom waves will be warm,

and in a single jump he'll reach the path above the clouds.[24]


FATHER *speaks*: Son, the poet Shao Yong[25] put it well: "One must settle one's doubts without delay."[26] If you're indecisive when a decision is needed, you'll suffer the troubling consequences. I will go and inform your mother and ask her to pack your luggage and some supplies for the road. Call the *fumo*[27] over and send him to invite the dream interpreter to come and interpret the dream.

ZHANG XIE: Yes, Father, you are very right. This is truly what is meant by "decisive."


FATHER: Son, if you want to go, you must not miss the chance.

ZHANG XIE: The stranger the dream, the greater the fortune.

FATHER: When the time to drink wine comes, we must drink.

*Together:* And when it is time to raise our voices in song, that we must also do.


*All exit.*

# ACT 3

*The* DAN *role acting as* POORLASS *enters and sings:*
(*Dasheng yue*)
In the village no one wants to smile at me,
or could know of my melancholy.
Wandering with slow paces
along paths of mulberry and hemp,
I am alone, vexed and troubled.

*Sings again:*
(*Daodao ling*)[1]
Poor I may be,
yet so delicate,
with these two combed eyebrows.
Sometimes, I privately recall my parents,
and teardrops fall, wetting my pretty face;
but who is there to know?
I am wanted by none.
I, myself, must hold fast to uprightness,
Even if it is something bitterly embraced.
There is no one for me to rely on.
It is my fate to weave hemp for others,
and all alone at night
I sleep in the old temple.

(*Same tune*)
No matter how much I worry about it,
it's simply that my fate is bad.
How many nights have I buried my resentment over this
    injustice?
I have endured a thousand kinds of sorrows,

and so much loneliness.
In vain my youthful years pass by.
I make do with my coarse shirt and cotton skirt,
but I long for a different kind of tune.
If you wish me well,
let me meet the man of my dreams,
that we may bind up our hair together,
and live as husband and wife until old age.

*Declaims:*
The old temple is deserted and desolate and I am afraid to return;
how long must I weep these tears alone.
Even the Yellow River will run clear one day,
so, surely I will meet with better times.

POORLASS *exits.*

# ACT 4

*The* MO *acting as a* SERVANT *enters and speaks:*

People in the south don't dream of camels,
While those in the north don't dream of elephants.

Nighttime dreams all arise from one's own mind. Scholar Zhang has asked me to invite the dream diviner. Here is a small room with an old four-leaf gate and a black cloth curtain where written in large characters it states: "Divines dreams like a god." There is a sign that says in bold characters "Listens to voices and does phrenology." Let me call him. Is the master in?

*The* CHOU *as the* DREAM DIVINER *answers from backstage*: Who is it? Who is it?

SERVANT: I've a small matter I want to bother you with.

DIVINER: What a fluke! In twenty-four months not a single person has come to my door.

SERVANT: You're in big demand![1]

*The* DIVINER *comes out*: When a monk sees a Buddha, he fetches a torch and lights incense.[2]

SERVANT: Greetings, Master.

DIVINER: Not to you, sir. Sir, do you wish to choose a mate, select an auspicious day, have me read your bones, analyze your voice, crack the tile, read the tortoise shell, toss the coins, or foretell your future?

SERVANT: All this says is that you have no specialized skill. That scholar Zhang sent me to invite you over to interpret a dream.

DIVINER: In the whole of Chengdu Prefecture, it is said I have no match.

SERVANT: Why don't you try wrestling?

DIVINER: Let's take a turn around the block.

SERVANT: What for?

DIVINER: Because in two years I haven't stepped outside my gate.

SERVANT: That's exactly twenty-four months.

*The* DIVINER *shouts*: Chen the voice expert is unbeatable.

SERVANT: Until I speak about *you*!

DIVINER: I need six cash now, and that is already a discount price.

SERVANT: You're far too cheap.

DIVINER: Other diviners call me an earthly immortal, and when I get it right, the people cheer.

SERVANT: Master, just wait a little while I call that scholar Zhang. Ah, but I hear the sound of footsteps. He's coming.

ZHANG XIE *enters and sings:*

(*Xidi jin*)

I have heard that you can tell one's fortune by listening to the tone
    of his voice.

Unmatched in the world, your fame has reached the imperial city.

For long have I heard your illustrious name,

    and I have a dream I wish to tell you.

*The* DIVINER *peers at the* SERVANT *and speaks:* Welcome, noble sir.

SERVANT: Open those dead eyes of yours. Scholar Zhang is here.[3]

DIVINER: Where? (*They make gestures.*)

SERVANT: Not in vain are you called Chen the voice expert!

ZHANG XIE: I want to have a dream interpreted.

DIVINER: Before we talk about the dream, let's hear the sound of
    your voice.

ZHANG XIE: Fine.

DIVINER: Your voice is very clear, and your timbre beautiful. It
    seems that in your previous life you were not of the human race.

ZHANG XIE *and* SERVANT: So what was he?

DIVINER: Let's just talk about you, Zhang Xie. You lived in the
    Country of Swallows.[4] In your former life you were a swallow.

SERVANT: And what do you predict for him?

DIVINER: Two lines in the diviner's manual put it well.

SERVANT: What do they say?

DIVINER: If you were not a swallow in your former life, how could
    you have made those beam-curling sounds?[5]

SERVANT: I'll beat the dust out of you.[6] And while on the subject,
    can you rub my skull and foretell my future?

DIVINER: You want phrenology?

SERVANT: If I may trouble you.

*The* DIVINER *touches the* SERVANT's *head*: This is a fine piece of bone!

SERVANT: What's your interpretation?

DIVINER: You are not from a first wife.

SERVANT: Was I born a concubine's son?

DIVINER: No. Not a concubine's son either.

SERVANT: What then?

DIVINER: Your parents could never have had a child, so with infinite schemes they scoured the land for you and raised you.

SERVANT: Amazing! How can you see that?

DIVINER: Nothing odd about it! This bone of yours is a begging bone.

SERVANT: The better to beat you with, you bone-head!

DIVINER: Let's decipher the dream now. How old are you?

ZHANG XIE: Eighteen.

DIVINER: Forty-eight?[7]

SERVANT: Your sole care is to get through midlife.[8] He's eighteen.

DIVINER: At what hour were you born?

ZHANG XIE: Around midnight.

DIVINER: Midnight, that's the third watch; just the time for crooks.

SERVANT: Yes, we should keep an eye on you!

DIVINER: Sir, let's hear your dream.


ZHANG XIE *sings*:

(*Same tune*)

In the dream it was not yet the fourth watch.

When I passed over two mountains,

I caught a glimpse of a person who looked like a tiger,

who wounded me in the arm and leg.

*The* DIVINER *sings*:
(*Chuan baolao*)
You were between two mountains;
mountain upon mountain makes the word "exit."[9]

*The* SERVANT *speaks*: A couple of mountains make the word "exit."

    *The* DIVINER *continues the song*:
    You came upon a person dressed in a tiger costume.
    Now, white tigers flourish only in the western regions,
    but the western regions are lands of rivers.
    Sir, when you depart you must head north;
    inevitably there will be
    some tumbles and falls that will make you sick oozing pus and blood.
    But a thousand *li* beyond, there will be a "leopard change,"[10]
    and all at once you'll become noteworthy
    and be celebrated upon your return.

    *The* SERVANT *sings*:
    (*Same tune*)
    For a long time I have heard said,
    heard said, that you could interpret dreams,
    but I never imagined your interpretations would be so strange.

    ZHANG XIE:
    So, once I leave home,
    when I'm a thousand *li* away,
    since no misfortune will come my way, I need not be doubtful at all.

    DIVINER:
    Good times will always follow the bad,
    and you'll be above the clouds,
    so don't worry about it.

*The* SERVANT *assents:*

Fine! Now if you could also solve my dream,

I'd be much obliged.

*The* DIVINER *speaks:* You too want to have a dream interpreted. What is it about?

SERVANT: Last night I dreamt that I saw a snake. It had a dragon's head and horns.

DIVINER: Strange! A snake with a dragon's head is called a "snake entering the dragon's den." Come now, use this sash as the dragon's head and this one as its tail and stand with your head up and feet apart.

SERVANT: What for?

DIVINER: Like a convict on display.

SERVANT: You convict carcass![11]

DIVINER: The diviner's manual has four lines, which are to the point.

SERVANT: I'm eager to hear them.

DIVINER: It says that: "When snakes turn into dragons in dreams, it's no idle matter. Where there is no calm, you will find calm."

SERVANT: Thank you very much.

DIVINER: Now you are still a snake in the green grass, but it won't be difficult for you to become a dragon one day and fly, swish, swish, swish.

SERVANT: There is a road in the sky.

ZHANG XIE: I'm very much obliged to you, sir.

DIVINER: The dream interpretation fee!

SERVANT: Six cash.

DIVINER: The voice listening fee!

SERVANT: More! Another six cash.

DIVINER: The phrenology fee.

SERVANT: Here are six cash more.

DIVINER: Fortune-telling, matchmaking, and choosing an auspicious day.

SERVANT: Stop it!

ZHANG XIE: It has been a most enlightening visit.

DIVINER: This morning I came to interpret a dream and met a noble gentleman.

SERVANT: How many people have lost their way in the world!

*Together*: In the tip of a finger all returns to the great way.[12]

*All exit.*

# ACT 5

ZHANG XIE's FATHER *enters and sings*:
(*Xingxiangzi*)
To change our social status,
we must tell our son
that it can only be done by studying the Classics.

*The* JING *acting as* ZHANG XIE's MOTHER *enters and continues the song*:
If you are only a foot away from the door,
You have not been gone long.
All because our son
wants to leave,
I secretly shed tears.

*The* MOTHER *speaks*: Hey! Ask the *fumo* to come over.
*The* SERVANT *enters and speaks*:

If there is conflict, don't squabble over it,
because when it's all is over, your mind will cool down.

I hadn't done a thing when I heard this "Hey!" calling me. I'll just
ignore her.

*The* SERVANT, *standing, turns his back to the* MOTHER.

MOTHER: Hey! Ignore her! Ignore her!

MOTHER *pulls the* SERVANT *by the ear*: Who did you mean?

SERVANT: I said nothing!

*The* MOTHER *makes a gesture.*

FATHER: Mother, why are you so angry?

SERVANT: Her ladyship always behaves this way.

MOTHER: My son wants to leave and I'm miserable. Don't you
think it's enough to make one anxious?

SERVANT: What do you want me to do?

MOTHER: Go and call my son. Ask him to come over.

SERVANT: Enough, enough. The whole day filled with this wran-
gling; if I don't take notice, it'll go away.

MOTHER: If you don't listen it'll go away! Damn it if you find my
house depressing![1]

SERVANT: You bicker too much!

*The* SERVANT *exits.*

ZHANG XIE *enters and sings*:

(*Wuling chun*)

Alone, I'll leave Sichuan without a traveling companion;

on the road, I will be lonely and frightened.

*The* MOTHER *continues the song*:

Today for the first time my son is leaving me.

*Together with the* FATHER:
Our thoughts are all of our son here.

*The* MOTHER *speaks*:

At night, wild birds rest in the same trees,
but at daybreak, each flies its own way.

Our son is going away and that's all well. It's just that there will
be no one to take care of our family. This old beggar is good for
nothing but eating, and steals my money for alms and prayers to
the Buddha. How can you call that a man?

FATHER: Alms! Alms! Don't ask about what I'll become!
MOTHER: You animal!
ZHANG XIE: Father, Mother, I've come to take my leave.
MOTHER: Son, once you are gone, who will collect the money people
owe me?
FATHER: Oh, that's great, great![2]
MOTHER: If we were like you, we'd just eat us out of our house!
ZHANG XIE: Mother, don't be angry!
MOTHER: Ask the *fumo* to come in.

*The* SERVANT *enters carrying an umbrella*:
Every five miles a single post.
Every ten miles a double marker.
I'll just rely on these few belongings.
MOTHER: Put them down lightly or you'll stumble and fall.
SERVANT: You bark like a mad dog.
*The* MOTHER *cries*: Son, before you go, help me settle a penalty for
those who owe me the interest.

FATHER: He needs to set an auspicious hour to leave, yet you go on with your idle prattle!

*The* MOTHER *sings*:
(*Fan Yingtao hua*)
Son, once you leave,
from time to time send us your news.

*Together*:
Don't allow this separation,
to cause us grief and consternation.
We'll look after ourselves,
but as soon as your exams are over, do come home.

FATHER:
Every day, we shall burn some incense and pray,
with the only hope that you, our son,
will attain your life's desire.

*Refrain*:
We hope that this time
your name will appear in the Golden List,
and you may snap the cassia twig in the moon.[3]

*The* MOTHER *speaks*: Son, once you go, see you get a whole branch full of flowers . . .
ZHANG XIE: A whole branch full of flowers.
MOTHER: Big like the ones in the camphor tree in front of the house. Buy a branch for me so that I can place it on my shoulders.
SERVANT: Oh, it's so tough for you!

ZHANG XIE *sings*:
(*Same tune*)
I am about to leave,
but I am afraid I will have no money for the road.

FATHER *and* MOTHER:
We will give you,
plenty of gold and pearls,
but don't be easy with the money,
we're afraid someone will cheat you.

ZHANG XIE:
Thank you for your great kindness.
Every single day I shall
pray to heaven and earth.

*Repeat the refrain.*

*The* MOTHER *speaks*: Son, if you happen to see a fine tooth comb, as
large as a flat carrying pole, bring it back for me to wear.
SERVANT: How would you wear it?

*The* MOTHER *sings*:
(*Same tune*)
Oh! And when you're gone,
I'll miss you terribly.

*Together*:
We can still
look after ourselves.
And we will stop worrying,
but frequently send us letters.

MOTHER:

If you're pestered by the servant,
you can curse him night and day.

SERVANT:

You're really absurd.

*Repeat the refrain.*

*The* SERVANT *sings:*
(*Same tune*)
I beg you let's leave early,
and find somewhere to spend the night.

MOTHER:

You lowdown ought-to-be-beaten filthy slave,
you good for nothing devil of a servant.
Let's have you go off with him,
and steal your food along the way.

SERVANT:

Now that the dream has been explained,
we must make sure that luggage, zither, books,
and all the rain gear are securely packed.

*Repeat the refrain.*

ZHANG XIE *speaks:* I'll bid farewell to my parents and be on my way.
FATHER: Son, take good care of yourself.
MOTHER: But before you go, let's call your sister to come and say
good-bye.
SERVANT: What a nuisance! Couldn't you have said so earlier!

MOTHER: Go and call her.

SERVANT: You are delaying our journey again; Miss, come and say good-bye to the top scholar.

> *The* CHOU *acting as* ZHANG XIE's SISTER *runs out and sings:*
> (*Same tune*)
> Brother, you're leaving
> and I've come to say good-bye.
> Whatever you find in the capital,
> that's a specialty and fun,
> buy some to bring back home.
> I'll wait for your return.
> Brother, bring me back
> a hawksbill comb,
> some flower embroidered slippers and a ribbon for my hair.

> SERVANT:
> No need to pay attention to this pettiness.

> *Repeat the refrain.*

SISTER *speaks*: Brother, dear brother, please, buy me a comb; please, buy the ribbons, brother.

SERVANT: Perfect for your good looks!

SISTER: And dear brother, please, if you see some high-grade ointment, bring some back.

ZHANG XIE: What for?

SISTER: So that I can plaster that tortoise-brain ointment on my twisted back.

SERVANT: Here we have another Hua Tuo.[4]

MOTHER: Let's go outside the city gates to see him off.

FATHER: Son, as soon as the exams are over, you must return home.

SISTER: And remember brother, to buy the hair ribbon.

MOTHER: We hope that you'll pass the exams the first time.

*Together:* Well before your parents reach old age.

*All exit.*

# ACT 6

POORLASS *enters and sings:*

(*Fengma'er*)

My parents passed away a long time ago;

so how would they know of my trials and tribulations?

All alone, my life depends on this old temple,

where in flowery mornings and moonlit nights,

oftentimes, tears fall quietly down.

*Speaks:* When I was young I lost my parents, and I don't have a brother. Not even a single distant relative or a clan member, not even a cousin. My ancestors left no property, and I scarcely possess any clothes. My three daily meals I earn weaving for people in the village with painstaking diligence. But as soon as it is dusk, I return to curl up in the desolation of the temple. It is cold and about to snow.

A single lamp may illuminate all the deities,

but still I am three cents too short to buy any oil.

*Sings again:*

(*Jie huanghua*)

It is my fate to be so very poor.

This life of mine has no value.

By spinning silk and weaving hemp,

I gain people's respect.
I am grateful that
the gods look after me,
and also that I have met Grandpa Li.
When at times I have no firewood or rice,
he quickly sends Xiao'er to bring me some.
Tonight the chilling northern wind is rising,
so terrible, how can I bear this freezing cold!

*The* MO *acting as a* VILLAGER *enters and sings*:
(*Same tune*)
In this deserted village the scene is sad and desolate;
in this lonely spot few pass by.
Master Li asked me to call on you,
so I've specially come to the old temple.

POORLASS:
Greetings[1] sir, but what did you come for?
Surely the road here must be dark.

VILLAGER:
Grandpa Li of the Eastern Bank,
has a small matter that requires your help,
and expressly sent me over.
You must go over early tomorrow morning.

POORLASS *speaks*: Thank you very much, Sir! Without his help, how
should I survive a single hour? I know, it must be either to stuff
the quilts or weave silk. Tomorrow early I'll be there.

VILLAGER: Miss,
Those who are lazy will always be poor,
better to be diligent than seek help from others.[2]

POORLASS: I know,

You can live in poverty in a bustling market and no one will visit you.

VILLAGER: But if you're rich, even though you're away in the mountains, you'll find relatives visiting you from distant parts.

*All exit.*

# ACT 7

ZHANG XIE *carrying his luggage enters and sings*:

(*Wangyuan xing*)

My home village gradually grows distant,

and Sword Pass is steep and the mountain top dangerous.[1]

Unaccustomed to this travel,

how can I dispel this gloominess!

From time to time I hear the cry of the gibbons on the cliffs,

Oh! When will I reach the capital

and tread the cloudy path to my heart's desire?

*Declaims*:

I spent years studying the classics,

in the hope of ascending the stairway to the clouds.

My straw sandals and leggings are caked with mud;

in the distance I gaze at Sword Pass among the towering

  mountains.

I must cross the Jialing River with its foaming waters,

clumps of reed flowers, and chilling wind.

Standing alone on the sandy shore I see a boatman;

dawn breaks in the nearby village, and suddenly the cock cries.

ZHANG XIE *exits.*

# ACT 8

*The* CHOU *acting as a* ROBBER *enters and speaks:*
I neither farm nor raise silkworms and I don't care to cut and gather firewood.

I hate dragging the plow or pulling the rake and I am equally lazy when it comes to bearing heavy or light burdens. I love to gamble and specially delight in drinking wine. Otherwise I have no plans, but when the wind is high, I set fire on the mountains; and when I want to show how tough I am, on moonless nights I slip across the river with a stolen ox. Untaxed salt and tea is my regular trade; flaying another man's ox and killing another man's dog is how I make a living. With a single carrying pole I can hold off a whole regiment in its camp, and with a single sword kill a whole patrol. If a string of porters in a government highway carry goods, I join with a band to rob them and then split the loot. But if it's just a trader, everything on his pole is mine alone. When there is no business, I let loose six or seven hunting dogs and they capture live deer and monkeys. And when I am lucky enough and manage to capture one or two tigers, I skin them to make a cloak and a hood. Deep in the forest, I dress up as a wild animal and hide by the mountain paths waiting for a traveler. Today the weather is cold, so I am looking for a big score. If the traveler is timid and weak, I will hit him with the back of the sword, but if he is stubborn and crafty, I will thrash him with my iron club. I won't even spare a ten-headed man-eating *raksha* and I'm not the least bit scared of the eight-armed Nezha.[1]

Even if you could employ the infinite strategies of Heaven, you'll find it hard to escape the trouble I'll give you now.

*The* ROBBER *exits.*

*The* MO *acting as a* TRAVELER *enters and sings*:
(*Sheng chazi*)
Mountains pile up layer upon layer,
and the river extends in the boundless distance.
My luggage and goods are all well packed,
but on my own are hard to handle.

*Speaks*: My shoulder pole has a load of hundreds of catties and on
my back I carry fifty. I can understand all the local dialects and
tell Sichuan goods from those of Guangdong. I will face mist and
fog and I'm never set back on account of the distance. Braving
rain and wind, I do not begrudge the fatigue of the road. I want
to cross over Mount Wuji, but alone I dare not. I'll wait for an
official caravan or a military escort before hurrying over.

Truly, I provide for hundreds of households.
I am just afraid that alone I will come to some mischance.

*The* JING *acting as a* TRAVELER *enters*: Hello! Traveler, it looks like
you are waiting to cross over the mountain? Hey, you!
MO TRAVELER: Hello there, fellow traveler!

*The* JING TRAVELER *and the* MO TRAVELER *hail each other*.

MO TRAVELER: Who is it? From a distance I couldn't tell, but now
he's closer, I can get a better look. Who is it?
*The* JING TRAVELER *returns the greeting*: We have not seen each
other for a long time.
MO TRAVELER: I don't know you.
JING TRAVELER: How can you not know me! Once in Chengdu, in
front of the Judicial Commissioner's *yamen* I beat a man selling
figurines of golden camels.

MO TRAVELER: Oh, that's right, I'm beginning to recall your handsome face.

JING TRAVELER: Who am I? I am a merchant, a prestigious merchant who travels everywhere. That person came to sell me some of those camels.

MO TRAVELER: I sort of remember; you were attacked by him.

JING TRAVELER: No, you're wrong.

MO TRAVELER: You were below and he was on top throwing punches.

JING TRAVELER: He did not land one single punch. I was below, my fists flying. (*Makes a gesture*).

MO TRAVELER: Why did you shout?

JING TRAVELER: I did not shout, when would I ever shout?

MO TRAVELER: How could you help it?

JING TRAVELER: In the greatest pain one is silent. I couldn't shout.

MO TRAVELER: All the same, you got a few punches and kicks.

JING TRAVELER: That idiot camel seller came and grabbed me around the waist and I got punched.

*The* JING TRAVELER *hits the head of the* MO TRAVELER.

MO TRAVELER: Hey, it's me!

JING TRAVELER: He tried to hit me, but I dodged out of the way and kicked him back.

MO TRAVELER: A devilish scuffle!

JING TRAVELER: So, who am I?

MO TRAVELER: I failed to recognize Mount Tai! Today I want to cross Mount Wuji, but I'm afraid of being ambushed and robbed, so I want to hurry over.

JING TRAVELER: Fine, fine, fine. You're lucky you bumped into me. Where are you from?

MO TRAVELER: I came from Zizhou. Where is your hometown?

JING TRAVELER: I'm from Chuzhou in Eastern Zhejiang. I'm known all over for my skills in boxing, wrestling, and fighting with the halberd and the club.

MO TRAVELER: What fluke! A complementary set of skills.

JING TRAVELER: Indeed, you're fortunate to have chanced upon my set of skills.

*Sings*:
(*Fu Xiangyang*)
One step after another,
one step after another,
I can barely lift my pole.
How on earth can I hurry?
I am drained of energy,
and drops of sweat drip from my brow like a curtain of rain.
There are still three thousand *li* ahead;
how am I going to carry on!

*The* MO TRAVELER *speaks*: Aiya! I cannot go up or down. Let's have a rest and sit down somewhere.

*The* MO TRAVELER *sings*:
(*Same tune*)
Farther away with every step,
farther away with every step.
We both set out on the road together,
but we could be bullied by someone.
Suppose we encounter a robber,
how should we handle it?
We'll take our poles, money, and goods,
and hand it all over to him.

*The* JING TRAVELER *speaks*: If a robber comes to steal our stuff, you just relax! I'll give you a demonstration of my club technique.

MO TRAVELER: Let's hear it.

*The* JING TRAVELER *brandishes the club*: This is the "Mountain Top" style; this is the "Foot of the Mountain" style; this is the "Boating" style; this is the "Underwater" style, and this is the one for you.

MO TRAVELER: What is that?

JING TRAVELER: To the ground! The "kowtowing" style!

MO TRAVELER: What crime have I committed?

JING TRAVELER: If I am attacked with a club, I'll wield my club, and if I'm attacked with a halberd, I'll thrust the halberd. There is the "Halberd for the Road" style, the "Halberd on Horseback" style, and the "Halberd on Board Ship" style. And how do I wield the club? I can wield it in a "Southern" fashion, "North-South" fashion, "Wide-Open Door" fashion, and "Door-Ajar" fashion. Though if a thief comes, I'll close the door.

MO TRAVELER: It's safer.

JING TRAVELER: As for club styles, there is the "Shandong" style and the "Grass" style. I am the Halberd-and-Club Officer of Wuyuan; the celebrated spear and club expert of the country's mountains.[2]

MO TRAVELER: Sounds like a lot of hot air.

JING TRAVELER: Who am I afraid of?

*The* ROBBER *runs onto the stage shouting*: Hey you! Stay where you are!

MO TRAVELER: Yuchi blocks Shan Xiongxin![3]

JING TRAVELER: Hey, You're the robber.

MO TRAVELER: Don't give the game away!

*The* ROBBER *shouts*: You fifty men in the forest, no need to come out, I'll handle them.

MO TRAVELER: What a fine pair these two make!

JING TRAVELER: And just who are you going to handle?

ROBBER: I'll handle you. Come on, try to resist me!

JING TRAVELER: So, you've come to rob our things!

MO TRAVELER: Even *I* know that!

ROBBER: If you want what's best for you, leave all your gold and jewels behind as a toll fee. Then I'll spare you.

JING TRAVELER: If you can last through a round of my club, then I'll let you have them.

ROBBER: Hey, don't go!

JING TRAVELER: I'm going nowhere. I'm not scared of you.

ROBBER: I'm not scared of two of you.

JING TRAVELER: I'm not scared of three of you.

ROBBER: I'm not scared of four of you.

JING TRAVELER: I'm not scared of five of you.

MO TRAVELER: That's the full round.

JING TRAVELER: If you want to fight, let's fight.

ROBBER: This place is too narrow, let's use the short club.

*The* JING TRAVELER *and the* ROBBER *stand staring doltishly at each other.*

MO TRAVELER: How come you're not moving? My apologies! I'll just pick up my stuff and leave.

ROBBER: Let me guess where you're going.

MO TRAVELER: You can certainly talk.

ROBBER: I'm contemplating which halberd technique to apply.

JING TRAVELER: And I'm meditating on what club method I'll use.

MO TRAVELER: I know! Sunzi's.[4]

*The* JING TRAVELER *and the* ROBBER *hit each other and make gestures.*

*The* JING TRAVELER *falls to the ground*: Gallant sir, please spare my life.

*The* ROBBER *hits him.*

*The* MO TRAVELER *pleads*: Please, spare his life.

ROBBER: Some guts you've got! But at least he fought me! I am taking all your belongings away, and if either of you make the faintest sound, I'll kill you.

> Those who cross this mountain,
> will certainly suffer a misfortune.
> From your past deeds,
> comes bad luck all at once.

*The* ROBBER *exits.*
*The* JING TRAVELER *calls from the ground.*

MO TRAVELER: You've deceived me!

JING TRAVELER: Aiya! Help!

MO TRAVELER: Sure! You talk about taking him on and you can't even do the "Open Door" style.

JING TRAVELER: I can only do the "Pounder" club.

MO TRAVELER: Still a blowhard! What a disaster! Our luggage and goods all have been stolen.

JING TRAVELER: Forget about the luggage and the goods, what hurts me is my stolen club.

MO TRAVELER: A personal treasure. Come on, get up.

> *The* JING TRAVELER *sings*:
> (*Fuzhou ge*)
> He has taken away
> all my goods,
> that I bought in Sichuan.
> My wife and son
> are expecting news from me at home.

*Refrain*:

Besides, snow keeps falling.

Where are we going to spend the night?

MO TRAVELER:

(*Same tune*)

He came to hit you,

but you would not yield,

and kindly pleaded with him to leave.

Wielding the halberd and the club,

you wanted simply to show your heroism.

*Refrain*:

Our goods have been stolen.

Where are we going to spend the night?

JING TRAVELER:

(*Same tune*)

The north wind is rising again,

but the paper thin blankets and jackets

we had in our luggage have all been robbed.

Our feet and hands,

our bodies all chilly like water.

*Refrain*:

Snow is falling again.

Where are we going to spend the night?

MO TRAVELER:

(*Same tune*)

You didn't strike back,

so you just withstood it.

He hit you and each time you first surrendered.
Neither in your pockets or mine
is any money or food left.

*Refrain*:
Our goods have been stolen.
Where are we going to spend the night?

*The* MO TRAVELER *speaks*: Let's go back down the mountain and rest.

JING TRAVELER: Let's go up.

MO TRAVELER: What for?

JING TRAVELER: The best time to go up is when you're empty handed.

MO TRAVELER: You must be joking. Let's go down.

JING TRAVELER: Fine, we'll go down.

MO TRAVELER: How so?

JING TRAVELER: Go down to borrow another club so that I can fight another round with him.

MO TRAVELER: You couldn't do it.

JING TRAVELER: I hope that you will remain a petty thief; surely your cronies will know how to deal with you!

MO TRAVELER: Just as blades of grass fear the frost and the frost the sun, evil people in the end are destroyed by evil people.

*All exit.*

# ACT 9

ZHANG XIE *enters and sings*:

(*Qi niangzi*)

The northern wind blows in all directions, the clouds droop low.

From the sky, snow flutters down.

Alone, I climb this towering mountain,

depleted of all strength.

Such is the pursuit of fame and wealth.

*Declaims*:

A gust of wind comes, and a blast of sand;

for a thousand mountains and ten thousand *li* not a living soul.

Sadly, I turn my head toward the road that leads to my native land,

as far as my eyes can see, dimly the sky extends.

As I climb up and down mountain after mountain,

forests of ancient trees grow among the labyrinthine peaks.

On the northern mountain slope, for a month the snow has not
    receded;

just tonight, snow is falling once more.

On the mountain ahead the smoke of a household rises;

with luck I could rest there tonight.

But it seems tonight I will have no shelter:

who will put me up for the night?

*Sings again*:

(*Putian le*)

Zhang Xie pleads to heaven above,

to take pity on my lonely self.

Since childhood, I have had the benefit of a strict father,

who instructed me in the Six Arts,[1] the civil and military arts,

because he always wanted to raise his status in life.

Today, I am on my way to sit for the exams, but it's getting dark
and snow keeps falling as I climb this mountain road.
Looking all around me, I find no place to rest.
If tonight I have to rest on this mountain,
please don't allow this body of mine,
to fall prey to wolves and tigers.

*The* ROBBER *enters and crouches on the ground.*

ZHANG XIE *speaks*: A strange gust of wind, like the sound of a cloth
tearing. Oh, a wild animal, an evil creature. I must be respectful!

I have no intention of harming the tiger,
but the tiger seems to want to harm me.

*The* ROBBER *stands up*: Hey, you wretch! I am a hometown hero and
a bandit. I would not let an official caravan go down the mountain, or a military one go by untouched. But you look like a
licentiate, so I suppose you're no merchant. I'll spare you a taste
of my iron club, just leave me your pearls and jewels as a toll fee.
ZHANG XIE *cries*: Gallant sir:

*Sings*:
(*Liangcao chong*)
My surname is Zhang and my personal name Xie.
I live in Sichuan.
I am a student,
on my way to sit in for the imperial exams.
I have some travel money
that I need for my daily sustenance.
I beg you to take pity on me and be considerate.
Spare me,
so that I have enough for the road there and back.

*The* ROBBER *speaks*: Sure!

> The moth is attracted to the flame
> and throws its life away.

Hey! You fifty men in the forest, no need to come out.

ZHANG XIE: This is terrible, terrible.
ROBBER: What is this?
ZHANG XIE: A sword.
ROBBER: And this?
ZHANG XIE: A rod.
ROBBER: And this?
ZHANG XIE: A club.
ROBBER: Which one do you want?

> ZHANG XIE *sings*:
> (*Hu daolian*)
> I have only a few coins,
> to use as traveling money,
> barely enough for the road.
> Besides, my family is far away,
> so please be understanding,
> help me.

> (*Same tune*)
> Please don't take them away.
> Just imagine how cold I shall be.
> Besides, there is no inn ahead.
> I've met with bad luck.
> I hope that you sir, today,
> will be good to me.

*The* ROBBER *speaks*: What a cunning act! Strip off your clothes!

ZHANG XIE: Please gallant sir, be kind to me; it's cold.

ROBBER: Give me all your gold and pearls, and you'll come to no
  harm. The slightest delay and I'll kill you with one blow.

> ZHANG XIE *sings*:
> (*Same tune*)
> I have just a few jewels
> to pay for my traveling expenses,
> and return to Sichuan.
> If you want to split it evenly,
> I'll give you half.
> Please, be kind!

*The* ROBBER *speaks*: You give me half and I'll give you half a beating.

ZHANG XIE *falls to the ground.*

> ROBBER:
> Half your jewels and you can go free;
> this mountain is called the world's trap.
> If King Yama sets your death at three,
> the fourth watch you will never see.

*The* ROBBER *exits.*

> *The* MO *acting as a* LOCAL GOD *enters and sings*:
> (*Linjiangxian*)
> The sound of torn cloth, the cry of a man;
> a robber has beaten the gentleman to the ground.
> The local mountain god sheds a stream of tears.
> Graduate Zhang,

you're unsuited to put up a fight against his powerful presence,
you should have restrained yourself.[2]

*Calls*: Top graduate, wake up!

ZHANG XIE *sings*:
(*Tangduo ling*)
He has robbed me of my traveling money,
and my flesh is all cut up.
My body chilly like water, I have no padded jacket,
and what's more, tonight I have no place to stay.
I am ready to leave for the Yellow Springs.

*The* LOCAL GOD *sings*:
(*You hetao*)
Sir, now make an effort and sit up.
Listen to me:
how could you cross on your own,
and bring upon yourself this disaster?

ZHANG XIE:
How could I have imagined, rash fool as I was,
that my body would be hurt with two blows and a smack?
Tonight, this heavy snow is going to freeze me to death.

*Refrain*:
It was my pitiful fate to run into him,
for how can one escape from a predestined enemy?

ZHANG XIE:
(*Same tune*)
Today I suddenly met you, old fellow,

going down the mountain.
Could you assist me and let me stay in your place
for the night?

LOCAL GOD:

Now he has asked, I shall have to let my secret out.[3] I am the local
mountain god; because I pitied you, I made myself manifest to
give you a few words of advice.

*Repeat the refrain.*

LOCAL GOD:
(*Same tune*)
Now, when you go back down the mountain,
there is a house
with a double leaf crimson door which, although dilapidated,
has mandarin duck tiles.

ZHANG XIE:
(*Same tune*)
But how do I know they'll let me in?
Thank you, venerable god, for helping me.
Tonight you've spared me a lot of anxiety.

*Repeat the refrain.*

ZHANG XIE:
All I can do is put up with these injuries,
and go down the mountain.
Your words, venerable god, have convinced me,
that I was a little too rash.

LOCAL GOD:

The doors are tied with straw, which you can undo,
and in no time someone will come and receive you.
Don't worry about how you're going to get across.

*Repeat the refrain.*

*The* LOCAL GOD *speaks*: Hullo, who's coming there?

ZHANG XIE *turns around to look.*

LOCAL GOD:

I see that your menacing dangers have been removed,
and once more you're treading the auspicious clouds.
From the Void spreads out a plucking cloud-hand,[4]
to lift you from the entanglements of this world.

*The* LOCAL GOD *exits.*

ZHANG XIE: I thank the power of the god.

Now at the foot of the mountain, I try to knock at the door.
In great profusion, flurries of snow fill the sky.
In Luoyang, the boundless flowers are lovely and bright,
but I will not reach it by spring.

ZHANG XIE *exits.*

# ACT 10

*The* JING *acting as a* MOUNTAIN GOD *enters and sings:*
(*Chu duizi*)
Auspicious clouds are sent down especially,
for a traveler who was robbed by a bandit.
The traveler is Zhang Xie, whose promising name
has already been inscribed in the cassia record.[1]

Tonight he has no place to stay and comes to knock on our door.

*Speaks:* I live at the foot of Mount Wuji. Near and far, all have heard
of my reputation. My divine presence has been manifest for
eight hundred years, and three times a day people come to burn
paper money. I take special care of the wild and fierce beasts
and also watch over the crops and the harvest. But how would I
know the taste of chicken? And I don't care for pork or mutton.
When I am presented with offerings, these are mostly bean buns
or sticky rice cakes. In the netherworld I am a local hegemon. I
resemble a clay statue and yet look like a living god, and I can
sing and speak too. Times are unlucky for Zhang Xie who has
been frightened by a robber. As a mountain god, I can't do anything but accommodate him in this place of mine for the night.
When Poorlass comes back, she'll probably not let him in, so
I'll have to explain these unusual circumstances to her. Judges of
good and evil who dwell at the foot of my altar, make yourselves
visible and come to my ministry to assist me.

*The* MO *acting as a* DIVINE JUDGE *enters and sings*:
(*Wufang gui*)
A shout,
just like a peel of thunder.
The shout turns out to be,
that of my superior god.
I don't know what the matter is
or why he calls me so fiercely.
I wonder what has people so startled?[2]

*The* MOUNTAIN GOD *sings*:
(*Same tune*)
At the foot of Mount Wuji,
there is a robber.
He has taken all of Zhang Xie's possessions,
and left him not a single cent.
He has beaten and lacerated him,
but this Zhang Xie is destined to be an imperial graduate.
I wonder if you people can comfort him?

*The* DIVINE JUDGE *speaks*: Venerable god, what do you think?
MOUNTAIN GOD: Let's move my altar for him to sleep.
DIVINE JUDGE: With piles of brocade quilts no doubt.
MOUNTAIN GOD: But to make him sleep with Poorlass would be
    extremely inappropriate.
DIVINE JUDGE: So he still knows something of worldly matters.
MOUNTAIN GOD: The paper stove is dirty inside, but he can sleep
    under the altar. Let me think: the door outside is broken and
    looks bad. Call that little demon to come over here and both of
    you turn into a pair of doors.
DIVINE JUDGE: How can a judge pose as a door?
MOUNTAIN GOD: Call that young fiend and we'll discuss it.
DIVINE JUDGE: Where's that young demon? Come at once.

*The* CHOU *acting as a* SMALL DEMON *enters and sings*:
(*Same tune*)
I am on duty today
as leader of the group;
I've no idea what meat
or wine taste like.

MOUNTAIN GOD:
Sure! As if your taste buds had no standards.

*The* DIVINE JUDGE *speaks*: What has he been eating?

*The* MOUNTAIN GOD *continues the song*:
The entire hall his bad breath fills.

DIVINE JUDGE:
Of your own kind speak no ill.

*The* MOUNTAIN GOD *speaks*: Top graduate Zhang Xie has been robbed of all his belongings, and has suddenly arrived here. I am in distress. The outside gate is in shambles, so I am sending both of you to pose as doors. Hurry up, now!

SMALL DEMON: I can only do one side of the gate; who's going to do the other?

MOUNTAIN GOD: The judge will be on the left and you'll be on the right. With one hand each hold firm [the door frame]. If someone suddenly arrives and knocks at the door, you must not say a word.

DIVINE JUDGE: Act stupid!

SMALL DEMON: Venerable god, listen, to pose as temple doors is common enough, but I am worried that someone may come and pick us up to use as latrine doors.

DIVINE JUDGE: What a perfumed head!

MOUNTAIN GOD: Hold the door in a manner that is familiar to Poorlass: when you open it, make it creak and when you close it, make it tight. At the slightest sign of disobedience you'll get ten blows of the iron hammer.

SMALL DEMON: Only the iron hammer or will you use nails?

DIVINE JUDGE: To nail you to death!

MOUNTAIN GOD: Let's see, try it once.

*The* DIVINE JUDGE *and the* SMALL DEMON *pose as doors. They make gestures.*

ZHANG XIE *enters and sings*:
(*Wu gongyang*)
At the foot of Mount Wuji,
no one knows where I come from.
I've been stripped of my clothes,
and my wounds are exposed.
Snow is falling again;
the crimson doors are closed, and the scene is so frightening.
I've reached the old temple so I'll try to open the door.
I might as well spend the night here.

*Sings again*:
(*Same tune*)
Venerable god, listen to me:
Think of this talented scholar from Chengdu Prefecture.
I was on my way to the capital
in search of scholarly honor.
But while I was crossing this mountain,
a robber stole all my valuables.
He also injured me badly and now I need to rest.
So I ask you for my sake to open these crimson doors.

MOUNTAIN GOD:

(*Same tune*)

Master Zhang, I am most clever.

DIVINE JUDGE:

He can speak. Is that not clever!

ZHANG XIE *continues the song*:

Thank-you, venerable god, for making

manifest your perspicacity.

SMALL DEMON:

Both sides of the crimson gate

open and bolt again.

DIVINE JUDGE:

How can doors talk?

*The* MOUNTAIN GOD *speaks*: Master Zhang, just go under the altar

and sleep for the night.

ZHANG XIE *continues the song*:

Thank you, venerable god.

ZHANG XIE *speaks*:

Luckily I managed to open the temple gate,

but my chest is filled with pain, hunger, and cold.

Tonight, I'll sit inside the room behind closed doors,

and no harm should come from Heaven.

ZHANG XIE *exits*.

SMALL DEMON: You're quite right! But in fact, disaster does come from Heaven.

MOUNTAIN GOD: Quiet! How can doors speak!

SMALL DEMON: Quiet! How can gods sing arias!

DIVINE JUDGE: Both of you shut up.

SMALL DEMON: The two of us and you, doesn't that make three?

DIVINE JUDGE: My teacher must be here.[3]

MOUNTAIN GOD: I am afraid that if Poorlass comes back and hears you speak, you'll scare her away. If she returns to Grandpa Li's house you'll just stir up trouble. So let's all keep quiet; hold back your tongues and be still.

DIVINE JUDGE: Poorlass is coming back, so be quiet.

MOUNTAIN GOD: Close the doors, wait until she gets here and knocks.

DIVINE JUDGE: Be quiet!

SMALL DEMON: Let's all be quiet!

POORLASS *enters and sings*:
(*Xinshui ling*)
The northern wind is freezing cold, the clouds hang low,
looking into the distant sky, snowflakes flutter and fall.
Trudging through the snow, I return
with the aid of a lantern
to keep me company in my solitude.

*Speaks*: I have not been told of any work to do, so there's certainly no hope. Who has pushed open my temple gate? Today is not a prayer day. It's locked inside. (*She calls out*) Open the door! (*She hits the back of the* SMALL DEMON.)

SMALL DEMON: Bang, bang, bang.

DIVINE JUDGE: They've just struck the second watch.

DAN *calls out*: Open the door!

*She hits the* SMALL DEMON's *back repeatedly.*

The SMALL DEMON *shouts*: Change hands and hit the other side,
would you?
DIVINE JUDGE: Shut up!

POORLASS *sings*:
(*Jiang'er shui*)
Who has entered my temple
and bolted the door?

*The* SMALL DEMON *speaks*: It's not a big bolt.
DIVINE JUDGE: I think it's your husband who bolted it.

POORLASS *continues the song*:
Forced to stand alone in the snow,
while this hissing northern wind cuts through my body,
[freezing] as if I had been thrown into that river.
Who can have come to stay here?
Hurry, open the door,
don't leave me standing here.

POORLASS *hits the back of the* SMALL DEMON *and calls out*: Open the
door, open the door!

*The* SMALL DEMON *groans in pain.*

DIVINE JUDGE: Why do you have to make such a noise?
SMALL DEMON: It's the door's creaking song.

ZHANG XIE *enters and sings*:
(*Same tune*)
People on the road cannot sleep,

so come to this place to lodge for the night.

If I open the door, I am afraid that the wind will blow in and I
won't be able to sleep.

*He moves the bolt on the door and opens it.*

SMALL DEMON: Creeeeaaak.

DIVINE JUDGE: Here you go again.

> The SMALL DEMON *continues the song*:
> This is the one the bandit robbed.

DIVINE JUDGE: Mind your own business!

SMALL DEMON: As the door god, wouldn't I know?

> ZHANG XIE *continues the song*:
> My clothes are all torn and my body freezing.

> MOUNTAIN GOD:
> Judge and demon,
> soften your stern expression,
> and come to stand here.

*The* DIVINE JUDGE *speaks*: It's all your fault.

SMALL DEMON: Our great lord knows; it's freezing cold outside, so
he called us in.

DIVINE JUDGE: As if this were the stove room.

POORLASS: Venerable god, I want to question him, so please soften
your stern expression.

MOUNTAIN GOD: My superior won't let me stand in front of her.

DIVINE JUDGE: Let's show a little respect.

SMALL DEMON: Tonight this Mr. Bowman will lean on his bamboo
cane and hammer his fists.[4]

DIVINE JUDGE: It's better than a wrestling match.

MOUNTAIN GOD: You two doors, come inside the temple.

SMALL DEMON: So that she is free to question him.

DIVINE JUDGE: I beg you, sir, to sweep away the snow in front of
the main gate.

*Together*: And don't mind the frost atop other peoples' houses.

*The* DIVINE JUDGE, MOUNTAIN GOD, *and* SMALL DEMON *all exit.*

POORLASS *sings*:
(*Daolianzi*)
Noble sir,
Where are you traveling to?
I do not know how you got such injuries,
but the sight of you breaks my heart.

ZHANG XIE *sings*:
(*Suonanzhi*)
I am,
a licentiate
recommended by local officials from Chengdu to take the imperial
exams.
I had the means to go to the capital,
but the journey was so long.

POORLASS:
I suppose that while you were climbing
this mountain
called Wuji,
you were cheated by someone?

ZHANG XIE:

(*Same tune, new opening*)[5]

While I was climbing this mountain,

a robber in a tiger's skin,

stole my meagre belongings,

and hit me,

and lacerated my body until I was soaked with blood.

Today I came to this place

and all of a sudden met you.

I don't know who you are,

but I hope you will take pity on me.


POORLASS:

(*Same tune*)

I come

from a wealthy family,

but because of fires and floods, we fell on hard times.

When I was still young, my parents passed away,

and I don't have older or younger brothers.

I have been living in this temple,

for five or six years.

Now I've met you,

in such a piteous state.


ZHANG XIE:

(*Same tune, new opening*)

Every day at home,

I studied the books of the ancient sages.

When snow like this fell,

we mostly drank Yanggao,

leisurely sipping the frothy wine.

We composed poems
or went to look for plum blossoms.
I never tasted
this kind of hardship!

POORLASS:
(*Same tune*)
Sir, please do not
bring up those times.
At present everything is bad for us.
You have no clothes or bedding,
and these I cannot provide.
But as for food,
I can feed you.
And when you need to sleep,
just go to bed.

ZHANG XIE:
(*Same tune, new opening*)
I will just go to rest,
and tomorrow I will not get up.
My whole body is red and swollen,
so tonight I'll curl up by the paper-money furnace,
to avoid the wind and rain.

POORLASS:
I will bring you
some porridge,
and provide you
with an old, thin bed cover.

ZHANG XIE *speaks*: I am concerned that I have no food or clothes.
Who could have known that today misfortune would cross my path.

> POORLASS: People in distress must not tell their worries to other
> people in distress.
> *Together*: When you tell others of your troubles, they'll toss and
> turn.

*All exit.*

# ACT 11

*The* MO *acting as* GRANDPA LI *enters and sings*:
(*Douye huang*)
The first snow announcing a fertile year falls nonstop.
I feel we are going to have a bumper crop.
I am most moved
by the goodness of our emperor.

*The* JING *acting as* GRANDMA LI *continues the song*:
Husband, this morning I burned some incense to thank the deities;
I only hope that we two,
will live briefly in peace until our hair turns white and our teeth
yellow.[1]

GRANDPA LI *speaks*: You mean "fate"; there is no one who can
escape it.
GRANDMA LI: Husband, I've been living at the foot of Mount Wuji
seventy or eighty years and seen some families go under. I don't
know how we've managed, in this house, to fill our bellies with
boiled wheat and taro stew for so long.

GRANDPA LI: As if those were delicacies! Tell me, who have you
seen go under?

GRANDMA LI: Take the case of that Poorlass. She came from the
Wang family, the ones called the Wealthy Wangs. But both parents died, and fires, floods, and thieves destroyed their family
livelihood. Now, of that whole family there is only that girl left
in the old temple ready to continue the family line.² But, you
old rogue, you really know no shame!³

GRANDPA LI: What shame do you have?

GRANDMA LI: I have money!

GRANDPA LI: What money have you?

GRANDMA LI: What do you mean I have no money? Yesterday
I sold a pig, three chickens, eight pounds of taro roots, and a
basket of big water chestnuts.

GRANDPA LI: You sure have money, Landlord King of Pearls.

GRANDMA LI: Of course! I have money in the house, I have fields
outside the house, a garden at the back of the house, a boat
beside the house, and Heaven above the house.

GRANDPA LI: A masterful calculation!

GRANDMA LI: And I have the power!⁴

GRANDPA LI: We're doing quite well. Why did you just bring up
Poorlass?

GRANDMA LI *sings*:
(*Tete ling*)
Normally she weaves hemp and spins cotton,
and that is how she makes a living.
But these days it has been snowing,
and you've not taken care of her.
Call Xiao'er to take her
a bottle of wine,
a peck of rice,
and a piece of bean curd.

GRANDPA LI *speaks*: Don't give it to her, don't give it to her.

GRANDMA LI: You old beast! How can you not give it to her!

GRANDPA LI: I'm just afraid it'll leave a bad smell in her mouth.

GRANDMA LI: If she's hungry, she'll cook the rice, if thirsty she'll make the bean curd into soup, and when she's cold she'll drink the wine. What bad smell will it leave in her mouth?

GRANDPA LI: I guess you're right. Ask Xiao'er to come here.

GRANDMA LI *calls*: Xiao'er, Xiao'er.

> The CHOU *acting as* XIAO'ER *enters and sings*:
> (*Same tune*)
> Whenever you have nothing to do, you call for Xiao'er.

GRANDPA LI *speaks*: What?

> XIAO'ER *continues the song*:
> But today I am doing nothing.

GRANDPA LI *speaks*: You're really lazy!

> XIAO'ER *continues the song*:
> One tender chicken,
> and a bottle of unstrained wine.
> I won't go to buy oil,
> or carry water,
> or pick vegetables,
> or look after the water buffalo.

GRANDPA LI *speaks*: Fine, fine! So today you don't need to eat either.

XIAO'ER: If you don't let me eat, I'll go and boil some taro porridge.

GRANDMA LI: Bring me a bowl, my boy.

GRANDPA LI: Neither of them ever goes short.

GRANDPA LI *and* GRANDMA LI *sing together:*
(*Same tune*)
The heavy snow turns our bodies to ice;
and earlier on we were thinking of Poorlass.
At times we rely on her
to weave hemp and spin cotton for us.
So we want you to bring her,
some bean curd,
some wine,
and some rice.

XIAO'ER *speaks*: Bring this to that lowlife Poorlass? I'm not going.
GRANDPA *and* GRANDMA LI: Why are you insulting her?
XIAO'ER: I'm accusing her.
GRANDPA *and* GRANDMA LI: What do you have against her?
XIAO'ER: Once I saw her standing in front of the temple, so I asked her: "Poorlass, you're so lonesome, and since I am so fair and pure . . ."
GRANDPA LI: If it were not for your black mouth.[5]
XIAO'ER: " . . .wouldn't you just marry me?" But that girl insulted me; bullied me saying I was just a kid.
GRANDPA LI: Next year you'll be forty.
XIAO'ER: Forty-one.
GRANDPA LI: I know.
GRANDMA LI: All right, all right. In that case I will find you a bride.
GRANDPA LI: What's that?
GRANDMA LI: He can't have managed to seduce Poorlass.
GRANDPA LI: Just think it over.
GRANDMA LI: Son, for my sake, take it over to her.
XIAO'ER: I just won't go.
GRANDPA LI: Mother, I have a rationale. Just tell him that one day you'll find him a bride. He'll take it then!

GRANDMA LI: Yes, you're right. *Calls*: Son, take it over and one day I'll make clothes for you to dress up, and I'll find you a wife.

XIAO'ER: Mother, you definitely must procure a wife for me.

GRANDPA LI: She is not marrying your land.

GRANDMA LI: Come on, come on, I'll go and get some rice, wine and bean curd and send you off to your ruin.

XIAO'ER: If I can have a wife I'll go!

GRANDPA LI: Then hurry up! Once there you must repeatedly express your mother's intentions.

XIAO'ER: I am just afraid that the snow outside the village is deep.

GRANDMA LI: It will keep on falling.

*Together*: It's truly more precious than gold from Yueyang.

*All exit.*

# ACT 12

ZHANG XIE *enters and sings*:

(*Ku xiangsi*)

Who knows how far I am from my parent's home,
so how can they know of their son's helplessness?

POORLASS *enters and continues the song*:

I heard you heave a long sigh,
and it made me cry.

ZHANG XIE *sings*:

(*Shizi xu*)

I regret that my time hasn't yet come;
at home and on the road
things have not gone well.

POORLASS:

I am not wanton, I am simply taking care of myself,

waiting to see what the Creator of All Things disposes.

ZHANG XIE:

I can rely only on my education.

POORLASS:

And I make a living doing needlework.

*Together*:

We must accept adversity;

there must come a time when things go our way.

POORLASS:

(*Same tune, new opening*)

In my humble opinion—

If one does not suffer a misfortune, there is no need to console
   oneself.

Rest and get better;

there is nothing else to discuss.

ZHANG XIE:

For now, all I have is a thin cotton robe, yet snow keeps falling,

and I am starving.

POORLASS:

Morning and night I will provide a little porridge for you.

ZHANG XIE:

And my clothes are all in tatters.

*Together*:
Somehow we'll get by,
we will find a solution.

ZHANG XIE:
(*Same tune, new opening*)
Listen,
I have never known anything like this;
normally I am dressed in formal cap and gown.

POORLASS:
There is nothing we can do now, but when the time is ripe for
    success,
surely it will be better than this.

ZHANG XIE:
Without travel money, how can I go to take the exams?

POORLASS:
You must stop worrying and wait for better times.

*Together*:
As the saying goes, good things
never come in haste.

POORLASS:
(*Same tune, new opening*)
As I see it,
with your fair complexion,
there will surely be a green official gown for you to wear one day.

ZHANG XIE:

Thank you for saying so.

How can I ever forget your kindness?


POORLASS:

All I can provide for you is coarse food and rough clothing.


ZHANG XIE:

I am sincerely touched by your good heart.


*Together*:

Perhaps in a former life

we were destined to meet.


POORLASS *speaks*: Who is coming?


XIAO'ER *enters with a carrying pole and sings*:

(*Zizi shuang*)

One picul, two piculs of rice and cereals,

one load.

Two buckets, three buckets of this stinking stuff,

also one load.

Four bundles, five bundles of firewood,

another load.

A jar of bean curd and a jar of wine,

one more load.


POORLASS *speaks*: Xiao'er, it's snowing hard. Why did you come?


XIAO'ER *sings*:

(*Shuang quanjiu*)

Father and mother,

have asked me to tell you this:
here is some wine and rice
I've brought for you.
If you want it, keep it,
if not, I'll take it back.

POORLASS *speaks*: I am so grateful to Grandma and Grandpa Li that, considering the heavy snow, they asked you to bring this over. How could I turn it down?

XIAO'ER *puts the bundle down and speaks*: Here you are, Poorlass.

POORLASS: Xiao'er, there's a scholar here, please welcome him.

*Xiao'er bows.*

ZHANG XIE *speaks*: Young brother, whose son are you?

XIAO'ER: Young brother? I'm your big brother, I'll be forty-one this year.

POORLASS: This is the son of Grandpa Li.

XIAO'ER: Poorlass, where is this "poor brother" staying?

POORLASS: Xiao'er, don't say such things!

ZHANG XIE: Miss, my body is hurting, I'll go inside.

POORLASS: Scholar Zhang, go to the western gallery, find something to eat, and go to sleep.

XIAO'ER: These two get on so well, truly Heaven matches the poor with the poor.

ZHANG XIE: Today, I've been fortunate to receive your help, you've kept me from sinking into the mire.

ZHANG XIE *exits.*

XIAO'ER: Who is this poor brother?

POORLASS: Xiao'er, he's a good person. Don't offend him.

XIAO'ER: You're Poorlass, he's Poorlad.

POORLASS: He is a licentiate who while crossing Mount Wuji was attacked by a robber. Now he's come to my temple to rest, first because of the heavy snow, but also because his wounds have not yet healed. When he is recovered, I will send him to pay his respects to Grandma and Grandpa Li.

XIAO'ER: I have some good news for you. (*He laughs.*)

POORLASS: What is it, Xiao'er?

XIAO'ER: I . . . (*He laughs.*)

POORLASS *laughs*: Tell me!

XIAO'ER *makes a gesture.*

POORLASS: What is it? Why don't you say it?

XIAO'ER *laughs*: If I do, I'm just afraid you'll beat me.

POORLASS: I won't beat you. Tell me.

XIAO'ER: All right, I'll tell you.

POORLASS: Go on.

XIAO'ER: My father and mother want us to be married.

POORLASS: Want us to . . . ?

XIAO'ER: . . . be married.[1]

POORLASS *spits*: You scoundrel! You ignorant, stupid fool, insulting me like this! Take that, you bastard! (*She hits Xiao'er.*)

XIAO'ER *shouts*: A fine thing! Headman![2] She's beating her husband, a wife is beating her husband!

POORLASS: Pervert! Me marry you! You wouldn't even do for the bones of an ox; you're more like a ghost than a man.

XIAO'ER: I look like a ghost? Ghosts have red hair!

POORLASS: Breast milk is still dribbling from the corners of your mouth, and you still have baby hair. How dare you come here and say this!

XIAO'ER *spits*: Wench, how can baby hair be this long? If you won't
  marry me, I'll starve you to death.

POORLASS: I am going to tell your parents.

XIAO'ER *stops* POORLASS: Don't! Spare me, wife.

POORLASS: So, you're frightened.

GRANDPA LI *enters*:

> The sword beheads the dishonorable man,
> while gold is awarded to the virtuous one.

I asked my son to bring some things over, but he hasn't yet returned.
  Why is there quarreling here?

POORLASS *sings*:
(*Zhu nu'er*)
I am so grateful to you, Grandpa and Grandma Li,
that in this heavy snow you kindly sent these goods to me.
I also thank Xiao'er, who braved the snow to come here,
but he's just such an ignoramus.
You know,
just tell me it's not true!
how can you give him to me as my husband!

GRANDPA LI: Miss,
(*Same tune*)
Just now he wouldn't bring the rice and wine,
so my wife teased him,
saying that one day she would marry you to him.
He was delighted and braved the snow to bring you the wine.
Don't say
it's not so.
You bully him by saying he is not presentable.

XIAO'ER *speaks*: Daddy, she bullied me, I'm telling you.

POORLASS: What are you talking about?

> XIAO'ER *sings*:
> (*Same tune*)
> Just now, when I brought the bundle to the front of the temple,
> I saw a bastard pestering her.
> She was singing some *ladida* tune,
> and made a fool of me.
> Don't say
> it's not so.
> How is she fit to be a wife?

GRANDPA LI *speaks*: Why don't you examine yourself a little. *Calls*: Young woman, who is this person?

POORLASS *speaks*: Even when there is no snow, I'm aware of your affection for me. He is a licentiate from Chengdu who is on his way to the capital to take the imperial exams. When he arrived at Mount Wuji, he was beaten by a bandit with an iron club and robbed of all his possessions. He has no clothes to wear, or food to eat, and no medicine to cure his wounds, or money to go home. At night he has no quilt to cover him, and besides, it is difficult to rest in the temple. Just now, while I was questioning him, your son brought over wine and rice.

XIAO'ER: When the wench goes to court, she'll confess. I'm one who can raise a racket!

GRANDPA LI: You're just too unreasonable, son. Go back now.

XIAO'ER: I'll go back and tell mother that I don't want you as a wife.

GRANDPA LI: She won't be upset.

XIAO'ER: Don't be mean to me. I can read the *Meng Qiu*[3] and I also can look after the water buffaloes.

GRANDPA LI: Be careful, or you'll fall off one.

XIAO'ER:

There are always places to fish,

but they are not along the shallow shores.[4]


XIAO'ER *exits*.


POORLASS *calls out*: Scholar Zhang, Grandpa is here. Find some
support and come out to greet him.


ZHANG XIE *enters and sings*:

(*Xiayun feng*)

Relaxing my knitted brows,

and opening my pain-filled sick eyes,

I force myself to hobble over the passageway.


POORLASS:

Scholar Zhang, please pay your respects to Grandpa.


GRANDPA LI:

I have long heard of your virtue,

but since I did not know you were here,

I did not come to pay my respects.


ZHANG XIE:

Snow was falling,[5]

and in my sickness,

I couldn't find an inn.


GRANDPA LI *sings*:

(*Heyan kai*)

I am old and my step is unsteady,

So lately, I rarely go outside.

I didn't know you were here.

POORLASS:

How could we, under such rain and snow,

so copious and threatening,

leave this place even for a moment.


ZHANG XIE:

Because I was robbed by a madman,

and beaten, I have been weeping continuously.


POORLASS *and* GRANDPA LI:

Sir, it is probably because your clothing is so thin,

and that you feel so terribly cold that you look like this.


ZHANG XIE:

(*Same tune*)

From the way you two speak to me,

it's as if we met in a previous life,

like old friends.


POORLASS:

Grandpa, please don't let Grandma know.

Perform a virtuous deed—

if you have some old clothes, please give them to him.


GRANDPA LI:

I have some coarse gowns,

I'll give you to wear.


ZHANG XIE *and* POORLASS:

Thank you so much, Grandpa.

Then I will be able to change these blood-stained clothes.

GRANDPA LI *speaks*: Although I am just a peasant from a remote village, I know something of the ways of the world. Normally, would I give one string of cash to those who kowtow to me, and five hundred cash to those who pay lip service to me? Not at all! In the cabinet, my clothes are your clothes and the money in the purse is ours equally.

ZHANG XIE: That shows your magnanimity, sir.

POORLASS: I have been in this temple for almost seven years. If it were not for Grandpa's protection, who would now take care of you?

ZHANG XIE: Thank you, Grandpa. I am not inconsiderate,[6] and there will be a day when I will repay you.

GRANDPA LI: I must return now,

and bring you some clothes that will help you bear this fierce cold.

DAN: If it were not for Grandpa, on whom could we rely?

SHENG: In the end there will be just retribution.

*Together*: It's only a question of when it will arrive.

*All exit.*

# ACT 13

*The* TIE *acting as* SHENGHUA *enters and sings*:

(*Jin qianzi*)

With peach cheeks and apricot face,

I am caught unaware, and the time has come for me to tie up my hair.[1]

In the painted hall, along with my companions,

We hear the songs of reed-pipes from another courtyard,

and the overflowing sounds of the flutes and the strings.

Instantly, my heart is at ease,

and I remain leaning on the eastern balustrade of the little tower.

*Sings again*:

(*Shang gonghua xu*)

For me, Shenghua,

in all four seasons,

nothing perturbs my heart.

Unless I go along to the imperial garden with my companions

to enjoy a happy celebration among the fragrance of flowers.

But just think!

When it comes to coiffures, make-up, and needlework,

what do I know!

I entrust my cloud-like hair and powdered face,

to my servants.

And when I look at myself in the mirror,

this made-up face is entirely their work.


(*Same tune, new opening*)

In the daytime,

we often joke,

and play in the Happy Spring Terrace.

I know intimately the rich and powerful houses,

and among them we are honored as the first.

But I am moved

when my emperor summons me,

to go to the Jasper Pool.

As spring passes, I can detect the scent

of the summer month lilies.

And when we set out in small boats,

for fun, we sing the songs of the water-caltrop pickers.


(*Same tune, new opening*)

As autumn arrives,

the moon atop the mountain shines full

on the tall ornate tower.

Wearing red skirts to the feast,

the whole night we do as we please and go late to sleep.

In winter we enjoy the snow,

and place sprigs of plum blossoms in a vase.

Sitting in a circle in the heated hall,

we drink the fragrant Yanggao wine.

You must know that I am rich and noble,

and naturally fine and delicate.

Even without rouge and powder on my face, I am still quite
charming.

*Speaks*: From ancient times, it is said that:

the people of Jing don't value jade,

nor do mermaids value pearls.[2]

Those who come from rich and noble families do not appreciate the
happiness of this life. Papa is Military Affairs Commissioner
Wang Deyong, but people call him the Black Prince. Mama is
Lady of Two States, from the Liu family. You can imagine how
much honor and wealth she enjoys. In court, father is called
the Crimson Prince. At times I have been summoned by the
emperor and allowed to wear court dress. Don't ask me to turn
my face so you can steal a glance. Truly, in the thirty-six palaces,
there is no match to my beauty.

SHENGHUA *exits*.

# ACT 14

ZHANG XIE *enters and sings*:

(*Bomei ling*)

My worries are many and my resentments great;

I have experienced no end of ordeals.

Fortunately, I can rest my bones and cease worrying for a few days.

POORLASS *enters and continues the song*:

I've heard that recently you are well,

and this makes me quietly happy.

*Together*:

Once again the snow has cleared and the rain has ceased.

ZHANG XIE *sings*:

(*Hong shan'er*)

Walking alone along the western corridor, my soul is about to
   break.

I feel lonely and desolate;

how can I bear it! All before me has turned into resentment and
   gloom.

POORLASS:

This village is isolated and forlorn,

and people are few.

Morning and night, I sit and stroll alone,

and thus I spend my days.[1]

ZHANG XIE:

(*Same tune, new opening*)

As soon as dusk sets in,

the roar of tigers and the cry of gibbons rise.
With your soft and delicate demeanor,
why don't you wed a good husband?


POORLASS:
How can you be so foolish and confused!
For one, even if you overlook my unsightliness
I don't have a cent to my name.
Besides, I have no relatives,
so who would take care of you?[2]


ZHANG XIE:
(*Same tune, new opening*)
I have been sick,
but I am slowly recovering from my wounds.
All the same,
I cannot return home.
You have no husband and I have no wife.
so why don't we get married?[3]
I am full of learning,
and one day I will succeed,
and be appointed to stand by Phoenix Pool.
As soon as I pass the exams,
I will take you to my hometown.
It is better than staying in this temple.
Wouldn't that be wonderful!


POORLASS:
(*Same tune, new opening*)
You are so shameless!
And much too frivolous!
How can you talk like this?

If you marry me it will simply arouse people's suspicion,
and stir up gossip.
Like water, I am completely pure;
without the slightest stain.
Please sir, leave this place immediately.
Do not remain here.

POORLASS *exits*.

GRANDPA LI *enters and sings*:
(A *zhuan* tune)[4]
Let me inquire, sir:
[A gentleman] recommends people with the proper etiquette,
and dismisses them with the proper etiquette.[5]

GRANDMA LI *enters and continues the song*:
My Poorlass,
why was she wiping away her tears and leaving in such a hurry?

ZHANG XIE:
Let me explain, Ma'am:
Since I still can't go home,
she has no husband, and I am alone,
I asked her to marry me.
But wiping away her tears,
she scolded me.

GRANDPA LI:
(*Same tune*)
Wife, hold on!

GRANDMA LI:

Scholar, what you say is very odd.

Do you want

me to act as go-between?

I'll ask her to come back,

and talk her into changing her mind.


GRANDPA LI:

My wife wants to arrange your marriage.


ZHANG XIE:

I'll trust you, sir, to advocate for me.


GRANDMA LI *calls* POORLASS *to come out*:

Don't be angry.

Come back and let's talk this over.


POORLASS:

Let me explain:

(*Jin lianzi*)

The temple door was closed,

yet you opened it and stayed here.

You had no means of survival,

so I helped you.

But this is most unreasonable!


GRANDPA *and* GRANDMA LI:

If you speak so impulsively,

he'll just drift away.

ZHANG XIE:

(*Same tune, new opening*)

In this place, I have no one to rely on,

and fortunately Poorlass has no husband.

GRANDPA *and* GRANDMA LI:

You are right.

The way we see it,

your spirit is so frank,

you will make a good couple.

POORLASS *sings*:

(*Zui taiping*)

Tomorrow then,

we will kneel to pray in front of the gods.

To learn if the gods allow this marriage,

we will look for the divination blocks.[6]

ZHANG XIE:

What you say makes sense.

GRANDPA LI:

No need for us now to act as go-betweens.

GRANDMA LI:

Husband, bring out a pig's head to offer to the local god.

*Together*:

When destiny unites couples, we celebrate.

GRANDPA LI:

(*Coda*)

Only these words ring true.


GRANDMA LI:

Please Zhang Xie, don't double-cross us.


ZHANG XIE:

One day I will succeed.


GRANDMA LI *speaks*: Tomorrow Grandpa Li will arrange some
    sacrifices for the gods (*laughs*) and I'll come prepared with a big
    open-mouth (*laughs*).[7]

GRANDPA LI: You're such a glutton. What's so funny?

GRANDMA LI: When you act as go-between, you have to put on a
    smile from time to time.

GRANDPA LI: But you overdo it!

GRANDMA LI: Small wonder people say:


> If a good couple happens to be poor,
> The go-between won't utter a word.

ZHANG XIE: If people are destined to meet, they will do so from a
    thousand *li*.

*Together*: But if this is not their destiny, even though they stand
    face to face they won't meet.


*All exit.*

# ACT 15

*The* WAI *dressed as* LADY WANG *enters and sings*:
(*Nü guanzi*)
Our position is of the highest rank,
hairpins and tassels indicate our status,
and we hold the insignia of power.
Ours is a highly cultured family;
high officials in red and purple robes line up behind our gates.
Besides, our relatives
all come from powerful families.
My husband is the Military Affairs Commissioner at court;
and we have a single daughter who has just come of age,
but she is yet unmarried.
Such worries
trouble my mind.
but I have no way to solve them.

*Sings again*:
(*He chongtian*)
Sighing deeply,
I suddenly realize that my daughter's marriage is yet unsettled.
Her figure slender and full of grace,
with peach cheeks and an apricot face.
Each day she is richly attired in pearls and jade like a goddess,
with a jade-fairy mien.
She is skilled at all the arts,
just look at her literary talent;
In the whole city, she is the most desirable bride.

(*Same tune*)

My daughter has just come of age,

and I am touched that my emperor has proclaimed this on
numerous occasions.

To make a good marriage,

it must be to the top graduate,

although she would be no disgrace as an imperial bride.[1]

Nor is she attached to anyone,

and has both honor and glory.

I'll see if this year,

I can find her a good husband.

*Speaks*: Daughter, your father is Military Affairs Commissioner at
court and your mother the Lady of Two Estates. How can we
not find you a good match?

She must marry a scholar.

and we will not ask whether he is wealthy or poor.

As long as the wind and moon of the Five Lakes is there,

We need not worry where to drop the line.

LADY WANG *exits*.

# ACT 16

*The* MOUNTAIN GOD *enters and sings*:

(*Ti yindeng*)

Of all the meat-eating gods in these parts, I am the most
efficacious;

for a hundred years, they've all said I respond to their requests.

Year after year, I see to it that the households that sacrifice to me
have no troubles.
With offerings of four or five plates of sweet sesame cakes,
and one or two hundred cash in paper money,
how can a god show its divinity or make its power felt?

*Speaks*:

To those who do good I send down one hundred blessings;
and to those who do evil, one hundred misfortunes.[1]

I have heard that Zhang Xie is a candidate of this enlightened
dynasty, minister material for the empire. He wants to marry
Poorlass. (*Laughs*) With me on their side, nothing will go
wrong, but without my help, the match would be delayed for
many years. On Mount Wuji I am the great king, who happens
to act as a matchmaker. I am known as the King of the Matchmaker Sprites.[2]

GRANDPA LI *enters and sings*:
(*Daying xi*)
Today we've set the table,
(*Assents*) Ah, yes!
And there are some things we must see to.

*The* MOUNTAIN GOD *speaks*: We must? You're not coming to ask me
empty handed?
GRANDPA LI: Listen to this:

*Sings*:
Wait a while and you'll see a pig's head arrive.

*The* MOUNTAIN GOD *laughs and points at* GRANDPA LI *saying*: This
hungry crow loves it!

*Sings*:
Pour a little wine and make sure you fill it up.

GRANDPA LI:
I suppose Zhang Xie and Poorlass will ask for the divination
   blocks.
They're becoming husband and wife;
it is their destiny.
Please, see that you attend to it.

MOUNTAIN GOD:
There is a pig's head;
let's see if it's a pig's head or a dog's head.

XIAO'ER *enters and sings*:
(*Lülü jin*)
Hey daddy, you've never seen
such a big pig's head.
Soon, when thanks have been offered to the gods,
I'll run off with it.

GRANDPA LI:
In a while, after they are married,
we must drink some wine.

MOUNTAIN GOD:
The deity has been waiting for a long time;
how can they take so long?[3]

GRANDPA LI *speaks*: You're so impatient! Ask scholar Zhang and
the girl to come out.

MOUNTAIN GOD: Pour the wine!

GRANDPA LI: No, it's not ready yet.


ZHANG XIE *enters and sings*:

(*Si yuan chun*)

You may want to give up, but I will not.


MOUNTAIN GOD:

Hurry, come below my altar to eat pig's head.


POORLASS *enters*:

If the divination blocks do not favor it,

how will I survive?


ZHANG XIE:

A gourd keeps a man at sea afloat,

and only when the gourd sinks, will I part with you.


*The* MOUNTAIN GOD *speaks*: I'm just like a minor god, never full and
never warm.


GRANDPA LI: The nobles are inside.[4] Scholar Zhang and you, young
lady, please pay your respects to the god as if the god is present,
and listen to me invoke him.[5]

XIAO'ER: Daddy, I'll pour the wine.

GRANDPA LI: We're not ready yet. Wait until I summon the god.

MOUNTAIN GOD: Just pour a little now.

GRANDPA LI: Shut up!

XIAO'ER: Daddy, hurry up and call the god, I want to eat meat.

GRANDPA LI: You won't go short! My god is awe-inspiring.

*The* MOUNTAIN GOD *opens his eyes wide in an imposing gesture.*

XIAO'ER: You can't compare with the Bright Horse King.[6]
GRANDPA LI *assents*: The incense is rising.
MOUNTAIN GOD: Pour the wine into the cup.
GRANDPA LI: Did you hear that, Xiao'er?
XIAO'ER: The deity wants some wine poured.

*The* MOUNTAIN GOD *agrees.*

GRANDPA LI: The incense is fragrant.
MOUNTAIN GOD: A piece of meat is missing from the cup.
XIAO'ER: I've stolen half.
GRANDPA LI: What? Xiao'er!
XIAO'ER: The deity says he won't eat fat.

> *The* MOUNTAIN GOD *declaims*:
> Fat I don't dislike,
> But lean is my delight.
> From the top of the head to the soles of the feet,
> Every bit of it smells so sweet.

GRANDPA LI: My god is efficacious.
MOUNTAIN GOD: And don't we know how efficacious he is!
GRANDPA LI: So when will our temple custodian grow fat?[7]

*The* MOUNTAIN GOD *steals wine and meat and makes a gesture.*

GRANDPA LI: Please scholar Zhang, say your prayers and make your wishes.

ZHANG XIE *sings*:

(*Juhua xin*)[8]

Powerful gods please listen:

I live in the prefecture of Chengdu,

but ever since I was young, I have applied myself to the classics.

I was going to the imperial city

when I was robbed on the way.

I had money enough for the journey,

but it was all stolen.

With one blow I was thrown to the ground;

yet put up with the snow and sought refuge in this temple.

Affected by endless grievances

I could not sleep peacefully.

Unexpectedly, I met Poorlass. She was without a husband,

and I without a wife.

Now we want to finalize this predestined bond.

I offer the gods some unstrained wine.

GRANDPA LI *speaks*: Dismount your horse and drink the soup.[9]

Let the wine be offered for the first time. Xiao'er, pour the wine.

XIAO'ER: I've already poured it.

GRANDPA LI: No you haven't, how can you say you have? You're so dishonest. (*He beats Xiao'er.*)

XIAO'ER: But daddy, I did pour it.

GRANDPA LI: Be quiet and pour again!

XIAO'ER *weeps*.

GRANDPA LI: What is that sound?

MOUNTAIN GOD: There's no meat.

XIAO'ER *agrees*.

GRANDPA LI: There's no meat, and you still agree!

XIAO'ER *pours wine and the* MOUNTAIN GOD *surreptitiously drinks it.*

GRANDPA LI: Please Miss, come and say your prayers and make your wish.

> POORLASS *sings:*
> (*Second tremolo*)
> When I was still young,
> both my parents passed away.
> I have slept alone in this temple for six or seven years.
> As for matters of clouds and rain,
> how would I know
> such things?[10]
> By chance I met Zhang Xie,
> who wants to become my husband.
> God, you are wonderfully efficacious.
> Shed your light on these blocks so that we may be united;
> if not, we'll immediately part ways and that will be the end of it.
> I know not why,
> but silently I feel half-crazed.
> Fill yet another cup,
> that I may offer the gods this unstrained wine.

GRANDPA LI *speaks:* One cup has been poured; the wine is offered a second time. You're still not pouring the wine. I'm going to beat you, you reprobate.

XIAO'ER: Daddy, I poured the wine. Don't beat me. See, the corners of my mouth aren't wet, so it must be the deity drinking it. This time look carefully.

GRANDPA LI: All right, pour the wine again.

XIAO'ER *sings*:
(*Interlude* [*Xiepai*])
Choking and speechless, I quietly wipe away my tears,
when I poured wine, no one drank it.
The parrot cup is deep.
As the cup is inclined,
it breaks into droplets.

The MOUNTAIN GOD *steals the wine*. GRANDPA LI *catches him and sings*:
I've just seen his wondrous power:
one pours, the other one drinks.

MOUNTAIN GOD:
You've presented your sacrifices scrupulously.
Thank you for your three offerings, but I have not eaten them.

GRANDPA LI *speaks*: As if you hadn't.[11]

The MOUNTAIN GOD *continues the song*:
Zhang Xie is Poorlass's destined match;
they formed a bond in a previous life,
and in this life they meet again.
Within the embroidered curtains,
they'll be like fish in water.[12]
They've been allowed to tie together the lover's knot,
and forever be united.

ZHANG XIE *and* POORLASS *sing together*:
(*Final tremolo*)
Just as the phoenix and the simurgh sing in harmony,
we support each other at the edge of the sky.
United like a pair of *qianqian* birds,[13]

frolicking like a pair of mandarin ducks.
With tenderness and love,
we will grow old together,
and closely follow each other.
I'll entrust you
to my heart.

GRANDPA LI:
The gods are singing, the ghosts dancing,
and in our village we are all merry,
and wish to look after each other in conjugal happiness until the end.

*Together*:
I will go to the moon palace and snap the cassia twig.
Already united in mutual bliss,
what a sweet taste all this has!

*The* MOUNTAIN GOD *speaks*: Now they are married.

GRANDPA LI: Yes.

MOUNTAIN GOD: So it is proper for the local god to return to the rear hall.

GRANDPA LI: The Great King returns to the clouds.

MOUNTAIN GOD: Actually, I am going to look for that wife of yours.[14]

GRANDPA LI: What for?

MOUNTAIN GOD: So that she can join in the feast.

GRANDPA LI: You want to eat more!

MOUNTAIN GOD: Three offerings! Three offerings! And I still have not seen meat or wine.

GRANDPA LI: You can only speak of food.

*The* MOUNTAIN GOD *exits*.

XIAO'ER: I'm off to slice a little meat.

GRANDPA LI: I'll go and get your mother.

ZHANG XIE *and* POORLASS: We thank you for marrying us.

XIAO'ER: I'll go and get the platter and you go and get mother.

GRANDPA LI: On this day of joy, we begrudge the briefness of the night.

*Together*: Yet when in times of leisure we feel lonely, we resent the long days.

GRANDPA LI *and* XIAO'ER *exit.*

POORLASS *sings*:

(*Tianzi sai Hongniang*)

At first my heart was lonely,

but then, unexpectedly, I met you.

How could we know of our destiny,

or that I was going to be united with you,

and fly together like the phoenix and the simurgh?

*Refrain*:

We hope to live for a hundred years in constant harmony,

and not leave each other for a moment.

ZHANG XIE:

(*Same tune*)

Honor and disgrace are determined in a former life.

All we can do is conduct ourselves correctly.

He who wears an official cap must not deceive others.

If I do anything like that,

I will suffer for it all my life.

*Refrain*:

We hope that at the first leap he will pass the dragon gate,[15]

and return home with honor.

POORLASS:

(*Same tune*)

No one knew of my poverty or hardship,

but now I can briefly relax my frown.

Sir, you must never

forget my kindness,

or when you came into the temple.

*Refrain*:

Our desire is to look after each other forever,

like fish in water.

ZHANG XIE:

(*Same tune*)

I am well versed in the classics, ritual and music,

how could I let you down!

Put your mind at rest,

I will not trouble my wife, or let her down,

trouble you or let you down.

*Refrain*:

We want to remain constant as in the beginning,

and be together until the end.

ZHANG XIE *and* POORLASS *speak*: We've caused Grandpa Li a lot of

trouble! He came so early.

XIAO'ER *enters and sings*:
(*Saihong niang*)
I was already quite depressed
to see Poorlass getting married.

GRANDPA LI *enters and continues the song*:
Inhuman wretch,
spare us the hypocrisy.

XIAO'ER:
Wait until I'm drunk,
then I'll curse him!

GRANDPA LI *speaks*: If you do, I'll certainly beat you.
ZHANG XIE: Is Grandma Li coming or not?
GRANDPA LI: She's here already.
GRANDMA LI: She came barefoot.

GRANDMA LI *enters holding a pair of shoes and sings*:
(*Same tune*)
It's because my feet are small,
and fit on a three-inch lotus.[16]

GRANDPA LI *speaks*: You mean one foot three inches.

GRANDMA LI *continues the song*:
There is a puddle of water
three feet wide in front of the temple gate.

GRANDPA LI *speaks*: Yes, there is a puddle of water.

GRANDMA LI *continues the song*:
So I took off my embroidered slippers,
and played the boat.

GRANDPA LI *speaks*: Who anchored you?

GRANDMA LI: Let me put on my slippers, prostrate myself, and pay my respects to the god.

ZHANG XIE: We're indebted to you, Grandma, for arranging everything and helping us both.

GRANDMA LI: Congratulations!

POORLASS: Thank you, Grandpa and Grandma Li.

XIAO'ER: I'm going home.

GRANDPA LI: Why?

XIAO'ER: I have no choice! He could have added two more words.

ZHANG XIE: What words?

XIAO'ER: "Thank you Grandma, Grandpa, *and* big brother." It would have been so much better!

GRANDPA LI: You're insufferable!

GRANDMA LI: Grandpa, today we've warmed up some wine to celebrate the occasion. We don't care whether it's cloudy or not.[17] We need stools to sit on and a table to eat at.

GRANDPA LI: What stools or tables do we have here?

GRANDMA LI: If this is to be called a celebration, how can there be no stools or tables! Call Xiao'er, he'll act as a table.

GRANDPA LI: Good idea!

GRANDMA LI: Son, you look like . . .

XIAO'ER: What do I look like? I look like a bridegroom!

GRANDPA LI: With that face! You look just like a table!

XIAO'ER: I'm a man, how can I pose as a table?

GRANDMA LI: I'll give you some fruit.

GRANDPA LI: And I'll get you some wine.

XIAO'ER: Ok, I'll do it!

GRANDPA LI: Very enthusiastic!

XIAO'ER: If I get to drink wine, then bring it over.

GRANDPA LI: Sure.

XIAO'ER: If I get to eat meat, then bring it over too.

GRANDPA LI: Sure.

XIAO'ER: If I call you, it's because I am hungry.

GRANDPA LI: I know, but I'm just instructing you to act the table.

XIAO'ER *bends over.*

ZHANG XIE: Grandpa Li, where did you get the table?

XIAO'ER: I'm the table.

GRANDPA LI: Be quiet!

*They place some plates and food on* XIAO'ER *'s back.* GRANDMA LI *picks up the wedding cup, Poorlass the bottle of wine, and* XIAO'ER *secretly eats the food. They make gestures.*

> ZHANG XIE *sings:*
> (*Pai ge*)
> I thank you
> Grandma and Grandpa Li, for coming.
> Thank you ever so much for the generous help.

> POORLASS:
> Since I was a girl I have received your kindness,
> and now I am married.

XIAO'ER *speaks:* Daddy.

GRANDPA LI: Do me a favor and be quiet!

XIAO'ER: I'm hungry and my waist aches!

GRANDPA LI: I'll give you something for your rheumatism.

> GRANDMA LI *continues the song:*
> Five hundred years ago,
> it was already written down.
> Today, I just came to give you encouragement.

XIAO'ER *eats secretly again.*

GRANDPA LI *and* GRANDMA LI *sing together:*
We urge you to drink a cup, don't refuse.
May you live in marital harmony for a hundred years.

POORLASS *speaks:* Let's drink.

*She continues the song:*
I urge you Grandma,
to drink some unstrained wine.
even if it makes you tipsy.

ZHANG XIE:
I thank you so much,
for the kindness you have shown us.
How could we ever forget your favor and equanimity?

GRANDPA LI:
(*Same tune*)
The two of you from now on,
must cherish each other.
And you must remember everything the classics have taught you.

GRANDMA LI:
As a couple you both are
so exceptional,
my goodness! You're quite the couple!

GRANDPA LI *speaks:* To know oneself is to know others.

XIAO'ER *continues the song*:
To act as a table,
I have to bend my waist and my head is low down.
If there is any wine, get a cup,
and give the table a drink.

GRANDPA LI *speaks*: Quiet!

POORLASS *sings*:
(*Hong xiuxie*)
Where is Xiao'er speaking from?

XIAO'ER:
Underneath the table.

GRANDMA LI:
I'll pick up the table and have a look.
Oh! how odd!

XIAO'ER *stands up*. GRANDMA LI *asks*: Where has the table gone?

XIAO'ER *continues the song*:
Mother, the table
has been borrowed by someone.

GRANDPA LI *asks*: Borrowed for what?

XIAO'ER *continues the song*:
For funerary rites.
They said it was nice and clean,
and they would use it.

GRANDPA LI *speaks*: What do you mean, nice and clean?

ZHANG XIE *and* POORLASS *sing*:
(*Guagu ling*)
Tonight we have enjoyed ourselves to the full.

GRANDMA LI:
When I drink wine I need to drink my fill.

XIAO'ER:
We've drunk more than ten bowls,
and licked the dishes clean.

GRANDPA LI:
Wife, son, you're both much too silly!

ZHANG XIE *and* POORLASS:
In the whole village, we are the only ones who married.

*Together*:
In a former life, our present destiny was formed.
All night long we drank the fragrant wine,
all night long we drank the fragrant wine.

ZHANG XIE *and* POORLASS *speak*: Thank you very much, Grandma
and Grandpa, we've given you so much trouble.
GRANDMA LI *and* GRANDPA LI: Seek happiness and live your lives
as best you can.

ZHANG XIE: We'll care for each other for some days, and then
I shall leave for the imperial city.
GRANDMA LI: It's not right to think of abandoning her.

GRANDPA LI: Don't hanker after your hometown as the place to live.

*Together*: Where you receive great kindness, that is your home.

*All exit*.

# ACT 17

LADY WANG *enters and sings*:

(*Feng rusong*)

The eastern wind blows gently bursting open the palace peach
    blossoms;

the last traces of snow are finally melting.

Willow buds brush the ground with a golden hue.

SHENGHUA *enters and continues the song*:

I wander deep in thought[1] in this desolate courtyard.

As I stroll past a string of lit lanterns,

the scene in the garden grove is like a painting.

LADY WANG *sings*:

(*Zhu Yingtai jin*)

Deep inside the painted hall,

everyone is quiet,

and spring enters the tips of the apricot blossoms.

The timely rain clears,

and white butterflies and yellow bees,

follow each other at this time of budding blooms.

SHENGHUA:

Green watercress

and emerald water lilies are swayed by the wind;

and fish sport in the pond.

*Together*:
Along the painted corridor
people stroll, laughing merrily.

LADY WANG:
(*Same tune, new opening*)
And now,
by the foot of the white-washed wall
are half-hidden winding paths;
what a marvelous scene.
In the secluded pavilion of the small court,
like a group of sylphs,
richly adorned ladies calmly sit in a circle.

SHENGHUA:
I can hear
the call of the flower vendor crossing the bridge to the West,
peddling his exotic blossoms vying in beauty.

*Refrain*:
The confused warbling of orioles,
noisily flying across the tree tops.

LADY WANG:
(*Same tune, new opening*)
In the clear dawn,
the servants with abandon,
shout back and forth, playing the "Flower Game,"
losing earrings and dropping hairpins.[2]

*Refrain*:
Stepping on the swing
and laughing out loud, unreserved.

SHENGHUA:

Exquisite peach blossoms,
open all at once like a burning sky,
and baby birds call now and then.
Looking at this scene,
my heart is troubled.

LADY WANG:

(*Same tune, new opening*)
You have lost your smile;
my child, cease this idle worrying,
and calm your concerns.
What good ever comes in haste?
Among this year's virtuous scholars,
we shall choose a young man.

SHENGHUA:

This vexation
is not because I want to marry.
Let me explain:

*Refrain:*[3]
I am sad
that my youthful glow will wane.

LADY WANG *speaks*:

Men take wives,
and women are married off.

This is the year of the examinations. Your mother will look for a talented and handsome official and you shall be married.

SHENGHUA: I am extremely grateful, mother!

LADY WANG: Find someone who is both talented and of good
  repute.
SHENGHUA: I care not if he is poor so long as he is accomplished.
LADY WANG: Countless are the sons of noble houses who die of
  hunger.
*Together*: Yet how many humble cottages produce great men.

*All exit.*

# ACT 18

ZHANG XIE *enters and sings*:
(*Shuidiao getou*)
I've pored over myriads of volumes,
and write as if divinely inspired.
As for my career,
I never thought so many obstacles would lie in the way.
Recently, I was forced to marry Poorlass,
but it was not part of my life plan as a scholar
and once more it sets constraints on myself.
The best thing is to go to the capital,
take the exams and win first place.

POORLASS *enters and sings*:
(*Heye pu shuimian*)
When you came here,
I just felt love be born in my heart.
Now that the snow has cleared,
you've decided to leave the temple.

*Refrain*:

Who was to know that in a former life

we were already betrothed?

When will we be able to cast aside the bounds

of poverty we endure?

ZHANG XIE:

(*Same tune*)

When I arrived here, I was moved by my wife,

so we made a lifelong pact of marriage.

Rather than stay confined here,

it is better to go to the capital and snap the cassia twig.

*Refrain*:

When I have won glory,

I shall have achieved my aspirations.

Yet without traveling money,

how am I to rise in the world?

POORLASS:

(*Xiaoshun ge*)

I was in very low spirits

when I met you,

and just think how poor we both are.

Since here you have no one,

and I have no relatives,

no one will come to our aid.

When you leave, I'll be the same as before;

I will be very lonely.

*Refrain*:

How are you to find money for the road,

money to go to the capital?

ZHANG XIE:

(*Same tune, new opening*)

If I leave today,

when will I be able to pursue our love,

win glory for my family,

and bring honor to myself?

And for you I wish,

for you I wish that when the time comes,

you will be conferred a title.


*Refrain*:

Joyfully united, happily married.

Happily married and joyfully united for a lifetime.


POORLASS:

(*Same tune*)

I will

leave the temple and go

to ask for a loan from Grandpa.

They'll give it to me as your traveling expenses.

I also need to buy some silk for garments,

and stuff it with old cotton.

I am afraid that if the spring is chilly,

you will not be properly dressed.


[*Refrain*:][1]

I'll prepare some clothes,

so you won't feel cold on the road.


ZHANG XIE:

(*Same tune, new opening*)

I hope that you can borrow it,

so do go and ask.

I'm afraid that I'll be short of money,
or that halfway there I will have to skimp and scrape.
Who will provide more money then?
I really hope that you
will somehow be able to persuade them.

*Refrain*:
Persuade them to add some more,
and when I come back I will repay it in full.

POORLASS *speaks*:

Underneath a great tree,
Frost never forms on the grass.

I will go and ask for help from Grandma and Grandpa Li. But
what profits have peasant families?
ZHANG XIE: Also, we need to give them something as surety. If we
give them much it may help, but if we give them too little, it will
be of no use.
POORLASS: I know. Grandma Li has often said that she wants hair to
make a wig, but I am just afraid that I won't be able to part with it.
If I take some from all around the top of my head and give it to her,
considering how much I can ask for, it should be enough.
ZHANG XIE: Good idea.

POORLASS: By nature, peasants have always been thrifty folk.
ZHANG XIE: We haven't planned for traveling expenses there and back.
POORLASS: We know that "up the mountain it's easy to catch a tiger."
ZHANG XIE: But "it's hard to ask someone for help."

*All exit.*

# ACT 19

GRANDPA LI *enters and declaims*:

After much rain [the rain] is beginning to clear and the wheat
harvest is rich.

I've just bathed and I'm clothed in white hemp.

I hear the sound of the pawlonia leaf-flute as smoke rises from the
stoves.

Paper mulberry and *cudrania* buds grow as hoopoes fly.

I have heard that licentiate Zhang is taking leave of his wife and
going to sit for the imperial exams. I do not know whether this
is true or not, so let me go over to ask my wife.


GRANDMA LI *enters and sings*:

(*Ma pozi*)

In the second month of spring, the scene is beautiful;

the delicate seedlings begin to sprout.

From time to time, I walk over to the top of the field,

where schools of tadpoles swim in the water.

I lean over and scoop a bowl,

then hurry over to buy some oil.


GRANDPA LI *speaks*: What do you want the oil for?

GRANDMA LI: I'll buy thirty cash of sesame oil, fry the tadpoles and
eat them with a bowl of barley.

GRANDPA LI: Nauseating!

GRANDMA LI: If it nauseates you, eat some salted plums.

GRANDPA LI: If I eat them, I can relieve myself. Wife, do you know
something? That scholar Zhang wants to go to take the imperial
exams.

GRANDMA LI: Surely Poorlass is going too?

GRANDPA LI: How could she? But here she comes.

POORLASS *enters and sings*:

(*Yin ling*)

He has met with so much loneliness,

and I have met with so much loneliness.

In the second month I enjoyed the quiet,

but now again I feel depressed.


GRANDPA *and* GRANDMA LI:

We have heard that your husband,

now wants to leave for the capital.


GRANDPA LI:

(*Same tune*)

He has no other prospects,

and you have no family,

so how are you going to arrange for the traveling expenses?


GRANDMA LI *looks elsewhere, and* GRANDPA LI *pulls her around*:

Hey you, turn around and look.


POORLASS:

If he is to leave now,

without money for the road, how is he to cope?


GRANDMA LI:

(*Same tune*)

If he wants to go, it's your problem;

if he doesn't, it's also your problem.

Why tell me,

and then tell my husband again?

GRANDPA LI *and* POORLASS:
For the time being,
we can only rely on you, Grandma.


GRANDMA LI *speaks*: It's all right for her to say that she relies on me,
but what about you!
GRANDPA LI: I'm not like a folding chair.[1]


POORLASS:
When the river is narrow, the water runs fast.
And when people are pressed, they come up with plans.


Zhang Xie is a scholar. Although he has already received
Grandma's help, he is still hoping for your assistance. "If you
must seek help, seek it from a notable person."


GRANDPA LI: "If you help someone, you should help someone in
urgent need."
GRANDMA LI *laughs*: Ask anybody. Just because I paint my lips and
powder my face, wear a skirt and a gown, does that make me a
notable person? Maybe this old beast has some money!
GRANDPA LI:


People seek help from others,
just as birds seek the forest.


Whatever money you have, just lend her some.


GRANDPA LI: "An honest man doesn't do anything underhanded."
How much money do you want?
POORLASS: I want about one hundred strings of cash.
GRANDMA LI: Gracious me! You'd have to sell your parents and
ancestors for the last seven generations!

GRANDPA LI: Look around for some money and lend it to her. When that scholar Zhang returns wearing the green official gown, he surely won't have forgotten Poorlass.

POORLASS: And I will never forget Grandpa and Grandma.

GRANDMA LI: Husband, go and collect fifteen strings of cash to give her.

GRANDPA LI: All right.

GRANDMA LI: I'm not boasting, but that box is truly great?[2] Now, you old beast . . .

GRANDPA LI: I have nothing at all![3]

POORLASS *sings*:
(*Dianzi yin ling*)
Let me pay my respects,
and please listen to me:
Grandma Li you've given us your support,
and I wish to stand by your side in your old age.
But now that Zhang Xie has recovered,
it is better that he sets out as soon as possible.

*Refrain*:
He will return having attained his goal,
only someday,
he will return to the old temple wearing his green gown.

GRANDMA LI:
(*Same tune*)
I have a treasure,
which I did not tell you about.

GRANDPA LI *speaks*: I don't know what you mean.

GRANDMA LI *continues the song*:
If you knew,
You would have already borrowed it from me.

GRANDPA LI: Could it be the pearl that glows in the dark?[4]

POORLASS *continues the song*:
Grandma, give it to him,
and entrust him with it.

*Repeat the refrain.*

GRANDPA LI:
(*Same tune*)
For the old road to the capital,[5]
whatever the travel expenses,
Grandma, give it to her now,
so that he'll set out on the road promptly.

POORLASS:
I am not a stranger bothering you
for this morning's support.

*Repeat the refrain.*

POORLASS *speaks*: People who help others are few. Grandma, if
you have any valuables, lend us some. We need another fifteen
strings of cash.
GRANDMA LI: I only have a couple of things.
GRANDPA LI: Might it be a wool robe?

GRANDMA LI *spits*: You have one of your own!

POORLASS: Grandma, is it a leather cloak?

GRANDMA LI *spits*: He has one of those at home!

GRANDPA LI: You're putting it on to me! Well then, if it's not wool or leather then it must be silk.

GRANDMA LI *spits*.

GRANDPA LI: Then what is it? Tell us!

GRANDMA LI: When I married you a long time ago, I had nothing with me but a couple of, a couple of . . .

GRANDPA LI: Of what?

GRANDMA LI: Of water buffalo skins.

GRANDPA LI: They're good for making drums, that's all.

GRANDMA LI: And for making shoes, too.

GRANDPA LI: That's obvious.

POORLASS: I have heard Grandma say many times that you wanted my hair, but I could not part with it. Today I have cut some locks of my hair and brought them to you thinking that you may want to make them into a hairpiece. If you can give me some cash for it, that would be wonderful.

GRANDMA LI: Fine, fine, that's just what I wanted, but the color isn't right.

GRANDPA LI: But it's so very black!

GRANDMA LI: It doesn't matter. It needs some red in it.

GRANDPA LI: You want to look like a ghost?

GRANDMA LI: I'll give you a few ounces of silver coins. When he succeeds, you can repay me. Go and fetch half a bowl of wine.

GRANDPA LI: Certainly, I'll add some [money] too.

GRANDMA LI *talks under her breath*.

POORLASS: Thank you very much, Grandpa and Grandma.

GRANDMA LI *picks up the wine cup and sings*:
(*Tianzi yin ling*)
With this cup of home-brew,
I thank you for cutting off your hair.
My hair bun
should certainly increase in value.

POORLASS:
I suppose the road is long,
and we need money for the expenses.

GRANDPA LI *and* GRANDMA LI *sing together*:
When you return to the temple, you must tell him
that both Grandpa and Grandma expect him
to become the top graduate this year.

POORLASS *pours wine for them and speaks*: Thank you very much,
Grandpa and Grandma. I am very grateful.

*Sings*:
(*Same tune*)
I don't have much capacity for wine,
with one cup, a peach-blossom flush.
Joined in an earlier life,
we formed a bond because of grandma.

GRANDMA LI:
I don't feel like going out,
and I won't be able to give him a farewell feast.

*Repeat the refrain.*

POORLASS *speaks*: Thank you, Grandpa and Grandma. I shall be going now.

GRANDMA LI: Tomorrow as usual, you will be all alone by the bed curtains.

GRANDPA LI: Husband and wife are birds that perch on the same tree.

*Together*: Yet when death comes, each goes their own way.

*All exit.*


# ACT 20

ZHANG XIE *enters in an angry mood and speaks*:
Damn! Murder can be forgiven,
but not lack of manners.


Poorlass, that low-bred! I'll beat her more dead than alive. If it wasn't for the terrible plight I was in, I would have never gone near her. Truly:

You know in your heart she's not the right companion,
but in an emergency you go with her for a while.

She left this morning and hasn't returned all day. She doesn't care that I want to leave. Never mind. I'll go and look for a stick around here, just to show her that although she may not come to Han Xin's misfortune, she'll suffer Qu Yuan's sorrow.[1]

POORLASS *enters and sings*:
(*Lan hua mei*)
Early in the morning, facing the mirror I felt sad,

and this is not because of my father or mother,

or because I cut my hair, which will eventually grow again.

What made me so upset,

is who, if not I, will take care of you on the way?


ZHANG XIE *speaks*: Hey you, you tramp, when you walk, don't swing your skirt, and when you smile don't show your teeth. That is the proper way for a woman. You go off for the whole day, and return with your face all red. Where have you been drinking? I'm going to beat you, you tramp! (*He beats Poorlass.*)

POORLASS: You're unjust! Husband, Heaven can testify! The gods confirm it! Just let me explain.

ZHANG XIE: Be quick, and if you don't tell the truth, I'll beat you straight through tomorrow.


POORLASS *sings*:

(*Shizi xu*)

You are too impatient,

Just listen to me:

The day of your departure is just ahead,

and I spent the night worrying that you have no money for the road,

so I hurried to Grandpa's house to ask for a loan.

Grandma said she had no gold,

no goods to pawn,

or cash.

So I cut off my hair,

to get a little money.

Alas! She offered me a cup of wine as encouragement.


ZHANG XIE:

(*Same tune*)

If you lie to me,

you're truly in trouble.

And if you're hiding anything from me,

I'll beat you for your dishonesty.

Whomever bought someone else's hair?

This pair of eyes say you're a fool through and through.

So now, where did you get the money?

And that silver?

And where did you get the wine?

If what you say is false, I won't be blamed.

Close the temple doors,

I'm going to find out where you've been.

ZHANG XIE *beats* POORLASS.

POORLASS *sings*:

(*Linjiang xian*)

You deities in the hall, you all know,

that I did nothing wrong.

You are no man!

ZHANG XIE *beats* POORLASS, *who cries out*: Grandpa Li! Grandpa
  Li, come to my rescue!

ZHANG XIE: Why are you calling for Grandpa Li!

GRANDPA LI *enters*:

He has studied ten thousand volumes,

And knows a thousand stories from the past.

Licentiate, what are you two quarreling about?

ZHANG XIE: I was delayed here for a while and you helped me out.
For all this I am grateful. But this infamous tramp, knowing
that I was about to depart, spent the whole day out on purpose.

GRANDPA LI: You're leaving?

ZHANG XIE: I do want to go, but even if I want to go, I have no luggage. For the sake of my career, the Creator of Things granted
me your help, and I will never forget you and Grandma. But
today, she was gone the entire day only to return with a flushed
face. Tell me, where were you today?

POORLASS *sings*:
(*Naizi hua*)
Grandpa,
Grandma said that she wanted some hairpieces,
so all I could do was cut off some hair.
Grandma was very pleased,
And invited me for a cup of unstrained wine.
For no reason at all he started hitting me,
as if
I had ruined his plans.

GRANDPA LI:
(*Same tune*)
Grandma has been wanting hair buns for over eight years,
so the minute she caught sight of so much hair, she was really
    pleased.
The silver and the wine came from our house.
So stop this nonsensical fight and control your anger.
And listen,
how are your family plans ruined?

ZHANG XIE *sings*:

(*Same tune*)

I want to go to the capital,

and I have been waiting from morning until now.

If my wife loves wine and is greedy for pleasure,

in the long run what does this accomplish?

And so I started thinking,

my wife had ruined my family plans.

POORLASS *enters and makes some gestures.*[2]

ZHANG XIE *speaks*: So that is what happened. According to what Grandpa says, I almost misjudged you.

POORLASS: Husband, you are a person in search of success and fame; don't act like this.

GRANDPA LI: No more idle talk. My wife has asked me repeatedly to inform you that she won't be able to send you off.

ZHANG XIE: I will go and bid her farewell in a moment.

GRANDPA LI: There really is no need.

ZHANG XIE: My wife will depend on you in every way. When I make the slightest headway, I'll certainly repay you.

GRANDPA LI: Oh, don't mention it!

POORLASS: Once you are gone, I will greatly miss you.

ZHANG XIE: I shall write, but the mountain roads are so remote.

GRANDPA LI: I hope to see the victory banner.

*Together*: And we shall all listen for good news.

GRANDPA LI *exits*.

POORLASS *sings*:

(*Zui luopo*)

Dearest, your behavior was such

that I feel uneasy at heart.


ZHANG XIE:

I felt nervous in my desire to leave.

I did not see you return,

and then I noticed your face looked unwell.


POORLASS *sings*:

(*Si huantou*)[3]

When you first came into my temple,

you did not show such a temper.

Now that we're husband and wife,

you treat me with such disrespect.


ZHANG XIE:

You forget to mention you disappeared for the whole day,

and I've been waiting since morning.


*Together*:

Clear as water,

and bright as the moon.

When anger explodes, resentment is born.


II. POORLASS:

I understand that you

feel pressed to leave,

but that would not have been possible,

had I not sold my hair.

ZHANG XIE:

This must be a good omen.

POORLASS:

When you attain fame and rank,

don't do what you did just now, and be so wickedly shameless.

III. ZHANG XIE:

Let the gods listen to me:

If I were to fail in gratitude to anyone, would it be to you?

POORLASS:

You must remember the past,

*Together:*

when by the paper-money furnace your clothes were stained with
    blood.

POORLASS:[4]

Don't be like Wang Kui, that ingrate,

who drove the messenger with a letter from the hall.[5]

*Together:*

That sort of person,

that sort of heart.

I will wait for news from you.

IV. ZHANG XIE:

After I am gone,

I expect you won't be moved by spring passion.

POORLASS:

On a moonless and dark night,

Jiang and Fei, the river goddesses, met a kindred spirit.[6]

For many years, I have lived in this lonely temple, cold and
cheerless.


*Together:*

Tonight once again, under the quilt I will sleep alone,

and as before, my eyes brimming with tears.


GRANDPA LI *enters and sings:*

(A *Zhuan* tune)

Grandma knows,

she knows that you are going to the capital.

Despite all her farming chores,

she did come especially to send you off.


GRANDMA LI *enters and continues the song:*

Listen,

I want nothing else but that you remain deeply attached to each other,

yet there is something I want to bother you with.

When you pass through Huzhou,

buy a mirror for me so I can powder my face.


GRANDPA LI:

You're so inconsiderate!


ZHANG XIE *and* POORLASS:

(*Same tune, new opening*)

Grandma, don't worry,

I am a simple person,

and if you want a mirror,

Would I dare to come to your door without one?

GRANDMA LI:

Farewell then.

You and I have been invited tonight

to the village on the other side of the river, to pray to the local god.

GRANDPA LI *speaks*: It's all for food.

GRANDMA LI *continues the song*:

You are asking

why I am so stingy?[7]

GRANDPA LI:

You're outrageous!

GRANDPA LI *and* GRANDMA LI *exit*.

POORLASS *sings again*:

(*Jiangluo qun*)

When you leave today, I will be—oh, how sad!

I have some money,

but how would you know I scraped it together to help you.

ZHANG XIE:

Your only reward is to waste away—oh, how sad!

*Together*:

Quietly, we wipe away our tears.

ZHANG XIE:

In this moment, my heart is—oh, how sad!

Touched by such simple earnestness.

POORLASS:

And you still cannot discern whether I'm good or bad—oh, how sad!

*Together*:

For that we need the gods.

POORLASS *sings again*:

(*Huhuanzi*)

With a steadfast heart I shall wait patiently;

there will come a day when I see my beloved again.

That day, when we meet once more,

we will speak again of our past love.

ZHANG XIE:

But presently—oh, how sad!

I simply want to go to the capital.

POORLASS:

I fear only that once you acquire honor and rank,

you will find my station too humble.

ZHANG XIE *sings*:

(*Coda*)

Such people are condemned to an early death!

*Together*:

If you too look three feet up, you see the gods.[8]

Both of us will fly apart—oh, how sad!

ZHANG XIE *speaks*: Tonight, my pillow will be soaked with tears.

POORLASS: I hope only that you will be among the top graduates.

ZHANG XIE: In front of my horse the runners will cry "Here comes
the top graduate."
*Together*: What a handsome husband he will be.

*All exit.*

# ACT 21

*The* MO *acting as an* ASSISTANT *enters and speaks*:
He holds a position of the highest rank. His nickname is the Black
Prince. At the head of the eight great ministers, his office stands
above all others. In the painted hall all is calm and quiet, and the
stately room is imposing. The hanging embroidered curtains screen
the spring wind, and along the sumptuous stairs lingers a faint fragrance, but no human traces. The Military Affairs Commissioner is
going up to the hall. Tell the assistant to take up his post.

*The* CHOU *acting as Military Affairs Commissioner* WANG DEYONG
*enters and sings*:
(*Dou heima*)
The emperor's virtue is so vast it surpasses that of Yao.
Happily we experience times of great peace.
I am the highest ranking Military Affairs Commissioner,
of this enlightened dynasty.
Pure is my conduct,
striking my bearings
and upright my arguments;
this is what scares people most.
If the "vinegar" is good,
I can drink five bottles.

WANG DEYONG *speaks*: My name is Wang Deyong, and I am the Military Affairs Commissioner. Who doesn't know the name of the Black Prince? I have no male descendants, just a daughter whose childhood name is Shenghua. She has just come of age but is still not betrothed. This is the year of the great national examination and I intend to summon the top graduate as my son-in-law. Yet I wonder what fate will bring. I shall just wait for my wife to come out, and discuss this matter with her. Assistant, bring some chairs.

ASSISTANT: Sir, the main hall and the library are both too far away. I won't have time to bring them over.

WANG DEYONG *shouts*: Hurry up and bring them over!

ASSISTANT: But sir, you are usually so patient.

WANG DEYONG: Not these days. (*He pulls the* ASSISTANT *until he falls.*) Since there are no folding chairs, I'll use you instead. (WANG DEYONG *sits on the back of the assistant. The* ASSISTANT *shouts.*) Don't shout! In ancient times, Minister Feng walked to the Tiny Hut in the Rear Flower Garden and sat in meditation for fifteen days.[1] Can't I sit for a day and a night?

ASSISTANT: Oh, dear me!

WANG DEYONG: Assistant!


*The* ASSISTANT *assents.*


WANG DEYONG: Do you need me to help you?

ASSISTANT: I beg you, sir, please do help me.

WANG DEYONG: I suppose five or ten strings of cash could be called help.

ASSISTANT: Indeed.

WANG DEYONG: All three teachings—Confucianism, Buddhism, and Daoism—offer help. As a licentiate, if you were appointed an official you couldn't do that.

ASSISTANT: Why not?

WANG DEYONG: Because licentiates have to study and use classical language, and wear tall scholars' hats and leather boots that have a heavy tread. Since you can't do such things, you can't become an official.

ASSISTANT: That's right, I couldn't.

WANG DEYONG: As a Daoist priest, if you were made a deacon, you couldn't do that either.

ASSISTANT: Why couldn't I?

WANG DEYONG: Because Daoist priests have to seek out and learn from the immortals how to dash off talismans and charms.

ASSISTANT: No, I couldn't do that either.

WANG DEYONG: As a monk, if you were made an abbot in charge of a large Chan monastery, you'd probably remain a plain monk and never make abbot.

ASSISTANT: How can I be compared to a plain monk?

WANG DEYONG: If you aren't one, what are you doing here learning how to bow down?

ASSISTANT: You asked me to pose like this.

*The* ASSISTANT *gets up and* WANG DEYONG *falls on his back.*

ASSISTANT: Now you've fallen on your back.

WANG DEYONG: Come on now, call my wife and young mistress Shenghua.

ASSISTANT: Yes, sir. Turning at the head of the stairs, I go up to the hall. Behind the screen, the corridor is deep and silent. In front of the painted hall, the heavy curtains hang to the ground. You must watch your step to be an assistant.

WANG DEYONG: Go inside and pass on the message. What are you doing standing out here?

ASSISTANT: But where do you want me to go?

LADY WANG *enters and sings*:
(*Fen die'er*)
In the deep and secluded courtyards,
spring is a vexing season.

SHENGHUA *enters and continues*:
In the inner chambers there is no hint of love.
Walking along the fragrant banks,
frolicking in the garden,
how I long for such diversions.

WANG DEYONG:
Child listen to me,
this concerns you.

WANG DEYONG *speaks*: Daughter, you've done wrong!
SHENGHUA: Papa, I've done no wrong.
WANG DEYONG: You haven't? Some days ago you took all those
hungry fleas from my jacket and boiled them to death!
ASSISTANT: You never reflect on your own faults.

WANG DEYONG *sings*:
(*Zhuma ting*)
Look at my daughter:
You look like the moon goddess Chang'e, but even prettier.
Your papa has no sons,
so when we turn old we can only rely
on you, our only child.

LADY WANG *and* SHENGHUA:

We still don't know what Papa's fine idea is.

Please hurry up and disclose it to us.

WANG DEYONG:

You must do no wrong to others;

do not let our daughter's youth slip by.

LADY WANG:

(*Same tune*)

For such a delicate and loving daughter,

we need a scholar as our son-in-law.

In our family, we have been nobles for many generations,

so how could she be fated to marry

an ordinary person?

WANG DEYONG:

Among the five hundred names, there are many talented ones;

Daughter, pick a handsome one.

LADY WANG:

Father, what kind of talk is this;

if it is not a top graduate, how can it be a match?

SHENGHUA:

(*Same tune*)

The whole array of high officials

cannot compare with the green gown of a top graduate.

Besides, I come from a powerful and noble household,

so if he is not the top

how can we associate with or admire him?

LADY WANG:

Our emperor will select worthy gentlemen this year.

We must give our child one with an auspicious future.

*Together:*

We can put up a lot of money,

to secure the top graduate as our son-in-law.

*The* ASSISTANT *speaks:* Sir, how much will you offer for a son-in-law?[2]

WANG DEYONG: I shall give on arrival a tip of ten thousand strings.[3]

*The* ASSISTANT *assents.*

WANG DEYONG: And another ten thousand when he dismounts.[4]

*The* ASSISTANT *assents.*

WANG DEYONG: Plus soup and wine, accepting the silk whip, and
    procession money, they're ten thousand each.[5]

ASSISTANT: Sir, where is all this money going to come from?

WANG DEYONG: The City God Temple will pay.

ASSISTANT: But that's paper money.[6]

WANG DEYONG: Come, this year you can select one and make your-
    self a little money. Make sure the top graduate is not over thirty,
    and bring him back as a husband for our Shenghua.

ASSISTANT: Yes, sir.

WANG DEYONG: Truly:

What need have scholars for good matchmakers,

when in the books there are beauties with faces like jade.

ASSISTANT: Is it not "there are beauties"?[7]

WANG DEYONG: Yes.

ASSISTANT: So, correct me.[8]

> SHENGHUA: Papa, we must both be of the same age or it won't do.
>
> LADY WANG: If he has talent, do not object that he is just a poor scholar.
>
> WANG DEYONG: A literary master calls on other literary masters.
>
> *Together:* Great men mix with other great men.

*All exit.*

# ACT 22

ZHANG XIE *enters and sings:*

(*Nü guanzi*)

In those days while I was stranded in the old temple,

I often walked along the grassy paths and dikes lined with willows.

Now, I can see in the high forests, among flowers and trees the
   oriole hatchlings call;

a wine shop pennant shows a branch of apricot flowers.

Weary of the hardships of the road,

I am afraid of dusk and resent the first morning light,

I ponder these things, aware that my heart is deeply troubled,

and in vain turn my head toward my home, but the road is long.

Cuckoo,

stop calling all night long.[1]

*Declaims:*

(*Shuidiao getou*)

Determined, I left my hometown,

all on my own, hoping to reach the court.

Along the road I met with disaster,

but how would I know I would meet Poorlass and linger on.

I remember wearing the brightly colored gown to enter the hall,[2]

and at the time of parting, the words of caution my parents gave me;

when I think about it, it was all good advice.

They asked me to dismount when I came to a bridge

and not to travel by boat at night.

Recently,

I have left the old temple,

and I am anxious.

Father and mother will be worried about me,

and I expect that Poorlass must be weeping streams of tears.

But I gave up all that,

and picked up my bundle and rain wear,

to cross over the towering mountains and ford the long rivers.

Truly:

Where wild geese cannot fly,

people are drawn by the thought of profit and fame.


ZHANG XIE *exits.*


# ACT 23

POORLASS *enters and sings*:

(*Fuqing ge*)

Ever since he left our home,

thoughts of our two months together like lovebirds

break my heart.

For long I've kept to my empty room,

and now, just as it was before,

it is as if I had never married him.

The swallows carry mud in their beaks

and search for their old nesting place still in couples.

*Speaks*:

North and south of the village, the sounds of the pawlonia-leaf
    flutes;

behind and in front of the mountain, white cabbage flowers.

This weather my beloved will not see. Full of unhappy thoughts,
    without a penny, and without even half nop bushel of rice to eat,
    all I can do is go over to Grandma's to weave hemp and ramie
    cloth in order to scrape together something to eat. Oh, what
    suffering! To buy spring clothes I have to pawn the summer
    ones, and as soon as the clothes are made, the season has passed.
    I have just now finished sewing a blouse for the spring. All over
    the mountain tops the cuckoo cries.


*She sings again*:

(*Yu meiren*)

Weaving hemp and ramie cloth, I ply the needle,

but I have no choice.

Often my tears do not dry,

for I fear that parting is much easier than reunion.


*The* JING *(*GRANDMA LI*) barks like a dog from backstage.*


GRANDMA LI *enters and speaks*: Xiao'er, go to the top of the field and
    look, I think someone is stealing our chickens! (*She clucks like a
    chicken.*) This damned Xiao'er, I can't see him anywhere. *Shouts*:
    Chickens, shoo! *Calls*: Oh dear! Miss Zhang!

POORLASS: Greetings, Grandma, I have not seen you for several
    days.

GRANDMA LI: Why haven't you come to visit?

GRANDPA LI *enters*: The ancients put it well:

> If fate means for us to eat porridge,
> we will forget to strain off the water when we boil the rice.

Your life has been so lonely, and when you finally wed, in less than two months he was gone again.

GRANDMA LI: He will soon come back. Why are your eyes so swollen?

POORLASS: Since Zhang Xie left, truly this peach blossom face of mine has been streaming with tears. I've wiped away thousands upon thousands.

GRANDMA LI: That's just it! My husband sometimes goes on business trips and is away for a week. I sit in my room and fret. My whole body gets dry and itchy. When your Zhang Xie left, did your body get dry and itchy?

GRANDPA LI: Just boil a pellet of honeylocust.[1]

POORLASS: How can you say such things! All I do is cry.

GRANDMA LI: When my husband is home, then I'm all right.

POORLASS: How so?

GRANDMA LI: Because when he is in the house, night after night he boils medicine to wash my scabies, so it does not itch.

GRANDPA LI: I just scratch her where she itches.

POORLASS *sings*:
(*Shang ma ti*)
My knitted eyebrows never ease;
and flowers I don't care to wear.
Thoughts of him make me weep, wetting my cheeks;
my fate is so twisted.
Just as we came together in harmony,
we met with a setback.

GRANDPA *and* GRANDMA LI:

We must wait

and when he becomes an official,

he must take us both along with him.

GRANDMA LI *sings*:

(*Same tune*)

I am personally happy

that you married.

We expect that after this journey,

he will soon snap the cassia twig in the moon.

A trousseau will be your lot,

of gold head dress and a rose-colored mantilla,

and I shall be named a lady.

*She points at* GRANDPA LI:

And my husband

will surely be named guarantor.

GRANDPA LI *speaks*: How would I be named guarantor?

GRANDMA LI: Because your grandfather was an intriguer, and your
father a servant, which makes you a guarantor.[2]

GRANDPA LI: You could hardly say we're three generations of
ministers.

GRANDPA LI *sings*:

(*Same tune*)

I'm not bragging,

but it is quite definite that he will pass the exams,

and return triumphant, clad in rich clothes.

It will be a time of honor and glory.

GRANDMA LI:

I'll be Grandma and you'll be the person on duty.

GRANDPA LI *speaks*: You've taken the best part again!

*Together*:

Then we will be happy,

buy candles and good incense.

And we shall all thank Heaven and Earth.

POORLASS *speaks*: I'm afraid that once he has passed the exams he
    will not return.

GRANDPA LI: You must compose yourself and count the days till his
    return.

GRANDMA LI: There will come a day when the Yellow River runs
    clear.

*Together*: Sooner or later everyone meets with good fortune.

*All exit.*

# ACT 24

ZHANG XIE *enters and sings*:

(*Wang wu xiang*)

My home is in Sichuan,

and when I look back, tears quietly fall.

How was I to know that along the way someone was to rob me,

or that I had no alternative but to marry Poorlass?

Luckily, I've escaped from that place,

and the capital

is right before my eyes,

all bustling with activity.

*Declaims*:

Being poor at home is not so bad,

but being poor on the road is dreadful.

I met with a vicious murderer,

and to go or stay was out of my control.

Mulling over things on the snowy road,

sleepless, I knocked at the temple's door.

Because Poorlass took care of me,

I had no choice but to marry her.

I craved warmth in rest and my fill in food,

so for a while my studies were neglected.

But once again I took the road to the capital,

and I've had to be careful with my expenses.

Now that I have reached the imperial city,

I feel my spirit renewed.

I will attain the top position.[1]

and assist our sage emperor.


STUDENT MO *and* STUDENT CHOU *enter together and sing*:

(*Sudi jin dang*)

Intent on reaching the clouds one becomes a scholar,

but how many autumns must pass reading beneath the lamp.

If at first try one attains the top graduate position,

we'll be able to display our hard-earned learning.


ZHANG XIE *speaks*: Greetings.

STUDENT CHOU: Greetings, honorable sir. May I ask your name?

ZHANG XIE: My name is Zhang.

STUDENT CHOU: You mean Zhang with the "bow" radical or the
  one with the characters "to stand" on top and "early" below?

ZHANG XIE: The "bow" radical.

STUDENT CHOU: The "bow"! That's Yuchi Jingde's weapon.[2]

STUDENT MO: If Shan Xiongxin could see you, he'd be trembling with fear.

ZHANG XIE: And your name?

STUDENT CHOU: Zilu.

STUDENT MO: We'd better put down some namecards.[3]

STUDENT CHOU: It's Zilu, but because last time I did not pass the exams, I changed my name to Luzi.

STUDENT MO: When did you grow those distinguished horns?[4]

ZHANG XIE: And your surname?

STUDENT CHOU: My surname is Hua, my full name Hua Luzi.

STUDENT MO: Hua Luzi, all you do is dirty people's doors.[5]

STUDENT CHOU: Sir, have you found a place to stay yet?

ZHANG XIE: No, not yet.

STUDENT CHOU: Those who travel together get to know one another, and rest for the night in the same place.

STUDENT MO: I'm lucky to get close to a nobleman.

ZHANG XIE: Sir, where can I find an inn?

STUDENT CHOU: It's just ahead, in the teahouse. You stay upstairs and I will stay downstairs.

STUDENT MO: As soon as he starts speaking, he sections off success and failure.

STUDENT CHOU: Only if you know how to get by without paying, can you be my friend.

STUDENT MO: You should befriend your betters.

STUDENT CHOU: This is the mill stand.[6] Those who sleep on the ground are like river water—they don't spring from the same source.[7] Here is the inn.

ZHANG XIE: Fantastic!

STUDENT MO: Sir, look at the teahouse, it's neat and tidy and the upper floor is spacious. In front of the gate you have a restaurant and a wine shop, and on the side there is a bath house and a rice shop. Outside the gates is the examination hall. If you want some excitement, there is the entertainment district: to the left you have the singing courtesans of the Mandarin Duck Towers and to the right the courtesan musicians of the Willow Flower Market.[8] You might as well stay here.

ZHANG XIE: Thank you so much, gentlemen. My arrival was a little abrupt and I've not had time to arrange a feast for you.

STUDENT CHOU: Oh, you're too kind, too kind! Since I have been renting this place I've discovered four advantages.

ZHANG XIE: Please, list them for me.

STUDENT CHOU: First, no one can bring a lawsuit against me.

ZHANG XIE: Why not?

STUDENT CHOU: Because since time immemorial people have been calling me a poor scholar.

STUDENT MO: It' better to kill oneself than to kill others.[9]

STUDENT CHOU: Second, mosquitoes and fleas can't do anything to me.

STUDENT MO: Why not?

STUDENT CHOU: Because I'm pretty thick-skinned.

STUDENT MO: Indeed, a skin fragrant like jade![10]

STUDENT CHOU: Third, hunger can't affect me.

ZHANG XIE: Why not?

STUDENT MO: I expect it's because you've gotten used to hunger on the road.

STUDENT CHOU: No, it's because I have a method of enduring it. When I am hungry, I tighten my belt and every time I tighten it, I belch. Burp!

STUDENT MO: He's hardly a bag of wine and meat.

STUDENT CHOU: Fourth, the innkeeper can't do anything to me.

STUDENT MO: Why not?

STUDENT CHOU: Because scholars aren't scared of innkeepers.

*The* JING *acting as the wife of the innkeeper enters and speaks*: A fine thing! Since the innkeeper can't do anything to you, the innkeeper's wife is needed. You owe me rent. (*She grabs the* STUDENT CHOU.) So I can't do anything to you? (*She beats the* STUDENT CHOU.)

*They make gestures.*

STUDENT CHOU: Spare me, Mrs. Innkeeper! Madam!

STUDENT MO: She has a lot of names.

INNKEEPER'S WIFE: You owe me thirty cash.

STUDENT CHOU: It's only twenty-nine!

*The* INNKEEPER'S WIFE *and the* STUDENT CHOU *fight.*

STUDENT MO: How much does he owe you?

INNKEEPER'S WIFE: Thirty cash.

STUDENT CHOU: Twenty-nine.

STUDENT MO: How many days have you been here?

STUDENT CHOU: Only a month.

STUDENT MO: A long month or a short one?

STUDENT CHOU: A long one.

STUDENT MO: Then it's thirty.

INNKEEPER'S WIFE: Give me the rent!

STUDENT CHOU: You're trying to take it by force!

STUDENT MO: Auntie, stop! If not out of respect for me, then at least out of respect for this official here. After all, he brought him over.

ZHANG XIE: Be patient, ma'am.

INNKEEPER'S WIFE: He's refusing to pay my rent.

STUDENT CHOU: She's robbing my money!

*The* INNKEEPER'S WIFE *sings*:
(*Ma lang*)
You cad! You dirty, lazy scholar!

STUDENT CHOU:
You cad! You dirty, lazy dog!

STUDENT MO:
There is no need for the two of you to fight.

ZHANG XIE:
Stop, both of you, and don't answer back.

INNKEEPER'S WIFE:
Thieving monkey!

STUDENT CHOU:
Monkey bitch!

ZHANG XIE *and* STUDENT MO:
As a favor to us, both of you stop!

STUDENT CHOU:
(*Same tune*)
I'm not paying any rent.

INNKEEPER'S WIFE:
I'll kick you out, and you can sleep in the pavilion on the bridge.

ZHANG XIE:
Listen to my colleagues' pleas.

STUDENT MO:

And stop using such indecent language.

STUDENT CHOU:

You're using your fists!

INNKEEPER'S WIFE:

Am I using my fists?

ZHANG XIE *and* STUDENT MO *together*:

Watch your language and stop fighting.

INNKEEPER'S WIFE:

(*Same tune*)

He owes me money. That's enough to make me angry

STUDENT CHOU:

How can I bear her insults?

STUDENT MO:

You're made for each other.

ZHANG XIE:

Yes, they are a fine pair, guest and host.

INNKEEPER'S WIFE:

I'll take you to court.

STUDENT CHOU:

I'll take *you* to court!

ZHANG XIE *and* STUDENT MO:

You both can probably spare a few coins.

STUDENT CHOU:

(*Same tune*)

I want you to take on this licentiate.

INNKEEPER'S WIFE:

I'll take care of him, but don't you dare come along.

STUDENT MO:

What a couple of poor, miserable bastards you are!

ZHANG XIE:

It's not important, so don't worry about it.

INNKEEPER'S WIFE:

I'm going to get my stick.

STUDENT CHOU:

And I'll get mine.

ZHANG XIE *and* STUDENT MO:

If you are going to fight, we'll have to leave.

*The* INNKEEPER'S WIFE *speaks*: Licentiate, welcome! You can stay
at my inn.

STUDENT MO: She's absurd.

STUDENT CHOU: This is none of your concern, sir. Why don't you
just rest here for a few days until you leave to take the exams?

STUDENT MO: It seems like you've both made your mark in the
world.[11]

ZHANG XIE: It's just a little rent. Be patient.

STUDENT MO: Scholars who curse each other make people ashamed of them.

STUDENT CHOU: Recently, I've learned the Black Tortoise method.

*Together*: Whenever you need to draw in your head, just draw it in.

*All exit.*

# ACT 25

LADY WANG *enters and sings*:

(*Tanchun ling*)

Every three years the finest are selected;

they are deeply learned men.

SHENGHUA *enters and continues the song*:

We still do not know

who passed as the top candidate.

When will I satisfy my hearts' desire?

SHENGHUA *speaks*: Welcome, mama.

LADY WANG: Child,

You see a saddle and you think of a horse,

and when you see an object, you think of its owner.

This year is the year of the great examination. If we don't find a top graduate now to become your husband, how much longer must we wait? *Calls*: Assistant come here.

*The* MO *acting as an* ASSISTANT *enters*:

In the morning I am a peasant in a hut,
and at dusk I ascend the emperor's hall.[1]

From earlier times until today, how many top graduates have there
been? My lady, young mistress, what are your wishes?

LADY WANG: For many years they have studied the civil and
military arts, and this year they will finally sell their skills to
the emperor. I intend to take advantage of the fact that my
Shenghua is now at her most charming to find her a husband.
I do not know what the Commissioner's orders are. Did he
tell you to arrange a decorated tower and to invite the new
son-in-law?[2]

*The* ASSISTANT *sings*:
(*Shenzhang'er*)
I am waiting to find out the results,
I am waiting to find out the results:
yesterday I received orders,
which are very strict.
The arrangement of the decorated tower has been completed
according to regulation.

*Together*:
Tomorrow a scholar will ascend the imperial hall,
and compete for the imperial salary.
But do we know the subject of the exams? What is the subject?

LADY WANG *sings*:
(*Dilou zi*)
Powerful houses and noble kin mix in infinite numbers.

*Together*:

They will certainly want to marry the top graduate.

SHENGHUA:

My allotment of happiness was determined in a former life.

*Together*:

It must be a young man.

ASSISTANT:

It was predestined, predestined,

and if your mind is firm and disciplined, it can cut through stone.

*Together*:

In front of the horse, in front of the horse,

the silk whip will be handed over to unite the lovers.

LADY WANG:

(*Same tune*)

There was no need to see who entered the examination hall some
    days earlier.

*Together*:

But we can see the procession through the streets and see who
    receives the silk whip.

SHENGHUA:

In the great houses for miles around, curtains are rolled up.

*Together*:

It must be to see the top graduate.

ASSISTANT:

In recent years, recent years,

many of the top graduates have been young.


*Together:*

In front of the horse, in front of the horse,

the silk whip will be handed over to unite the lovers.


LADY WANG *speaks*: He will change his white robes for the green
  gown.

SHENGHUA: If our fates match, I will be fortunate.

ASSISTANT: Then, a single scholar will be granted the emperor's favor.

*Together:* Indeed, the whole family will live off the imperial salary.


*All exit.*


# ACT 26


POORLASS *enters and sings*:

(*Huang ying'er*)

Since he left, I have received no news from him;

how lonely this makes me.

I don't know when he donned the green robe,[1]

gladdening my heart.

He is so talented and intelligent,[2]

he must have won the first place.

I'll soon get someone to go to Jiangling,

and find out who passed.

XIAO'ER *enters and sings*:
(*Wu xiaosi*)
A poor devil,
who called himself a scholar,
asked my mother to act as a go-between.
Once he left for the capital, he did not return.
It seems his wife is really dumb,
and only hopes for a "peel of thunder on the plain."[3]

POORLASS *speaks*: Xiao'er.

XIAO'ER *reacts with a doltish expression*.

POORLASS: Xiao'er, brother, what are you singing?
XIAO'ER: I was not singing.
POORLASS: I do have ears, you know. Keep on singing and let me
   listen.
XIAO'ER: You (*laughs*) have ears too? I'll sing, but don't think
   I made it up. Someone composed ten stanzas, but I can
   remember only two.
POORLASS: Sing and I'll listen.

   XIAO'ER *sings*:
   (*Wu xiaosi*)
   A poor devil,
   who called himself a scholar.

POORLASS *speaks*: This line must refer to scholar Zhang.

   XIAO'ER *continues the song*:
   Asked my mother to act as a go-between.

POORLASS *speaks*: You clearly made this up.

XIAO'ER *continues the song*:
Once he left for the capital, he did not return.
It seems his wife is really dumb,

*Speaks*: It says that because you wait for him you're dumb.

*Sings*:
And only hopes for a "peel of thunder on the plain."

*Laughs.*

POORLASS *sings*:
(*Same tune*)
Ever since he left for the capital,
I often shed tears.
The pain of separation is hard to bear,
and day and night I think about him, but there is no news.
I never thought you would make fun of me.
Sing the song and let me listen carefully.

XIAO'ER *speaks*: I didn't make it up. Two elder members of our
writing group composed it. There is still another stanza.
POORLASS: Go on, sing.

XIAO'ER *sings*:
(*Same tune*)
The couple met,
united in poverty,
but once he left, there's been no trace of him:
like walking on floating duckweed, holding on to the void.

I urge you, do not pursue him as a husband,

he's really a whirlwind.

POORLASS *sings*:

(*Same tune*)

Ever since I married him,

I have conducted myself with utmost sincerity,

but could he possibly be ungrateful?

As soon as he passed the exams and acquired fame,

sure enough, he betrayed me and sent not a word.

Across endless rivers and infinite mountains, I shall go to look for

him.

POORLASS *speaks*: Xiao'er, when are you going to Jiangling to pay

your taxes?

XIAO'ER: I'm on my way. But I'm afraid that the county magistrate

will send someone to follow me and give me fifteen whacks

with a stick.

POORLASS: Stop talking nonsense. When you go, if you see people

on the street selling the list with the examination results, buy a

copy and bring it back.

XIAO'ER: Does Jiangling have the exam results for sale?

POORLASS: Surely.

XIAO'ER: If I see one, I'll buy it and bring it back.

POORLASS: If he has passed, I shall stop shedding these pear-like

tears.

XIAO'ER: Beside the window unknown for ten years . . .

POORLASS: But as soon as he passes, he will be known to the world.

*All exit.*

# ACT 27

LADY WANG *enters and sings*:
(*Busuanzi*)
By the looming ten-foot decorated tower,
all the townspeople join the commotion.

SHENGHUA *enters and continues the song*:
Today the top graduate will parade through the streets.

*Together*:
What a splendid scene!

LADY WANG *speaks*: Daughter,

People don't react suddenly;
nor do things happen by chance.

I have heard that this year's top graduate is from Western Sichuan,
but I don't yet know his name. Let me call the assistant and ask him.
(*She calls*:) Assistant, come here.

ASSISTANT *comes out*:
With one imperial dispatch the emperor summons [all the
candidates]
and everyone hopes for the first position.

Madam, I was born and raised in the capital where the exams are
held once every three years and twice every five.[1] Of all the top
graduates I have seen, not one of them look as intelligent as
this year's candidate. I have heard that his ancestors come from
Western Sichuan and his family lives in Chengdu. At three he

could read and by five compose prose; his essays surpass those of Du Fu and Li Bo and his talent combines that of the Cheng brothers.[2] He has a noble mien and a free and easy disposition. His writing is unrestrained, like passing clouds, yet speeds faster than lightning. In front of the emperor, he answered the questions with great fluency. On the banner no other name appears but that of top graduate Zhang Xie.

SHENGHUA *sings*:

(*Fu malang*)

I know it is a scholar from Chengdu,

the one who among all five hundred candidates

has procured the first prize.

Today,

He will parade through the streets.

*Together*:

From the rows of noble houses,

People strive to catch a glimpse as the escorts call out "the top graduate is coming!"

SHENGHUA:

(*Same tune*)

My father is at court; what need have we for go-betweens?

He relies on me to hand over my silk whip

and choose a great talent.

The feast

will soon be arranged.

*Together*:

People fix their gaze on the top of the decorated towers,

and all the curtains are rolled up waiting to pick the top graduate.

ASSISTANT:

(*Same tune*)

Banners join the music in hurrying them along,

and guards run like bolts of lightning,

escorting the top graduate.

After he accepts the silk whip,

they will urge him to drink the three cups of wine.

*Together*:

The bridal chambers will certainly be open,

and with a mien like Chang E's,

they will crowd around the approaching top graduate.

LADY WANG *speaks*: My daughter Shenghua and I have ascended the tall, decorated tower. Assistant, when the top graduate comes, wouldn't it be best if my husband personally handed him the whip?

ASSISTANT: From ancient times, family members of officials have ascended the decorated tower and handed over the silk whip. If the talented candidate does not accept it, the next day His Excellency will think of another plan.

    LADY WANG: You are right. This time my daughter will marry the top graduate.

    ASSISTANT: In front of the horse, the escorts exhort the candidates to take the silk whip.

    SHENGHUA: No one is surprised that the scholars pass the exams early.

    *Together*: Because in the moon Chang E loves young men.

LADY WANG *and* SHENGHUA *exit*.

ASSISTANT: What need has a top graduate to look for a matchmaker when in the books there are maidens with faces like jade?
The Crimson Prince[3] and his daughter Shenghua have summoned the top graduate to be her husband. This can truly be
called "a young girl and a youth of well-matched appearance."
The top graduate will soon be here.

ZHANG XIE *dressed as a top graduate enters and sings*:
(*Pu suanzi*)
I have received the emperor's favor,
and all of a sudden I am dressed in the green official gown.
When I look back, my parents are thousands of miles away,
and I suppose they have already received the imperial stipend.

*Declaims*:
Leading the group of immortals to the heavenly palace,
amidst the clouds they all follow me.
I have already passed the third exam level
and reached the top branch of the cassia tree.
In the Bright Garden, no horse precedes mine;
in the Apricot Garden, all poems follow mine.[4]
A young man's ambitions must be thus,
my sleeves infused with the imperial fragrance[5]as the whole world
    knows.

SHENGHUA *holding the silk whip enters and sings*:
(*Same tune*)
A confused roar of exultation arises,
crowding around my outstanding husband.
Indeed, we are a destined match,
since he has taken the silk whip.

*The* ASSISTANT *sings*:

(*Dasheng le*)

Atop the decorated tower there is a delicate beauty,

and the house of the Crimson Prince is looking for a son-in-law.

ZHANG XIE *laughs*:

The phoenix perches only on the pawlonia tree,

so why worry about a higher branch?[6]

SHENGHUA:

Consider that my father comes from three generations of noble
　　officials,

and now he hopes that you, outstanding and virtuous as you are,

　　will pull the bridle and stop the horse.

ASSISTANT:

This is the most charming of places.

It is as if the immortals had happened upon it;

it is an image of Penglai.

ZHANG XIE:

(*Same tune*)

I am looking for fame, not for a wife,

and my heart is not yet inclined toward the joys of marriage.

When a powerful house rudely thrusts the silk whip upon us,

how can any beauty appeal to a man's fancy!

SHENGHUA:

I assume you have not been married before;

what obstacle is there to prevent you from accepting the silk
　　whip?

ASSISTANT:

It seems he is refusing.

How can we know, whether long ago, in a former existence,

they were in fact destined to meet?

LADY WANG *enters and sings*:

(*Same tune*)

Daughter, don't long for love's rapture;

marriage is determined in a former life.

ASSISTANT:

Don't insist on handing over the silk whip;

we must let the Commissioner know.

ZHANG XIE:

Although I have no wife, I have no choice in this matter;

father and mother are back home and still do not know.

*Together*:

Go and parade through the streets.

What has been determined in a former life,

is not to be decided now.

*The* ASSISTANT *speaks*: I must ascend the painted hall to inform the Military Affairs Commissioner.

ZHANG XIE: I am not looking for a wife, just for fame.

SHENGHUA: So naturally we were not a destined match.

*Together*: It is not that he has no feeling for me.

LADY WANG *and* SHENGHUA *exit*.

WANG DEYONG *enters*: Come in, come in.

ASSISTANT: My Lord, Crimson Prince, the top graduate is coming to visit.

WANG DEYONG: Top graduate, please remove your casual hat and wear only the official cap.

ASSISTANT: Wrong! He has to remove his official cap and wear his casual hat.[7]

WANG DEYONG: Wear your casual hat, and perform for us "Zhong Kui Chases the Small Demon."[8]

ASSISTANT: Let's have a little peace and quiet.

WANG DEYONG: Greetings, sir.

ZHANG XIE: Today I've come to pay my respects . . .

WANG DEYONG: Today you've come to pay your respects? I wish I had stolen a strip of calf leather. One half I'll use to stretch over a drum and the other half to make shoes.

ASSISTANT: What do you want to make shoes for?

WANG DEYONG: Because each pair can be sold for a couple of cash.

ASSISTANT: From the looks of it you'll only get one cash.

ZHANG XIE: I have just come to pay my respects, Sir, Commissioner . . .

ASSISTANT: Sir Commissioner wants me to catch a monk. With his bottom half I'll make a vegetarian dish and I'll use his bald pate as a pestle.

ASSISTANT: Sir, show some respect.

ZHANG XIE: I have just come to pay my respects, Sir, Commissioner; I came to wish you a thousand blessings.

WANG DEYONG: A thousand blessings! He wants me to grab a box of powder and a cake of ink. I will paint my mouth black and use the powder to paint a white deer on the door.[9]

ASSISTANT: Such disrespect!

*The* ASSISTANT *bows with both hands [to Zhang Xie] but* WANG DEYONG *instead responds to his greeting.*

ASSISTANT: Who asked you to open your mouth in the first place?

ZHANG XIE *sings*:
(*Shiwu lang*)
Thanks to your grace
today, by good fortune I don the green robe.

WANG DEYONG:
Just think how beautiful my daughter is,
her complexion as radiant and white as mine.

ASSISTANT *speaks*: What complexion?

*Continues the song*:
Below the decorated tower, the silk whip was passed on,
but the top graduate is not satisfied.

WANG DEYONG:
How can he bully us by refusing my daughter;
we lack good fortune.

ZHANG XIE:
(*Same tune*)
My family is from Sichuan,
and in all decisions, I will follow my parents' desire.

WANG DEYONG:
Look at my daughter with a delicate face like a flower;
how can she not marry the top graduate!

ASSISTANT:

Such matters require the agreement of both parties,

so why must *you*[10] decide about the silk whip?


WANG DEYONG:

I suspect that poor devil was not destined for us;

if he does not want the marriage feast, that is his choice.


WANG DEYONG *speaks*: To refuse the silk whip is most insulting.

ZHANG XIE: But I just want fame, not a wife.

WANG DEYONG: You've ruined a night of painted candles in the
bridal chamber.

*Together*: But you've managed to have your name inscribed on the
Golden List.


ZHANG XIE *exits*.


WANG DEYONG: Unfortunately he is the top graduate. That my precious daughter should marry such a miserable, miserable . . .

ASSISTANT: That doesn't sound so nice.

WANG DEYONG: No matter what, I won't give my daughter in marriage to him.

ASSISTANT: He doesn't want her either.

WANG DEYONG: He's just put on his green gown and left the Donghua Gate; he's a tattered lotus leaf.[11]

ASSISTANT: It's only good for wrapping gorgon fruit.[12]

WANG DEYONG: I shall not give him my daughter in marriage. That
scholar in his stepped-up hat leaving the Donghua Gate, in a
few years will be like an old flight of steps.[13]

ASSISTANT: It will be hard to go up or down.

WANG DEYONG: I will not . . .

*The* ASSISTANT *joins in*: Give him my daughter in marriage.

WANG DEYONG: Once he's tied his sash around his waist and left through the Donghua Gate, he's no better than a black python.[14]

ASSISTANT: What a poisoned remark.

WANG DEYONG *sings*:

(*Jiangtou song bie*)

You've just passed,

you've just passed,

and my daughter was to marry you.

The house of the Zhangs,

the house of the Wangs,

why didn't it happen?

It is just too strange that he did not take the silk whip.

I suppose he's just odd.

ASSISTANT:

(*Same tune*)

These matters of fate,

these matters of fate,

Have been determined for five hundred years.

He did not accept,

he did not accept,

I fear there will be no other alternative.

WANG DEYONG *speaks*: I'm afraid there will be no other alternative—unless it's not the top graduate.

ASSISTANT: That is right sir.

WANG DEYONG *continues the song*:

Since he's deceived us,

call my wife to come out to discuss this with me.

ASSISTANT *speaks*: Madam and Shenghua will be here in a moment sir.

LADY WANG *enters and sings*:

(*Jin jiaoye*)

He removed his white gown and assumed the green;

what a pity he did not consent to marry.

SHENGHUA *enters and continues the song*:

All of a sudden I think,

it must be I have no fortune.

WANG DEYONG *speaks*: Strange, really strange. "An assassin can be
forgiven, but a man with no manners is hard to endure."

LADY WANG: Husband, why did he not accept the silk whip?

WANG DEYONG: Because if he was benevolent, he would be able
to spread benevolence to others and turn the world into one
large family. But he is full of suspicions and will attract the
enmity of his own flesh and blood. It is clear that he will bully
his subordinates.

LADY WANG *sings*:

(*Dou kema*)

For some years, for our son-in-law

we wanted to attract a top graduate.

How were we to know that the newcomer

would so reject us?

Unwilling to accept

the silk whip from us,

he has made my daughter

weep endlessly.

*Refrain*:

Oh, how fate stings

by making our predestined love empty.

In vain has Chang E,

fallen in love with a young man.


SHENGHUA:

(*Same tune*)

From ancient times it has been said of sons-in-law,

that there are thousands from which to choose.

How were we to know that as soon as he passed

he was to be the top graduate?

I just expected

that we would be forever united.

He must come and take

this silk whip.


*Repeat the refrain.*


WANG DEYONG:

(*Same tune*)

Didn't you do it before?

Don't give him the silk whip again.

I shall dress up as you, my daughter,

and with my hands in my sleeves stand meekly by his side.


ASSISTANT:

Not too close,

or are the gods near at hand?[15]

WANG DEYONG:
If he does not take the silk whip,
I'll punch him.

*Repeat the refrain.*

ASSISTANT:
(*Same tune*)
Among all five hundred officials,
how could you pass unnoticed?[16]
And why bother
to marry a top graduate?

WANG DEYONG:
You have given me
a resolute heart
that will even cut
through stone.

*Repeat the refrain.*

WANG DEYONG *speaks*: Daughter, put your mind at ease. Whatever
his appointment, I will beg to govern the same district, and rest
assured that I'll deal with Zhang Xie.

LADY WANG: Daughter, don't be so despondent.
WANG DEYONG: This marriage chance is worth ten thousand in gold.
SHENGHUA: Like the fish that swallows the line along with the hook.
*Together*: It pierces the intestines and ties the heart in knots.

*All exit.*

# ACT 28

*The* JING *role as a* BOOKSELLER *enters and speaks*: List of the successful examinees for sale! List of the successful examinees for sale!

*Sings*:
(*Hua'er*)
For three cash you can buy the top graduate,
and all the five hundred candidates' districts and provinces.
Two copies will cost you six cash,
and if you want one thousand, it will be five strings of cash.

*Speaks*: If you see it and don't buy it, you'll regret it forever. All you know is that Zhang Xie is the top graduate, but if you don't know where the second and third graduates come from, buy a booklet and look it up. *Shouts*: List of the successful examinees for sale!

*The* MO *as a* CUSTOMER *enters*: I'll buy one.

BOOKSELLER: You can get it at the small shop by that field ahead.

CUSTOMER: Are they sold here?

BOOKSELLER: There!

CUSTOMER: Turn your head.

*The* BOOKSELLER *turns his head.*

CUSTOMER: You'll never learn, will you?[1] Where is the top graduate from? What is his name?

BOOKSELLER: His surname is Cheng and his name Du City.

CUSTOMER: Where does he live?

BOOKSELLER: In Xie County, in Zhang Prefecture.

CUSTOMER: Rubbish! Isn't he from the city of Chengdu and called Zhang Xie?

BOOKSELLER: That's right.

CUSTOMER: I helped him earlier on.[2] Who came second?

BOOKSELLER: Speedboat Zhou.

CUSTOMER: When the water rises, boats sail fast.[3] And the third?

BOOKSELLER: Dream Reader.

CUSTOMER: You know phrenology too.

BOOKSELLER: Give me three cash. I want to hit the road.

CUSTOMER: You can hit a great football.

*The* BOOKSELLER *shouts*: List of the successful examinees for sale! List of the successful examinees for sale!

XIAO'ER *enters running*: I'll buy one, quickly.

CUSTOMER: He really knows the way!

BOOKSELLER: A country hick! What is it you want to buy?

CUSTOMER: You still haven't left?[4]

XIAO'ER: I want to buy a list.

CUSTOMER: Buy a list?

XIAO'ER, *panting*: I'm just a country fellow and I can't say it.

CUSTOMER: The mute has a dream.[5]

XIAO'ER: There is a lady back home who has had no luck with love. Her husband went to the capital to take the exams and she gave me three cash to buy the "examinees."

BOOKSELLER: You mean buy the list of the successful examinees?

XIAO'ER: Yes, the list of successful examinees. I forgot the "successful" bit.

CUSTOMER: You can always borrow a candle to successfully light your way.[6]

XIAO'ER: So, can I buy the successful list?

CUSTOMER: The list of successful examinees.

XIAO'ER *laughs*: Now I forgot the "examinees."

CUSTOMER: Just like a stray dog.[7]

XIAO'ER: Give me a booklet; I have to go.

BOOKSELLER: Give me the money.

XIAO'ER: I've already given you the money.

BOOKSELLER: Give me the money!

XIAO'ER: Give me a list.

*The* BOOKSELLER *and* XIAO'ER *spit at each other. They make gestures.*

CUSTOMER: Both of you, stop it!

BOOKSELLER: He wants a booklet but doesn't want to pay!

XIAO'ER: He takes my money, but doesn't give me the booklet.

CUSTOMER: What is it that you both want! You need not pay anything, and you don't need to hand over a booklet. I'll give you a booklet. Now look kindly on each other and return home.

BOOKSELLER: You have cheated me out of three cash.

XIAO'ER: Then go and file a suit in the headman's court!

BOOKSELLER: Go back to your oxen!

XIAO'ER: You insult me just because of the way I'm dressed.

CUSTOMER: One of you is just as bad as the other. Go home and stop quarreling.

> BOOKSELLER: A guilty conscience will deprive you of half of your share of fortune.
>
> XIAO'ER: And if your behavior is bad, Heaven will give you a lifetime of poverty.

*All exit.*

# ACT 29

LADY WANG *enters and sings*:

(*Tuan shanzi*)

Heaven has not complied with our desires,

and left mother and daughter distressed.

SHENGHUA *enters and continues the song*:

Who would have thought he would not accept the silk whip,

that after all he would not become my husband?


*Together*:

This measure of good fortune

soon turned into sorrow.


LADY WANG *sings*:

(*Zui taiping*)

For long I intended,

and it was constantly in my heart,

to find you a husband.


SHENGHUA:

Who was to know that now

I'd feel like a lovebird without a mate?


LADY WANG:

Alas, it grieves me that he did not keep the silk whip,

that the feast in the painted hall was prepared in vain.


SHENGHUA:

I suppose my looks

did not even for a moment

please him.


LADY WANG:

(*Same tune, new opening*)

Hurt and grieving,

my daughter weeps,

as soon as she brushes off her tears

she begins to shed them again.

SHENGHUA:

In the mansions of the nobles,

there can be no one as melancholy as I.

Just think,

he said he had done much studying,

yet as soon as he passed, he rejected us.


*Together:*

But there is nothing to be done;

only sleep,

will allow us to forget for a moment.


LADY WANG:

(*Same tune, new opening*)

All day long,

I feel so agitated

Do not leave me;

I feel half out of my mind.


SHENGHUA:

If that day atop the tower we had not met,

how would I be so full of anxiety?

I am so depressed,

that my thoughts are making me sick.

I will surrender my life to the Yellow Springs.


*Together:*

Bullied by him,

we were embarrassed and humiliated.

What kind of life is this?

LADY WANG:

(*Same tune, new opening*)
Your father's intention
is to on your behalf
take revenge on Zhang Xie,
our present enemy.

SHENGHUA:

Today I feel
my heart so troubled that I cannot eat anything.
No one but me knows of this matter in my heart,
and I constantly and quietly shed tears.

LADY WANG *speaks*: Since he did not want to accept the silk whip,
the wedding was called off.
SHENGHUA: That we could do nothing about it was so shameful.
LADY WANG: In her eyes are seas and rivers of tears.
*Together*: And in her heart all the sorrows of heaven and earth.

*All exit.*

# ACT 30

POORLASS *enters and sings*:
(*Shanpo liyang*)
Did he pass?
Did he not pass?
Is he in the capital?
Has he returned?
These thoughts make me weep the whole day long.
Perhaps he did not pass and is ashamed to return?

Or perhaps he is offended by my poverty.
Since we parted,
since we parted, he has not sent me a word,
not a word.

GRANDMA LI *enters and sings*:
(*Same tune*)
Grandpa is really happy,
and I am also very happy,
our son has come back to report to us
and to inform Poorlass.
When Xiao'er went on some business to Jiangling,
he said Poorlass asked him to buy a booklet with the exam results.
He says that Zhang Xie is the top graduate.
I've specially come to congratulate her,
congratulate her.

POORLASS *speaks, putting palms together*: Oh, thank you! It's all due
to you, Grandma.[1]
GRANDPA LI *enters*:

Other mountains come up only to the foot of the tallest one,
and rivers seem shallow when they reach the sea.

There are many scholars in the world, but only our Zhang Xie is
top graduate. That's no small feat.
POORLASS: Greetings, Grandpa, I still don't know whether it's true
or not?
GRANDPA LI: Congratulations, Poorlass!
GRANDMA LI: When Xiao'er came back, the brute was still reading
it. Luckily, I can spot a good man when I see one.

GRANDPA LI: Anyone who can tell the good merchandise from the bad one will not be poor. (POORLASS *looks at the booklet*.) Zhang Xie is top graduate, and he comes from Chengdu.

GRANDMA LI: Earlier I asked him to buy a mirror for me. Now I'll get ten.

GRANDPA LI: Why do you need so many?

> *Grandma Li sings:*
> (*Ku jipo*)
> With two mirrors,
> I'll have some fun.
> I could pick one up in each hand,
> and look at myself at all times.
> I can look into my right hand mirror, then the one in my left hand.
> I can look into my left hand mirror, then the one in my right hand.

GRANDPA LI *speaks*: Whether you wear light makeup or thick, it'll make no difference.

POORLASS: Ask Xiao'er to come over. I want to ask him for the details.

GRANDPA LI: What do you want to ask him?

GRANDMA LI: Xiao'er has gone to the shop in the eastern village.

POORLASS: To buy what?

GRANDMA LI: To buy five hundred cash worth of powder and five hundred cash worth of rouge, in case Zhang Xie sends the mirrors.

GRANDPA LI: You've really bought too much.

GRANDMA LI: Too much! I'll pat it on here and I'll pat it on there, and it will be gone in a jiffy.

GRANDPA LI: You must have a pair of cymbals.[2]

POORLASS: Grandpa and Grandma, you're like my parents, and that is why I can tell you this: even before there was news of Zhang Xie, I had this idea: since he has passed the examination,

I will go to the capital and look for him, what do you think? I'm just afraid his tears may have been real, but his heart was false. He may have taken someone else's silk whip, otherwise he would have returned home. What do you think of this resolution of mine?

GRANDMA LI: You're right.

GRANDPA LI: It's all right to go, but you may not have enough money for the road.

POORLASS *sings*:

(*Chenzui dongfeng*)

I parted with Zhang Xie when he left for the capital,

and now who will care for me without Grandpa and Grandma to
help?

Since he has donned the green gown,

he can be seen with the powerful and wealthy.

GRANDPA LI:

If you don't go, you'll be wasting your time here.

*Together*:

I have neither father nor mother,

or brother or sister.

It is best to go to the capital,

and search for my husband.

GRANDMA LI:

(*Same tune*)

You have never traveled that road before,

how will you withstand the heat and the cold?

If you have no money for the road,

I can help you.

POORLASS:

After I return, I will never let you down.

*Together*:

I have no purse or jewel box,

or any friends.

It's best to go to the capital,

and search for my husband.

GRANDPA LI:

(*Same tune*)

If he does not keep you with him, it means he does not want you;

in that case you should return right away.

If you're not aware of this soon,

it will leave you alone and helpless.

GRANDMA LI:

Would he dare to simply betray Poorlass?

*Together*:

I have no box

or basket.

It is best to go to the capital

and search for my husband.

GRANDMA LI *speaks*: Luckily your husband is top graduate.

GRANDPA LI: I hope you find him and meet with no grievance.

POORLASS: I'll cling to him as close as a leech to the foot of an egret.

*Together*: When you go to the imperial court, we shall go too.

*All exit.*

# ACT 31

ZHANG XIE *enters and sings*:

(*Si niang'er*)

I am grateful for my emperor's favor;

I snapped the cassia twig and trod the clouds.

Gazing into the distance, I cannot see my home pass, and my

    native mountains are far away.

I will write a letter and ask for it to be sent

by a special envoy going on ahead,

to notify my parents.

*Declaims*:

To raise a child and not instruct him is the father's fault,

but if the child has the books and does not study, it's his own

    stupidity.

Suddenly my name is inscribed on the Golden List;

I am indeed like a priceless pearl.

In books there are verily houses of yellow gold;

in books there are truly a thousand bushels of grain.

In books blessings certainly pile up in mountains;

in books doubtless there are maidens of jade-like beauty.

In front of my horse, the guards shout "The top graduate is

    coming!"

Just as the finest talent chosen from the forest of scholars,

I have jumped the three-foot waves at the dragon's gate;

a sudden roll of thunder on the plain.

ZHANG XIE *exits*.

# ACT 32

LADY WANG *enters and sings*:
(*Maihua sheng*)
That day among rows of noble mansions,
we wanted to take a son-in-law,
but to our surprise he rejected us.

*The* JING *playing a* MAID *supporting* SHENGHUA *enters.*

    SHENGHUA *continues the song*:
    I, your daughter, bear my resentment,
    all day long displaying no feeling or emotion.
    How were you, my mother, to know
    that weak and weary I would inflict so much harm upon myself.

*The* MAID *speaks*: Madam, your daughter Shenghua is terribly ill. Medicine to her is like water splashed on the stones, like hot liquid sprinkled on snow. She seems ill, and yet it seems not like an illness, as if she were drunk or crazed. She heaves long sighs, her tears fall continuously, and she does not eat or sleep. I have helped her come out to dispel this sadness.

SHENGHUA, *acting as a sick person, stands up.*

LADY WANG: Daughter, you must calm yourself and do what I suggest.

    SHENGHUA *sings*:
    (*Yan guo sha*)
    The day I handed over the silk whip,
    I thought it was the perfect match.

But that youth, surrounded by the multitude,
his green gown highlighting his peach-blossom face,
cast me aside.

SHENGHUA *lowers her voice*:
People laugh at me for not being able to marry that top graduate.

*Refrain*:
People laugh at me for not being able to marry that top graduate.

LADY WANG:
(*Same tune*)
It's generally all a matter of marital fate,
daughter, do not worry yourself so.
There are thousands of noble and eminent houses,
and this scholar was not your destined match.
I suspect he will not have good fortune.

SHENGHUA *lowers her voice*:
People laugh at me for not being able to marry that top graduate.

*Refrain*:
People laugh at me for not being able to marry that top graduate.

MAID:
(*Same tune*)
Please daughter, little by little,
please daughter, give us a smile.
Don't let your knitted eyebrows pile up like distant mountains.
Eat something and pay no attention to all this;
I'm afraid you did not have a chance with this match.

SHENGHUA *lowers her voice*:
People laugh at me for not being able to marry that top graduate.

*Refrain*:
People laugh at me for not being able to marry that top graduate.

WANG DEYONG:
(*Same tune*)
Daughter, you must stop this endless weeping;
I will seek revenge for you.
I am not afraid of that top graduate!
Zhang Xie has been appointed to Zizhou as notary to the
administrative assistant.

SHENGHUA:
Alas! When I listen to your words, father, it breaks my heart.
People laugh at me for not being able to marry that top graduate;
People laugh at me for not being able to marry that top graduate.[1]

SHENGHUA *cries out and falls. Her* MAID *helps her up*.

WANG DEYONG *speaks*: My poor daughter! Quick! Cauterize her
heels.[2]

LADY WANG: Take her to her bedroom and look after her.
WANG DEYONG: We must hurry and find a doctor.
MAID: When you come through the door do not ask us how things
stand.
*Together*: One look at her face and you will know.

*The* MAID *exits helping* SHENGHUA.

LADY WANG: My lord, you should not have mentioned that Zhang
    Xie has been appointed as notary to the administrative assistant
    to Zizhou; it has affected our daughter.[3]
WANG DEYONG: That's got nothing to do with me. Tell an assistant
    to go and fetch well-known doctor, and to get medicine for her.
ASSISTANT: Sir, there isn't a single doctor who dares to treat her.

*The* MAID *enters running:*

Just as we cannot predict the weather above,
among people, fortunes change in an instant.

Madam, just as Miss Shenghua passed the screen, she collapsed,
    and when she returned to her room, her hands were stretched
    out. Her eyes were closed like a holy man sunk in meditation,
    and her eyebrows knitted like Xi Shi's with a stomach ache.[4]
    Her breath is faint, as if she were gasping for air, and her throat
    choked with phlegm. She has her teeth tightly clenched, and
    she is unconscious.

LADY WANG: What can we do about her?
WANG DEYONG: We must act soon if we are to save her.
MAID: The green dragon spirit walks with the white tiger.[5]
*Together:* There's no way to guarantee whether our luck is good or bad.

*All exit.*

*The* MO *role acting as the* ASSISTANT *enters:*[6]
As I see it,
Isn't it said that the nature of water has never been stable?
Some heads are square and some heads round.

That Shenghua girl was intent upon marrying top graduate Zhang
Xie, but that obstinate Zhang Xie wouldn't go along. The
Crimson Prince is Military Affairs Commissioner at court, but
still his daughter was not good enough for him. What do you
think of that? It seems that while gazing greedily at the autumn
moon up in heaven, the graduate lost the brilliant pearl on the
platter before him.

WANG DEYONG *enters*: Assistant.

*The* ASSISTANT *assents.*

WANG DEYONG: There was no saving my Shenghua. (*He makes a
crying gesture.*)
ASSISTANT: Sir, please calm down.
WANG DEYONG: Bring a chair over. My daughter's three spirits have
departed her pure body and her seven souls have taken leave for
the Yang Terrace. Please, take over my duties.
ASSISTANT: Yes, sir.

WANG DEYONG *sits down and sings*:
(*Taizhou ge*)
My child,
everyone said that as the daughter of a commissioner, you would
find it easy to marry,
that you were not to be compared to the children of the humble
people who marry those as poor as they.
My Shenghua had a very fair complexion,
her hair tied in a bun, long like a coiled dragon.
She had a small and delicate figure,
and often wore deep red.
Beyond the Donghua Gate, just east of the little tower nearby,

we welcomed the top graduate, and thought he would be happy to
 meet us,
that he would take up the silk whip without a single care,
but who was to know he would turn out to be a whirlwind?
Day after day, we argued until my ears went deaf,
and for two or three days, I could not eat a mouthful.
Who was to know that today she would be dead and gone?

WANG DEYONG *chokes and falls, and the* ASSISTANT *rescues him*: The
 Military Affairs Commissioner has choked and fallen. Quick,
 some cold water. *Calls out*: Sir, sir, Shenghua has come to!
WANG DEYONG: Awake! Tra-la!
ASSISTANT: A happy tune!
WANG DEYONG: Never mind my daughter, I'm almost dead myself
 because of you!

ASSISTANT:

 Whether people live long or die young, it is heaven's design;
 who knows when the water of the river Wei will break the bridge.

WANG DEYONG: Tomorrow I will submit a memorial and ask to
 be appointed to Zizhou. I wait only for a chance to avenge my
 daughter.
ASSISTANT: If you, sir, want to be appointed to Zizhou you will
 certainly succeed.

 WANG DEYONG: If I obtain my emperor's permission to go to Zizhou,
 I will surely avenge my daughter.
 ASSISTANT: Top graduate, there will come a day when we meet again,
 and you will be the one humiliated, not I.

*All exit.*

# ACT 33

*The* JING *acting as the* MOUNTAIN GOD *enters and sings*:

(*Wufang Shen*)

I protect the region,

as a local god,

and calm worries and anxieties.

If you're asking for blessings with nothing to offer, don't bother
    to pray;

if you come without meat or wine don't cast the divination blocks.


*Declaims*:

(*Wang Jiangnan*)

I've made my divinity manifest

for over eight hundred years.

Every year the village elders invoke me as their patron,

and I even acted as a matchmaker for Poorlass,

about which I am both pleased and resentful.

Zhang Xie has gone,

and has already snatched the first prize.

But that faithless lover has cut off relations,

while the lovesick Poorlass is longing for her lover's return;

yet I can say nothing.


GRANDPA LI *enters and sings*:

(*Wuye di*)

I heard you arise with the cock's crow.


POORLASS *enters and continues the song*:

Pattering down, two streams of tears fall.


GRANDPA LI:

Now your husband has donned the green gown in the capital.

POORLASS:
Still no letter from him;
in the end, it was nothing but lies.

*Together:*
You must leave the temple,
and try to find him in the capital.

GRANDMA LI *speaks:* Yes, Poorlass,

You should not seek him out in the dwellings of the nobles,[1]
or approach the houses of the lowly people.

By marrying that Zhang Xie, you've caused a foul mess.
GRANDPA LI: Stumbled in a ditch.

GRANDPA LI *sings:*
(*Wufang shen*)
Venerable god,
today Poorlass
is going to the capital.

POORLASS:
I'm afraid that Zhang Xie has already rejected me,
so I hope that your abilities will protect me all the way to the
    capital.

*The* MOUNTAIN GOD *sings:*
(*Ting qian liu*)
Zhang Xie left for the capital,
passed the exams but sent no news.
What is the point of asking me for divine assistance,
when it's all come to naught?

POORLASS:

God, I must leave today.


*Together*:

These days,

I'm afraid that gradually we will grow distant.


POORLASS:

(*Same tune*)

If he has let me down,

he truly will not remember those difficult times.

If when I reach the capital he is still indifferent,

my efforts will all have been in vain.


MOUNTAIN GOD:

In the end there will be reunion.


POORLASS:

Since he is already an official,

I'm afraid that gradually we will grow distant.


GRANDPA LI:

(*Same tune*)

God, consider that she's all alone,

and not familiar with the ways of the road.

Today she is leaving the temple,

and I hope you do give her your support.


MOUNTAIN GOD:

When you see him, don't scold him too much.

*Together:*
If you anger him,
I'm afraid that gradually we will grow distant.

*The* MOUNTAIN GOD *speaks:* It's all very well if you leave, but who will close the doors of the temple for me?

GRANDPA LI: She's no Sun Jing.[2]

POORLASS: Good-bye, Grandpa, take care of yourself. I will go to bid farewell to Grandma and then leave.

MOUNTAIN GOD: No need, I'm your Grandma.[3]

GRANDPA LI: Don't disclose our trade secrets!

MOUNTAIN GOD: Oh, and by the way, "Although the Liang Gardens are fun for a time, it is no place for you to stay."[4]

POORLASS: Thank you, venerable god.

MOUNTAIN GOD: If he does not take you back, return right away.

GRANDPA LI: Because if you stay too long, I'm afraid it may cause trouble.

POORLASS: White clouds have no feelings.

*Together:* Drawn out by a clear wind.

*All exit.*

# ACT 34

ZHANG XIE *enters and sings:*
(*Qingyü'an*)
I have just donned the green gown and received a great favor from the emperor;
I answered his majesty's questions with fluency and the imperial countenance was moved.

It would have been pointless to take the silk whip; what use would
    it be?
When I think of that Poorlass,
that we became love birds,
these days, the thought of it is hazy like a dream.

*Declaims*:
By a frozen window with determined ambition I passed several years;
suddenly, I succeeded in the examinations and won the first prize.
I've already shown my lifelong ambition to be a great man,
and should be able to occupy a prime minister's position.
Atop the tower there was a maiden with a face like jade,
but I thought in this life my allotted luck has been meager.
I judged more fitting to return home and pay my respects to my
    parents,
and present them both with the imperial stipend.
Is there a clerk there up front?

*The* CLERK *played by the* MO *role enters*:

The country is in order, and the Heaven favors us,
the officials are honest, and the people at peace.

Sir, what are your orders?

ZHANG XIE: Today I have been appointed as notary to the administrative assistant at Zizhou. It is very far away, and I see no need
to send a letter. I shall ride my horse there. Transmit the following orders to the guards in the front office: if officials come up
to the *yamen*, always let them in, but if peasants or women-folk
want to come in, they must not be allowed to enter. The guards
must first inform me about them privately. If they go against my
orders, they will be bound and severely punished.

CLERK: Yes, sir.

ZHANG XIE: In serving as an official one still needs to bow and
    make calls on other officials;
or without expecting it, we may cause outside trouble.
CLERK: In worldly affairs, one must be a keen observer;
social relations should be meted out according to status.

*All exit.*

# ACT 35

*The* MO *and the* JING *acting as gatekeepers enter and sing:*
(*Zhao pixie*)
The top graduate is really a great talent;
facing the *yamen*, the gates are open.
If you still don't know how to read,
or you are a commoner asking for a meeting,
don't bother to come.

GATEKEEPER MO *speaks:*

Benevolence is not dominant in the military,
nor does righteousness rule among the rich.

The top graduate has ordered that we admit only ministers and
    court officials. All other people including peasants, people from
    out of town, and women are forbidden entry.
GATEKEEPER JING: Yes sir. And I won't let in pearl-sellers, match-
    makers, or midwives.
GATEKEEPER MO: I'm afraid you'll offend people.

GATEKEEPER JING: I truly have no consideration for others. I wouldn't even recognize my father if he came.

> POORLASS *enters and sings*:
>
> (*Xiqian ying*)
>
> Luckily I have arrived in the capital;
>
> across mountains and rivers, I've suffered a million sorrows.
>
> If only I could see my husband, it would ease my troubled mind,
>
> but I do not know where he hides at present.
>
> I've searched everywhere,
>
> but I cannot find him.

*Speaks*: Greetings! I have some questions to ask.

GATEKEEPER MO: Yes ma'am, what do you want? Go ahead, ask.

POORLASS: Where is the new top graduate staying?

GATEKEEPER MO: This is his temporary *yamen*. Ask that gatekeeper and he'll tell you.

POORLASS: Greetings!

GATEKEEPER JING: Oh, it's just a fake female.[1]

POORLASS: I have heard that this is the residence of the new top graduate.

GATEKEEPER JING: Yes, that's right, but now he is called Notary to the Administrative Assistant. What do you want? Are you selling pearls?

GATEKEEPER MO: Let her speak.

POORLASS: I have come especially to see the top graduate.

GATEKEEPER JING: If I'm to hand in their name cards, those who want to visit the top graduate must wear the purple robes.

POORLASS: But I am a woman.

GATEKEEPER JING: If you're a woman, why aren't your feet bound?

GATEKEEPER MO: You must look up at the top.

GATEKEEPER JING: I've looked up at her face.
GATEKEEPER MO: Like a tame dog.

> *The* GATEKEEPER JING *sings*:
> (*Zhao pixie*)
> Who dares report to the top graduate!
> When he's angry, he's vicious.
> If you really must see him,
> one method is just to shout "Greetings!"

POORLASS *speaks*: Greetings! Greetings!
ZHANG XIE *shouts from backstage*: What woman has entered the hall?
   Gatekeepers up front, why don't you stop her!
GATEKEEPER JING: Yes, sir. Did you hear that? Come on, off you go!
POORLASS: Let me tell him, I'm not just anyone.
GATEKEEPER JING: Tell me.

> POORLASS *sings*:
> (*Wu gengzhuan*)
> This top graduate,
> is my husband,
> and I am his wife.
> We were married for just over two months,
> but alas, we parted and he came to the capital.
> When I bought the examination booklet,
> and looked at the results,
> I saw my husband had passed first.
> Heedless of the long road ahead, I have come to look for him,
> but since you did not know that,
> you asked me to leave.

GATEKEEPER JING *speaks*: Your story is so sad!

> GATEKEEPER MO *sings*:
> (*Zhao pixie*)
> The orders of the top graduate are:
> if officials come there is nothing to be done.
> But if women and peasants get inside the hall,
> the gatekeepers will receive
> thirteen strokes with the cane.

GATEKEEPER JING *speaks*: Out you go! Off with you!

POORLASS: But I am the top graduate's wife.

GATEKEEPER JING: Take it easy, take it easy; I'm afraid that all those pearls on your headgear may fall off.[2]

GATEKEEPER MO: As they say, "People don't pick up what others have lost."

ZHANG XIE *shouts from backstage*: Who is making so much noise? Why don't you beat her out!

POORLASS: Top graduate, I am Poorlass, from Mount Wuji.

GATEKEEPER JING: Poorlass is a beggar woman. Beat the beggar woman!

GATEKEEPER MO: Don't be so blunt!

> POORLASS *sings*:
> (*Wugeng zhuan*)
> My husband
> is Zhang Xie.

GATEKEEPER JING *speaks*: You've used the master's personal name.[3]

> POORLASS *continues the song*:
> On the road, snow kept falling,
> your travel money was all stolen, not a cent left;

you had been beaten, and were covered in blood.

With nowhere else to turn,

in the temple

you curled up and slept.

I nursed you back to health,

and you passed the exams,

but showed no gratitude or righteousness.

ZHANG XIE *enters and speaks*:

Officials are strict and don't let a needle through,

but in private they'll let a carriage pass by.

I told you not to let just anyone enter, and you've let a woman into the hall!

GATEKEEPER JING: It's not my fault; she just came in.

GATEKEEPER MO: As if you could not push her out!

ZHANG XIE: Thirteen strokes for that gatekeeper!

GATEKEEPER JING *makes gestures*.

POORLASS: Top graduate, greetings! Don't be so angry. I have not prepared a visiting card to pay my respects to you.

ZHANG XIE: Look Poorlass, Wang Tong once said, "There is no greater disgrace than to know no shame."[4] Your appearance is squalid, your family poor, and people look down on you. You know nothing of the sacrificial rites. How could we be a compatible couple? Now I am rich and noble, and you are still called Poorlass. How dare you come and harass me, calling yourself my wife! Close the *yamen* doors, and if she does not go, drive her out!

ZHANG XIE *exits*.

*The* GATEKEEPER JING *beats* POORLASS.

> GATEKEEPER MO: If they are married, they must get a divorce.
> POORLASS: How will I ever wash away this humiliation?
> GATEKEEPER JING: You'd best hurry back to your mountain.
> *Together*: Dismiss matters and let His Excellency put an end to this.

GATEKEEPER JING: Thump! (*Makes the gesture of closing the doors.*)

*The gatekeepers* MO *and* JING *exit.*

POORLASS: That such a thing could happen!

> POORLASS *sings*:
> (*Same tune*)
> He is my husband,
> but he will not acknowledge me;
> as soon as he saw me, he hurried to close the door.
> If at the beginning I had closed the door and not let you in,
> you would have never had a chance of passing the exams.
> I have traveled more than a thousand *li*,
> to come here,
> in hopes that you would express some sympathy.
> Now I have to return but have no travel money,
> and tonight
> I have nowhere to go.
>
> (*Same tune*)
> Do you remember
> when you wanted to come to the capital,
> I sold my hair and gave you the money?

At the time you said you would never abandon me;[5]
it was all those good words that made me come here!
I have no money for the road;
I'll beg my way,
to my hometown.
I shall buy a stick of good incense and pray to Heaven:
"I want your deceitful heart
to be forever honored."[6]

*Declaims*:
Straight in the face those doorkeepers beat me
and then insulted me.
People can be good or cruel, but Heaven is never cruel,
and people can be evil or afraid, but Heaven is never afraid.

POORLASS *exits*.

# ACT 36

ZHANG XIE *enters and sings*:
(*Taishi yin*)
Last year I was in a hopeless situation,
and a robber stole my last possessions.
So I sought refuge at the desolate temple,
where Poorlass, instantly allowed me to stay,
and talked me into becoming her husband.
As soon as my name was announced, she expressly came to look
for me.
Had the nobles at court known,
they would ask, "Who is that person?"

*Speaks*: An ancient poem says: "Muddy waters cannot conceal Mr. Xu's dragon."[1] Poorlass does not have a single possession, not a penny in her bag. Even if I used "phoenix glue," once the string is broken how can we continue?[2] I am riding to take up my post and I will have to pass through Mount Wuji. There, I shall eliminate the source of the trouble and burn down the old temple. This meeting with Poorlass did not defeat her, so when I hit her, she'll remember how hard she has just hit me.

When the dragon comes to shallow shores, the frogs ridicule it; when the phoenix enters the deep forest it is mocked by the sparrows.

ZHANG XIE *exits*.

# ACT 37

POORLASS *enters carrying a signboard and sings*:
(*Yizhi hua*)
When I lived in Jiangling Prefecture,
we were a family of rich and eminent people.
When I was young I lost my parents,
and I have constantly been alone and miserable.
I went to the imperial city,
especially to look for my husband.
Unfortunately, he let me down,
and I have no money for the road.
How will I return home!

*Declaims*:

In a lonely and desolate temple I remained poor but honest,

untouched by the fates of marriage or the entanglements of the
world.

Because you alone came seeking refuge,

we married hoping to complement each other.

In the third month of autumn, you, talented youth, snapped the
cassia twig,

and across miles of open grassland I walked alone.

Today we met but you did not dismount your horse,[1]

so we each go our own way.


*Sings again*:

(*Jinqian hua*)

On both sides of the street the talented and virtuous,

all pity me.

Yet bearing this shame, I dare not protest my injustice,

poor and lowly as I am.

There is a road to my hometown, but no money for the journey,

so I express my grievances, hoping for some pity:

please, spare a couple of coins.


(*Same tune*)

On both sides of the street are officials,

with their wives.

I think of how we, husband and wife, will not reunite,

but broke apart.

You drove me out, so how could I stay?

There are one thousand *li* ahead and no money for the road:

please, spare a couple of coins.

*Declaims*:

I came here to look for my husband,

but what can I do about this meager fate and adverse conditions?

Every morning I will have to dust off the thick frost;

only when the spring wind comes, shall I open my eyes.


*Sings again*:

(*Manjiang hong*)

I hope, gentlemen, that you will help me with a couple of coins,

so that I can return home.


POORLASS *exits*.


# ACT 38

GRANDPA LI *enters and sings*:

(*Mian daxu*)

The scholar's wife has been gone for such a long time,

she must have reached the capital,

and they now both make a fine couple.


GRANDMA LI *enters*:

Remember me;

buy them and bring them back for me.


GRANDPA LI *speaks*: Wife, what are you talking about?


GRANDMA LI *continues the song*:

It's about those bronze mirrors he promised.

GRANDPA LI:

They won't be too happy about reflecting you.

There must be other types of local specialties.

GRANDMA LI:

But for painting one's eyebrows, how can they compare with a
mirror?

GRANDPA LI *speaks*: Remarkable! A Zhang Chang![1]

GRANDMA LI: Husband, on the track on Mount Wuji, there is a
woman walking ahead, and behind someone carrying a bundle
on the back. It must be Miss Zhang coming back.

GRANDPA LI: No, it's not.

GRANDMA LI: Yes, they are carrying something round.

GRANDPA LI: I can't see anything.

GRANDMA LI: It's a bronze mirror.

GRANDPA LI: No, it's not a mirror. It's only a fan.

GRANDMA LI: No, it's not a mirror or a fan; it's just a notice board.

GRANDPA LI: You're too crazy.[2]

GRANDPA LI *sings*:

(*Same tune*)

She left at the end of spring, when the cuckoos were singing,

but now the willows along the banks have withered,

and you can see the tender chrysanthemums open up several blooms.

I imagine that Top Graduate Zhang,

was really happy to see her,

and they have taken to each other like fish to water,

like glue to lacquer.

GRANDMA LI:

Neither of them remembered

that they had to buy a mirror and bring it back as a local specialty.

GRANDPA LI *speaks*: Wife, don't worry. She will remember to buy it and bring it back.

GRANDMA LI: I'm not a relative, but it feels as if I were.

GRANDPA LI: If you get a mirror, I won't stand a chance.

GRANDMA LI: If one's flesh and blood are like this . . .

GRANDPA LI: how much the more a mere stranger?[3]

*All exit.*

# ACT 39

POORLASS *enters and sings*:

(*Ku wutong*)

Who, who will believe me,

that my fate is so out of joint?

All the way I hurried to the imperial city,

through mountain roads full of steep and dangerous places.

When I departed, in the sky willow floss drifted;

upon my return, the leaves of the *wutong* trees are in a whirl.

I am ashamed as I look upon my hometown.

*Speaks*: It has been said from ancient times that "flowers are matched with flowers, and willows with willows." Since I am so ugly and poor, how could I attract a top graduate? Now I can thank heaven and earth that I have returned home. I will just tell Grandma and Grandpa that I could not find Zhang Xie.

Truly, one day the waves rose,

and once again the mandarin ducks flew their separate ways.


*Sings again*:

(*Yi qin'e*)

Like a mute who has eaten yellow oak,[1]

I keep this bitter pain inside.

I cannot swallow it, or spit it out,

like a fish that has taken the bait.


GRANDMA LI *enters and speaks*: Miss Zhang, you're back!

POORLASS: Grandma, greetings!

GRANDMA LI: Greetings!

POORLASS: I have not seen you for so long. Where is Grandpa?

GRANDMA LI: Husband, our young lady Miss Zhang is back.

> GRANDPA LI *enters*:

> I only wish for people to live a long life

> and together share the moonlight a thousand miles away.[2]


POORLASS: Greetings, Grandpa!

GRANDPA LI: You've come back.

POORLASS: I've just arrived.

GRANDPA LI: How many bundles did you bring back?

POORLASS: I came alone.

GRANDMA LI *astonished*: Top graduate Zhang did not ask you to stay?

POORLASS: It's a long story.

GRANDMA LI: Tell us.


> POORLASS *sings*:

> (*Ku wutong*)

> Ever since I left, on the road,

> I have been despised and slighted.

Distant rivers and towering mountains were fraught with dangers,
and when people saw me they would avoid me.
I reached the capital and inquired, full of expectations,
and thoroughly searched every one of the thirty-six alleys,
but I did not meet my beloved.

GRANDMA LI:

(*Same tune*)

I was looking forward to your return,
and thought you'd be the wife of an official.
But your skirt is threadbare, your shirt torn, and your face thin,
like someone right out of the poorhouse.

POORLASS:

I begged for food all the way back home because I had no money.

GRANDMA LI:

I don't see the mirror I was hoping for.
You've done a disservice to my delicate face.

GRANDPA LI:

(*Same tune*)

If he is still interested in you,
he will certainly find a way to see you.

POORLASS:

As we drift further and further apart, he may betray my vows of love.

GRANDPA LI:

I think that his feelings were rather shallow;
it's been almost a year since he left.

GRANDMA LI:

Even if he does not remember you, he must remember us;

I want to see the reflection of this delicate face.

GRANDPA LI *speaks*:

The gentleman seeks righteousness;

the petty man seeks profit.[3]

He is the top graduate, so he would never try to avoid you.

GRANDMA LI: Husband, let's say that he hasn't taken up his post, gone back to his hometown, or entered the court; he has simply gone to Huzhou.

GRANDPA LI: To buy a mirror for you.

GRANDMA LI: Obviously.

GRANDPA LI: To illuminate your face.

GRANDMA LI: Miss Zhang, you mustn't worry. Stay here at home for the time being. During the day you can spin cotton and at night weave some hemp; in autumn you can gather some firewood and when spring arrives you can pick some tea. In winter, as before you'll endure the cold and in summer you can go and catch black toads.

GRANDPA LI: These reveal your own skills.

GRANDMA LI: We'll choose a day for you to move back to your old temple.

POORLASS *sings*:

(*Wang meihua*)

I thank you, venerable god,

yet I have been so cruelly wronged by Zhang Xie!

I'm just like a mute

who has eaten a bitter melon.

Even today,

I cannot swallow or spit it out.

POORLASS *pays her respects (to the god).*

GRANDMA LI *stands facing* POORLASS.

GRANDPA LI *speaks*: She is praying to the god, so move on.
GRANDMA LI: Move on? I am the one acting the god.[4]
GRANDPA LI: Don't disclose your real nature.

> POORLASS: I tried hard, yet I did not find my husband.
> GRANDMA LI: Your face seems yellow, the color of squash.
> GRANDPA LI: One year of good intentions, and her complexion will look like jade.
> *Together*: After half a year journeying alone, the hair at her temples is turning white.

*All exit.*

# ACT 40

ZHANG XIE *enters and sings*:
(*He chuan*)
The time to take up my post has come.
Astride our saddles, holding the whip,
we move ahead along winding roads.
Spring has come to the willows along the dikes,
the ice melts and fish sport in the spring water.
Tall and craggy mountains,
and a sudden mountain creek—
how I delight in this glorious scene.

*Declaims*:

I could not spend the whole winter in the capital,

facing the wind, under the bright moon.[1]

At dusk I occupied myself with accumulating wine debts;

by day, I express my poetic feelings to those I meet in town.

Even though I passed and entered the civil service,

to rise to the top I must curry favor with powerful officials.[2]

But there is one other person, now far away,

about whom my humble heart is constantly ill at ease.

*The* MO *acting as* ASSISTANT *to* ZHANG XIE *enters*:

He has passed his exams

while his parents are still young.

*Greets politely*: Sir, are we leaving the capital today?

ZHANG XIE: Yes. Now that I've passed the exams I long for my home, but the road is long. On the one hand, I will ride a horse to take up my appointment, and when I reach my post, I'll decide what to do.

ASSISTANT: Yes, sir. *Calls*: Porter Li Sheng![3]

*The* CHOU *acting as* PORTER LI SHENG *enters and assents.*

ASSISTANT: Chen Ji.

*The* JING *acting as* PORTER CHEN JI[4] *enters and assents.*

ASSISTANT: Li Wang.

PORTER LI SHENG *assents.*

ASSISTANT: You again! His Excellency wants to leave the capital today. Each one of you carry a load.

PORTER CHEN JI: Shouldering a load is no problem.

PORTER LI SHENG: But what about our wages?

ZHANG XIE: You'll get three taels of silver a day each.

PORTER CHEN JI: And money for food?

ZHANG XIE: Two strings of cash a day.

PORTER LI SHENG: And wine money?

ZHANG XIE: A string a day each.

PORTER CHEN JI: Straw sandal money?

ZHANG XIE: Each one ten cash a day.

PORTER LI SHENG: Tips?

ZHANG XIE: When we get to a town, you will each receive five strings of cash.

PORTER CHEN JI: Money to cross the mountain?

ASSISTANT: What do you mean by "money to cross the mountain"?

PORTER LI SHENG: It is easy to walk on level ground, but crossing mountains and ridges is difficult.

ASSISTANT: Don't have such idle hopes.

ZHANG XIE *sings*:
(*Shangtang shuilu*)
I return to my hometown dressed in brocade.[5]

*Together*:
We are so pleased.

ZHANG XIE:
Leaning on the gate they await my return.

*Together*:
Your parents will be delighted.

ZHANG XIE:

All of you, do me a favor and hurry up!

*Together*:

Yes, sir.

ZHANG XIE:

We'll leave the city at once.

*Together*:

Without realizing it we've journeyed one *li* after another.

*The* ASSISTANT *sings*:

(*Same tune*)

I turn my head and look back at the imperial city.

*Together*:

Separated by riverside villages.

ASSISTANT:

One distant pavilion, one closer up.

*Together*:

Don't pour any wine!

ASSISTANT:

His Excellency wants you to hurry up.

*Together*:

Yes, sir.

ASSISTANT:

We are now leaving the city.

*Together*:

Without realizing it we've journeyed one *li* after another.

PORTER LI SHENG *sings*:

(*Same tune*)

We've walked so fast we're all out of breath.

*Together*:

And we're hungry.

PORTER LI SHENG:

But we still have not lit a cooking fire.

*Together*:

Let's rest a little.

ZHANG XIE:

If you don't keep going, I'll beat you!

*Together*:

Yes, sir.

PORTER LI SHENG:

We ford streams; to the east we cross a river.

*Together*:

Without realizing it, we've journeyed one *li* after another.

PORTER CHEN JI *sings*:
(*Same tune*)
Jiangling lies ahead of us.

*Together*:
But we've reached Mount Wuji.

PORTER CHEN JI:
It looks like we're are in the artery of the earth.

*Together*:
We care not that we are very far away.

ZHANG XIE:
If you move fast, you'll be given a reward.

*Together*:
Yes, sir.

PORTER CHEN JI:
A returning horse needs no whip.

*Together*:
Without realizing it we've journeyed one *li* after another.

PORTER LI SHENG *speaks*: Today we can go no further!
PORTER CHEN JI: And we have not seen any wine or food!
ASSISTANT: What's that?
ZHANG XIE: What is that place ahead?
ASSISTANT: This is Mount Wuji. This mountain is so tall it pierces the Big Dipper and [so large] it straddles all the way to the southeast. Eastward it reaches the Eastern Capital, and westward

it links up with Sichuan. For miles there isn't a single inn, and within half a day's walk there is no sign of human habitation. All you can see are the tracks of wolves and tigers and hear the mournful wind howling. At times the sounds of the gibbons rise under the bright moon. Let's eat and then move on.

ZHANG XIE: Porters, you'll each be paid two hundred cash.

PORTERS LI *and* CHEN: How about our wine? (*They nod.*)

ASSISTANT: Just be patient.

ZHANG XIE: Well then, as soon as you have finished drinking, take up your loads and we'll cross Mount Wuji. Then we must look for an inn. But we will not spend the night in a monastery or a temple. *Calls*: Assistant, get your sword and follow me.

ASSISTANT: Yes, sir.

PORTERS LI *and* CHEN: You drink a little wine and your face goes red.

ASSISTANT: Since when? Oh, His Excellency is slowing down, he's hesitating.

PORTER CHEN JI: When you're working hard, you need to get drunk.

ZHANG XIE: Here the wildflowers cover the ground.

*Together*: Just like the smell of local brew as it seeps out of the bottle.

PORTERS CHEN *and* LI *and the* ASSISTANT *all exit*.

ZHANG XIE:

A man with no hatred is no gentleman;
without venom one isn't a true man.

That confounded Poorlass came to the capital and for no good reason offended me. Now that I have arrived at this place, if when I see her she says a few nice things, I'll let it go, but if she's just as stupid, I'll kill her with a sword. And together with the temple, I will destroy everything.

I'm not a person to be provoked,[6]
but unfortunately her language incensed me.
This time I'll pull up trouble by the roots,
lest it sprouts again next spring.


ZHANG XIE *exits*.


# ACT 41

POORLASS *enters and sings*:
(*Tianxia le*)
As spring reaches the plain, days creep by;
the *Qiangqi* tea fields spread over mountains and valleys.
Secluded in the old temple, I have no companion,
and pick tea leaves to make a living.


*Declaims*:
Untimely, the spring has reached the plain,
and with a clap of thunder startled the branches at dawn.
The buds on the tip of the branches sprout forth the *Queshe* tea
    leaves;
wreathed in mist and fog I pick the leaves and return.
I live secluded in the old temple with no one to care for me,
so I will ask Grandma Li to come and keep me company.
I don't shrink from this work because it is too hard;
imperceptibly, my small basket fills with the spring wind.
I have finished weaving hemp,
and am done with picking mulberry leaves.
I have to go and call Grandma.
to help me pick the tea leaves.

*She calls*: Grandma.

GRANDMA LI *answers from backstage*: Who is it? Who is it?

POORLASS: Let's go together to pick tea leaves.

GRANDMA LI *enters*: Miss Zhang, I'm too busy! I'm too busy!

POORLASS: What are you doing?

GRANDMA LI: I'm binding my feet.

POORLASS: That takes no time. I'll wait.

GRANDMA LI: No, you go ahead. I'll come after I've had my breakfast.

POORLASS: Grandma, hurry up! Come to pick up the spring *Sheqian* leaves.

GRANDMA LI: Yesterday I picked a catty.


POORLASS: Don't brew this tea for just any guest.

*Together*: Only brew it for those who know tea.


GRANDMA LI *exits*.


POORLASS *sings*:

(*Qiujiang songbie*)

Walking slowly over the paths across the fields,

the first rays of dawn cast gold patterns through dark green willows.

The east wind is still bitter cold,

but when the bright sun rises, the cold will slowly recede.


ZHANG XIE *enters*:

I remember last year when I went to the capital,

I spent a long time weeping.

Once again I climb this mountain;

but now that my life is steadily more pleasurable,

from the depths of your misfortunes, my good fortune is born.

POORLASS:

(*Same tune*)

That person on top of the mountain,

looks like my scholar Zhang.


ZHANG XIE:

That person at the foot of the mountain,

in such simple clothes looks like Poorlass.


POORLASS:

Heaven has allowed that I meet my husband once again;

I will ask my beloved why he has been so unfair.


ZHANG XIE:

Poorlass is coming.


POORLASS:

It's scholar Zhang;

today we meet again!


POORLASS *speaks*: Graduate Zhang, is this a nostalgic visit to your
hometown?

ZHANG XIE: Listen Poorlass,

When a palace burns, you can't put out the fire with tears;

when the Yellow River breaks its banks, you cannot stop it with
your hands.

From now on there is no bond between us.

POORLASS: What do you mean there is no bond between us?

ZHANG XIE: If we did have it, why did you come to the capital to insult me?

> POORLASS *sings*:
> (*Guagu ling*)
> Please sir, cease your anger a moment,
> and allow me to speak:
> It was snowing when a robber stole your possessions,
> so you came to the temple where I rescued you
> and wore myself out for your sake.
> When you passed the exams, I rejoiced and went to the capital.

> *Refrain*:
> Why do you always get so angry?
> You won't come to a good end.

> ZHANG XIE:
> (*Same tune*)
> When you came to the capital,
> I did not ask you to stay
> but you had the temerity to say you were my wife,
> yet I had honor and wealth, while you were so poor.
> I never thought you would be so infatuated;
> let's find another way of closing the door.

> *Repeat the refrain.*

> POORLASS:
> (*Same tune*)
> My love was true,
> and with all my devotion I kept you company.
> I sold my hair for your traveling expenses,

and you inscribed your name in the Wild Goose Pagoda.[1]
I crossed mountains and rivers to get to the capital,
but you told your doorkeepers to beat me brutally.

*Repeat the refrain.*

ZHANG XIE:
(*Same tune*)
Keen to leave the capital,
I did not stop for a minute in any city or town.
We used to laugh together,
but your insults raised my anger.
I said it once and was very clear with you,
but now we meet again and you hurl insults in my face!

*Repeat the refrain.*

ZHANG XIE *speaks*: Poorlass, who keeps you company when you
    pick tea?
POORLASS: Grandma will come as soon as she's finished breakfast.
ZHANG XIE: Prepare to face my sword!

POORLASS *falls.*

ZHANG XIE:
With one stroke of the sword I have killed you;
and on the way to the Yellow Springs you will learn a sense of
    shame.
Disputes arise when people speak too much,
and worry is unleashed when you mind other's business.

ZHANG XIE *exits.*

GRANDMA LI *enters and sings*:

(*Bubu jiao*)

Clusters of beautiful flowers announce the early spring,

but flower buds on the tip of the branches are still few.

My husband is off to gather firewood,

and Xiao'er is at the end of the field

inspecting the rice seedlings.

I've seen that the tender tea leaves are particularly good,

so every day I go to check on them.

*Speaks*: At dawn, when I hadn't yet put on my trousers, Miss Zhang
came and asked me to go with her to pick tea. I wonder where
she is. *Calls*: Miss Zhang!

POORLASS: Grandma, help me!

GRANDMA LI: Where are you!

POORLASS: I've fallen into a pit.

GRANDA LI *looks and makes gestures*: Oh dear! Oh dear! What can I
do about you? Husband, hurry, over here!

GRANDPA LI *enters*:

When people are at peace, they don't speak;

when water is level, it doesn't flow.

Wife, what is the matter?

GRANDMA LI: Husband, Miss Zhang has fallen into a pit.

GRANDPA LI: What pit?

GRANDMA LI: A cesspool.

GRANDPA LI: It will raise a stench! Let me help you get her out.

GRANDPA *and* GRANDMA LI *sing*:

(*Daqiu chang*)

Poorlass,

you were picking tea;

how did you happen to trip and fall?

Perhaps someone tricked you;

your whole body is soaked in blood.


POORLASS *sings*:

(*Xiang bian man*)

Grandpa, Grandma stop,

let me relax and catch my breath:

I was alone, standing on a rock and reaching up to pick the tea,

when I lost my footing,

and slit my arm as if with a knife.


*Refrain*:

A single fall,

and our heart is tied in a thousand knots.


GRANDPA LI:

(*Same tune*)

Ever since you returned from the capital,

you have not had a moment's rest,

weaving silk and gauze without a break.

Such a fate!

Such evil times!


*Repeat the refrain.*

GRANDMA LI:

(*Same tune*)

You just stumbled and fell,

so how did you get yourself covered in so much blood?

You'd have done better just to break an ankle.

There are so many people who pick tea;

how can you be so clumsy?

*Repeat the refrain.*

GRANDMA LI *speaks*: Husband, husband, go and get a door leaf to carry her back.

GRANDPA LI: She's trying to show she's not badly hurt.

POORLASS: Grandma and Grandpa, please help me walk slowly back home.

GRANDPA *and* GRANDMA LI *and* POORLASS *walk*.

GRANDMA LI *sings*:

(*Jinpai lang*)

I'll help you all the way back.

*Together*:

We'll hold you all the way back,

and do our best through the mountain paths.

POORLASS:

I am just a wretched orphan.

*Together*:

Someone must have attacked you;

hold on, you are dripping with blood.

POORLASS:
(*Same tune*)
When will I recover?

*Together*:
When will she recover?
We need to find some medicine.

GRANDMA LI:
Child, don't worry.

*Together*:
Let's slowly return to the old temple,
and ask the god for help.

POORLASS *speaks*: For half a year, tears have streamed down my
    cheeks.
GRANDMA LI: When I think about it, your five elements must be in
    disarray.
GRANDPA LI: I doubt that we can blame it on your lack of decorum.
*Together*: This fall is clearly due to your bad fortune.

*All exit.*


# ACT 42

LADY WANG *enters and sings*:
(*Bo xing*)
Spring days are warm,
and the rivers and mountains are lovely.
I remember how my daughter longed for

days like this.

In the famous garden,

they pushed the swing and played the "Flower Contest."

Daughter, where is your soul now?


*Speaks*: Scholar Zhang, you should have known this day would come—soon you will regret you were not more careful earlier on. The house of the Military Affairs Commissioner had a daughter, and invited you to be her husband, but you simply refused. You left my daughter without a breath of life, and she soon departed for the Yellow Springs. Now you are on your way to Zizhou to take up your post, and my husband will be the censor there. Alas!


If in all your life you do nothing to furrow people's brows,

no one in the world will become your enemy.


*The* ASSISTANT *enters*: Servants.

WANG DEYONG *enters*: Turning around.

ASSISTANT: You shouldn't answer.[1]

WANG DEYONG: Assistant.


*The* ASSISTANT *assents*.


WANG DEYONG: Please call my wife.

ASSISTANT: Your wife is here.

WANG DEYONG: I didn't realize that was my wife; I thought it was an old woman selling medicinal plants.

ASSISTANT: Go ahead, take the lead and buy the herbs.

LADY WANG: Husband, we ought to take advantage of this auspicious day to leave for your new position.

WANG DEYONG: Assistant, call a maid to attend to my wife on the journey.

ASSISTANT: Yes, sir. *Calls:* Hurry out to the hall, maid.

WANG DEYONG: I have some matters that require your aid.

ASSISTANT: Sounds very much like rhyming.


*The* TIE *disguised as the* MAID *to* LADY WANG *enters and sings:*[2]
(*Linjiang xian*)
Deep inside the inner courtyards, the days are, oh—so long,


*The* JING *as the* MAID *to the deceased* SHENGHUA *enters and continues:*
Specks of willow floss strew my lapels.


WANG DEYONG:
Of all the servants, you understand matters best.


ASSISTANT:
Today we are leaving on duty for Zizhou,
and you shall go to attend on Madam.


LADY WANG'S MAID *speaks:* For long I have lived in the inner courtyards, ever keeping to the secluded boudoirs. But I'd like very much to go with Madam to her official post. Thank you, Madam!

LADY WANG: If only my daughter could be among us, I would be content.

SHENGHUA'S MAID *and* LADY WANG'S MAID *together:* Madam, don't bring that up.

ASSISTANT: Yes, watch your head.[3]

WANG DEYONG: Go and call the household carriage to go ahead.

Meanwhile, I will go and see to my horse.

ASSISTANT: Yes, sir.

LADY WANG *sings*:

(*Ma an'er*)

We sing the "Yang Pass" and pour the parting wine,

truly a lovely scene.

From the banks we see the mountain's layers of green,

and among them clusters of mountain wildflowers.


ASSISTANT:

I have heard your instructions,

and I will carefully serve Your Honor.


WANG DEYONG *sings the refrain*:

All of you climb into the carriage and leave first.

I'll wait for my horse

and hurry behind.


LADY WANG'S MAID:

(*Same tune*)

We sing the "Yang Pass" and grow despondent,

but all along the road, the scenery is magnificent.

Green water encircles dwellings

and slender willow boughs brush the delicate lotus leaves

   by the eddy.


SHENGHUA'S MAID:

The desire to leave is like a galloping steed;

we are now leaving the capital.


WANG DEYONG *sings the refrain*.

ASSISTANT:

(*Same tune*)

We sing the "Yang Pass" as we leave our home,

but the road to Zizhou extends far away.

The guards have already left,

so please ladies, quickly climb into your carriages.


SHENGHUA'S MAID *and* LADY WANG'S MAID:

The two concubines have already left,

and in a moment the master will follow.


WANG DEYONG *sings the refrain.*


LADY WANG *speaks*: Ten small carriages have already left.

WANG DEYONG: The embossed saddle follows rushing ahead.

LADY WANG'S MAID: On the trees along the post road orioles chirp
  tweet-tweet.

*Together*: The horses cross the bridge over the stream and trot ahead.


*All exit.*


# ACT 43


POORLASS *enters and sings*:

(*Jinchandao*)

Oh, God in Heaven!

For some years now I have felt so trapped,

and my thoughts are full of resentment.

Zhang Xie denied me what he owes me,

but this is my lot.

When snow fell and you had not a thread to wear,

you came to this old temple, weeping profusely.

I took pity on you,

gave you clothes to wear and food to eat.
And then you asked others to convince me
to marry you,
hoping to stay together for a hundred years.

(*Guo lülan ti*)
But your heart changed,
when you went to Bianliang, the capital.
You had no money for the road, so I cut off my hair,
and you left to take the exams.
All letters stopped,
and you cast me aside.
I went to the capital,
but how could I ever meet with you?
You expressly ordered the gatekeepers to treat me like dirt,
and now you have tried to kill me.
My fate is against me,
and your feelings so shallow.
My arm hurts all day long;
and nursing this grievance
morning and night I quietly wipe away my tears.

*Speaks*: Top graduate Zhang,

Today you have injured me,
and forgot how poor you were at first.
They say a sword will behead the dishonorable man,
and gold will reward the virtuous one.

POORLASS *exits*.

# ACT 44

*The* ASSISTANT *enters and sings:*
(*Santai ling*)
Tam, tam, the beating of drums;
dang, dang, the clang of the gongs.

WANG DEYONG *enters and continues the song:*
I hurry along on my horse.

ASSISTANT:
As he rides onward, the Commissioner's is in good spirits.

*Speaks:* The Commissioner and his horse are well suited.

WANG DEYONG: Watch out for the horse's hoof.
ASSISTANT: I'll fry it and sell it myself.[1]
*Together:* Bang, bang-ba, bang, bang, ba-ba-bang.
WANG DEYONG: I want a report, a report. Why in all this military
    retinue is there only one drum?
ASSISTANT: Sir, one drum has two sides covered with skin.
WANG DEYONG: Two sides like the skin on my lips.
ASSISTANT: I can see for myself.

*The* ASSISTANT *sings:*
(*Linli ji*)
Crossing mountains and fording rivers,

*Together:*
Crossing the bridge over the river, tra-la-la we go,
the horses walking.

WANG DEYONG:

I fear only a mean horse and a rough road:

It could kick you to death,

and I wouldn't even notice,

trample you to death,

and I wouldn't even notice.

*The* ASSISTANT *speaks*: Sir, this is Mount Wuji. At the foot of the
mountain is an old temple where we can rest a while.

WANG DEYONG: I doubt that my family will want to go in.

ASSISTANT: But look, sir, so many carriages are already in front of
the temple.

WANG DEYONG: I have good eyesight, so how come I can't see them!

ASSISTANT: Just trim your sails to the wind.

WANG DEYONG: Why not look for an inn, or a monastery or an
abbey? How can you ask me to bed down in a temple!²

ASSISTANT: Perhaps you want to have a prophetic dream?³ Sir, there
are no inns in these parts, and no monasteries or abbeys either.
Although this temple bears no imperial tablet, it has divine power
and is roomier than an official lodging. Let's rest a while.

WANG DEYONG: Yes, you are right.

ASSISTANT:

It's better to spend the night at a temple

than stay at the home of a villager.

WANG DEYONG:

When I hear the bells, I become aware of a temple hidden in the
mountains;

only when you reach the banks, do you know that the river divides
the village.

*All exit.*

# ACT 45

LADY WANG *enters and sings*:

(*Chuan bozhuo*)

We specifically came to Sichuan
because of our daughter.
In the midst of this grassy wilderness we can see an old temple,
which makes me sadder still,
and thoughts of my daughter make me weep.

*Declaims*:

(*Chang xiangsi*)

Good marriage fortune,
ill marriage fortune.
My daughter was still young, in the spring of her life;
how could she withstand meeting that top graduate?
Our child had a wretched fate;
our daughter had a wretched fate.
Riding back and forth, he did not take the silk whip,
and a deep longing for marriage met with a faithless lover.

*The* ASSISTANT *enters and speaks*: Madam, there are no inns ahead,
and we have left behind the last thatched cottage; it is hard to
find a place to stay among people's houses in the village, so let's
rest in this old temple.

LADY WANG: Is the master here yet?

ASSISTANT: The Commissioner is just dismounting.

WANG DEYONG: Bang, bang, ba, bang, bang. *Calls*: Prepare to
report!

ASSISTANT: To whom must we report?

WANG DEYONG: I've dismounted some time ago, and the music just keeps going "bang, bang, bang."

ASSISTANT: Fine. I'll report to you.

WANG DEYONG: Wife, look at the statue of the god in the hall; it's so lifelike.

LADY WANG: It is indeed.

WANG DEYONG: And look at the little demon; it's all of twelve feet tall.

LADY WANG: Indeed, very tall.

WANG DEYONG: Wife, if I can see the demon in front of my eyes, can you see it as well?

LADY WANG: You make me do so![1]

LADY WANG'S MAID enters: I have seen a strange thing, strange enough to prolong one's life.[2] Where is Madam?

LADY WANG: Maid, calm down and tell me what the matter is. Don't make such a fuss.

> LADY WANG'S MAID sings:
> (Tao hongju)
> When I went inside the temple,
> I saw a lovely girl but very poor.
> She looked just like Miss Shenghua,
>     but all covered in blood; her shirt was stained red.

WANG DEYONG speaks: (Spits:) You cannot have seen a roast!

ASSISTANT: Seen a ghost!

WANG DEYONG: Seen a roast!

ASSISTANT: You're so stubborn.[3]

LADY WANG: How can there be a girl in the temple? I'll go inside and see.

ASSISTANT: Madam, she is very poor, and her bedroom won't be very clean.

WANG DEYONG: Then call the maid to help her come out for us to see her.

LADY WANG: Maid, go and bring her out.

LADY WANG'S MAID: Yes, ma'am. She's the very image of Miss Shenghua.

LADY WANG *and* WANG DEYONG: What does she look like?

LADY WANG'S MAID: She's a match for the Goddess of the River Luo and the equal of the moon goddess Chang E.[4]

LADY WANG'S MAID *exits*.

WANG DEYONG: Wife, if she is pretty, we should take her with us. In the morning she can serve us our medicine, and in the evening wait upon us in the toilet.

ASSISTANT: You can't tell a good smell from a bad one.

POORLASS, *supported by* LADY WANG'S MAID, *enters and sings*:
(*Xiangliu niang*)
For decades I have lived in this temple,
but few people have come to inquire after me.
All alone I have lived,
with no one to rely on.

LADY WANG'S MAID:
Come out and try to make your bows,
and let Madam ease your heart a little.

POORLASS:
Greetings!
Greetings!
But I am so downhearted.

*Together:*
What is causing you so much distress?

WANG DEYONG *sings:*
(*Same tune*)
Her eyebrows and eyes
are the very image of my daughter's,
her body is as graceful, and her waist as fine.

LADY WANG:
At first glance,
I already feel pity for you.
Why is your face so drawn?

LADY WANG'S MAID:
And why, I wonder,
why
are your clothes soaked in blood?

*Together:*
Why are you like this?

POORLASS:
(*Same tune*)
As far as I remember, since I was young,
I have lived on my own in great poverty.
Because I went to pick tea,
and fell on my arm.

LADY WANG:
If you are all alone, how did you get porridge to eat,
and medicine to restore your good health?

POORLASS:
In the village up ahead is Grandpa,
who pities and cherishes me.


*Together:*
This was determined in a former life.


WANG DEYONG *speaks*: Miss, you are so lonely here. Why don't you follow us to my post and take care of our latrines? Our maid would be happy too.

ASSISTANT: What are you asking her to do?

LADY WANG: Husband, whatever her aspect,[5] just look at her face. Her spirit is so open and upright. How can you ask her to do such work? The only thing we can do is to adopt her as our own daughter.

WANG DEYONG: If you can leave this place and follow us, we will get a doctor to cure you and marry you to an official.

POORLASS: There is nothing to stop me from going. However, I have no luck, and I also need to ask Grandma Li, who lives in front of the village. If she consents, I will go.

WANG DEYONG: Maid, bring some porridge for her to eat. Assistant, go to the village and fetch Grandma Li.

ASSISTANT: Yes, sir.


LADY WANG'S MAID: Who was to know that today our noble Lord would be moved, and that she would part with the old lady and just go.

ASSISTANT: Generally, she seems to have a good disposition; even without make-up she is very charming.


LADY WANG'S MAID *and the* ASSISTANT *exit.*

WANG DEYONG: Girl, tell us who you really are.

> POORLASS *sings*:
> (*Taizi you simen*)
> I come from a wealthy family,
> and I was much loved by my parents.
> When I was young, they both passed away,
> leaving me in great poverty.
> I spin silk and weave hemp,
> and when spring comes I pick tea leaves.
> Unfortunately, I slipped and broke my arm,
> and there is no one to care for me.

WANG DEYONG *speaks*: My dear daughter, all over the neighborhood it is announced: if you sing "Taizi you simen" you're bound to bump into a procuress.[6]

GRANDMA LI *enters*: Clip-clop, clip-clop.

ASSISTANT *enters.*[7]

> GRANDMA LI *sings*:
> (*Same tune*)
> I see an official,
> perhaps he is a relative of yours?
> But you've been in this temple for five or six springs,
> and no one has come to care for you!
> Picking tender tea leaves on the mountain,
> you fell on your arm and hurt it.
> Listen, Madam, why not help her out;
> and why not rid her of her poverty?

WANG DEYONG *sings*:
(*Same tune*)
I am the Crimson Prince,
now assigned to the prefecture of Zizhou.
Poorlass is now in a desperate state,
and my daughter recently passed away,
yet her face manifests the same spirit.
So my wife wants to adopt her.
If you raise any objections,
assistant,
tie her to the front of the horse and we'll deal with her.


GRANDMA LI *bows politely and speaks*: Yes, I agree, I agree.
ASSISTANT: You wouldn't dare say anything else.


POORLASS *sings*:
(*E'ya man duchuan*)
But since my family was rich and noble,
How can I simply go with someone else?


LADY WANG:
Because you are on your own here,
and you have no one to rely on.


ASSISTANT:
Grandma come forward. You don't need to kneel down to pay your
    respects.


GRANDMA LI:
Greetings, sir. Let me inform you:
This Poorlass,
ever since she was young she has lived in this temple,
and day and night I have helped her.

WANG DEYONG:

(*Same tune*)

When I think of my daughter,

she was prettier than Poorlass.


LADY WANG:

In Zhang Xie's actions,

there is no difference between the two girls.[8]


LADY WANG'S MAID:

I will go and boil some porridge for her to eat.


WANG DEYONG:

Wait a moment, let me tell you:

it is better if we find you a doctor to take charge.


*Together:*

You will follow and serve us as a daughter,

and dress up in luxurious clothes.


LADY WANG'S MAID:

(*Same tune*)

I urge you, stop your musings;

if you come, your good fortune will follow.


*Together:*

You will have plenty of the very best,

clothes and delicacies to your heart's desire.


GRANDMA LI:

Since you were young I have cherished you,

so if you leave, I will go with you.

*Together:*
Since you are not yet recovered,

GRANDMA LI:
Grandma will take care of you on the road.

*Together:*
We will stay close together to avoid worries,
and as companions bring a little flavor to the road.

GRANDMA LI:
(*Same tune*)
My husband will not go with you;
he'll look after our child properly.[9]

ASSISTANT:
What utter foolishness.[10]

LADY WANG:
I am employing you
to take good care of her.

WANG DEYONG:
My own daughter was as beautiful as you.

*Together:*
Then she will marry a good husband.

LADY WANG:
Grandma, please go
to pack your luggage.

*Together:*
We shall add another sedan chair.


GRANDMA LI:
I will walk.


ASSISTANT *speaks*: On three-inch lotuses.


*Together:*
Clearly, it was determined in a former life
that in this life they meet again with her as their child.
LADY WANG'S MAID *speaks*: Madam, do not worry that the road is
   still long.
LADY WANG: Your mother was very lonely all day long.
POORLASS: Who was to know that this morning we would meet
   again?
WANG DEYONG: Your father will carry the sedan chair without
   complaint.
ASSISTANT: Sir, please be sensible and don't say such foolish things.
The old woman is in no mood to take care of all of us.


GRANDMA LI: How can one obstruct the river;
in the end it always runs to the sea and turn to waves.
ASSISTANT: When they reach *you*, they turn to waves.
*Together:* We once sailed a small boat over the ocean,
and now we are not afraid that the waves are high.


*All exit.*

# ACT 46

ZHANG XIE *enters and sings*:

(*Manpai ling*)

Intent upon studying the classics,

I wanted to change my status.

On the road to the capital, I was severely beaten,

my whole body thoroughly wounded,

and I married, which did not help my scholarly ambitions.

As I passed the exams, my name was inscribed on the Wild Goose
Pagoda,

and as a mark of my strenuous studying,

I stood first.

*Speaks*: Han Yu once remarked that "Sages are not found in every
age, and wise men appear only now and then." Take me, Zhang
Xie: alone I took the first prize and passed as top graduate. For
this, I have first to repay my debt to heaven and earth, second, I
want to thank our enlightened emperor, and third, I am grateful
for the favors I received from my father and mother. Luckily I
have been appointed to Zizhou, so I'll select an auspicious day
to take up my post.

Ten years under the window unknown by all—

but once I passed, I became known to the whole world.

ZHANG XIE *exits*.

# ACT 47

*The* ASSISTANT *enters and sings*:
(*Jin lianhua*)
Idly, I turn my gaze toward the capital.


LADY WANG *enters*:
The incense smoke rises evenly;
everywhere it is quiet and calm.


SHENGHUA'S MAID *enters*:
In the Wu River, the water flows clear and cold.


LADY WANG'S MAID *enters*:
Encroaching even upon the Milky Way,
the dark-green mountains of Sichuan.


*Together*:
We can only see the plank roads¹ reaching to the clouds,
and hear the cries of the wild gibbons.
These truly are like the patterns on curtains and screens.
Ai!


LADY WANG'S MAID:
(*Same tune*)
Our new companion resembles Shenghua, just as beguiling.


*Together*:
A peach-blossom face
and a small ochre mouth.

LADY WANG:

This morning, after combing her hair and binding her feet, she
surpasses even our daughter.

*Together:*
A magnolia,
she inserts to one side of her hair.
With golden phoenix hairpins,
and ornaments of kingfisher feathers;
she's as charming as our daughter!
Ai!

POORLASS:
(*Same tune*)
Suddenly, combed and washed, I feel bashful.

*Together:*
Give up your worries;
it's pointless to knit those brows.

WANG DEYONG *enters:*
Calmly follow mother and father, and be carefree in your travels.

*Together:*
Good fortune
converges now.
We shall persuade you to marry
a good husband,
and you will become even more fond of us!
Ai!

LADY WANG:

(*Same tune*)

Luckily, our daughter's wounds have dried.

*Together*:

From today,

she will always be well dressed.

LADY WANG'S MAID:

By the Imperial Aloeswood Pavilion, leaning against the rail.

*Together*:

Amongst the magnolias

and red peonies.

And amid the *Yao* yellows,

*Taihu* rocks—

What a brilliant sight!

Ai!

WANG DEYONG *speaks*: Daughter, calm down! Papa has been appointed to the district of Zizhou, but after two years we'll be back at court. If you have good fortune, I will find a match that will take good care of you.

POORLASS: I'm just afraid that my allotted luck is meager.

LADY WANG: Husband, you mustn't keep thinking of our daughter.

WANG DEYONG: When we return home, we will not see her powdered face.

*Together*: And when we leave, no one will ask us to quickly return.

*All exit.*

# ACT 48

WANG DEYONG *enters and speaks*: Assistant, come here.

*The* ASSISTANT *enters.*

On the Yangzi one wave chases the other,
newcomers push out the old.

ASSISTANT: Yes, sir. What are your orders?

WANG DEYONG: We have arrived in Zizhou, but officials from the *yamen* haven't yet come to present themselves. I want to see only the civil and military officers to find out how graduate Zhang is handling himself.

ASSISTANT: Sir, the streets outside are clogged with officials; their regalia fills the alleys. There is a constant hubbub resounding with the rattle and clank of carriages. The Five Grand Secretaries and the Eight Grand Officials in permanent residence are all represented, as well as those in the Six Ministries and the Three Bureaus. Of the civil officials, the Secretaries to the Regional Commanding Officers and the State Monopoly Agents are also here. I haven't yet let the Surveillance Commissioner and the Defense Commissioner and their retinue in to pay their respects. Why don't you just invite the two officials to visit?

WANG DEYONG: You're quite right.

THE JING *acting as* LIU TUNTIAN *enters*: Your humble servant is here.

ASSISTANT: Please, please come in.

WANG DEYONG: Please.

LIU TUNTIAN: Liu Tuntian is here to visit.[1]

ASSISTANT: His Excellency requests your presence.

*The* ASSISTANT *sings*:
(*Ye you hu*)
There are thousands of officials in the county.

WANG DEYONG:
Who is the first to pay his respects?

LIU TUNTIAN:
My name is Liu Tuntian.

*Together*:
Let's bow to each other and exchange pleasantries.

LIU TUNTIAN *speaks*: I have come promptly to pay my respects.
WANG DEYONG: It's my fault, I've been most impolite.
LIU TUNTIAN: In the past we painted a white deer on black doors.
 Among the dark clouds there was a road.[2]
LIU TUNTIAN *and* WANG DEYONG: When we bow to each other,
 we look like grain being poured into a sack.
ASSISTANT: When did you lose your coarseness?[3]
WANG DEYONG: Please sit down.
LIU TUNTIAN: There is nothing to sit on.
WANG DEYONG: Then pretend. (*Makes a gesture.*)
ASSISTANT: You're so disrespectful.
WANG DEYONG: I remember when we were small we used to ride a
 bamboo horse.
LIU TUNTIAN: In the blink of an eye we're white-haired old men.
WANG DEYONG: Assistant, this official composed three hundred and
 eight *ci* poems and has obtained the title of Secretary Tuntian.
LIU TUNTIAN: I can also declaim poems, compose *ci*, I excel at
 merry-making, play musical instruments, pull the crossbow, and
 kick the ball.

TOP GRADUATE ZHANG XIE ❧ 327

ASSISTANT: That makes you the head of the rakes.

WANG DEYONG: I remember one year you were really good at the crossbow.

LIU TUNTIAN: My technique is the best. To use the crossbow you need to look from behind the arrow, and when you fit the arrow you should not injure others. There are several other styles one can employ, so that if you lay a wager you can win nine times out of ten.

WANG DEYONG: And the year we played ball, do you remember that?

LIU TUNTIAN: You kicked the ball like a shooting star, following each step with a turn as if the moon were after you. I remember I kicked the ball in the "left" style and you kicked in the "right" style. I kicked left turns.

WANG DEYONG: I kicked right turns.

LIU TUNTIAN *and* WANG DEYONG *kick and fall.*

ASSISTANT: Gentlemen, a little decorum, please.

LIU TUNTIAN *and* WANG DEYONG: Chitchatting here we got distracted.

ASSISTANT: Too distracted.

LIU TUNTIAN *and* WANG DEYONG *kick the ball and make gestures.*

LIU TUNTIAN: I must leave now.

WANG DEYONG: Allow me to see you off.

LIU TUNTIAN: No, no, don't bother.

LIU TUNTIAN: *exits.*

WANG DEYONG: It wasn't a good idea to see this frivolous official. Let's invite an experienced official.

ASSISTANT: Why?

WANG DEYONG: So that I can inquire about the local sites.

ASSISTANT: Yes, sir.

*The* JING *acting as* VICE COMMISSIONER TAN *enters.*

ASSISTANT: Please, come in.

VICE COMMISSIONER TAN: The old general from Guanxi, Military
 ViceCommissioner Tan, comes to introduce himself.

ASSISTANT: Military officials must stand on the steps.

WANG DEYONG: This is a close friend; we can make an exception
 in this case.

VICE COMMISSIONER TAN: I'll stand guard.

 *Sings*:
 (*Wuyun mei*)
 I've come to present my respects.

WANG DEYONG:
 I have not seen you for a long time.

VICE COMMISSIONER TAN:
 I had urgent matters in Guanxi to attend to,
 and was unable to send you a letter.

WANG DEYONG:
 I've just arrived, and have had no time to greet you properly.

VICE COMMISSIONER TAN:
 Your arrival truly heartens me.

WANG DEYONG:
 I am sorry if I've inconvenienced Your Honor, I am at fault.

VICE COMMISSIONER TAN:
I am most grateful you allowed me to come.
(*They bow to each other.*)

WANG DEYONG *speaks*: Please, sit down.

VICE COMMISSIONER TAN *and* WANG DEYONG *mime sitting down.*

ASSISTANT: Have some tea.

VICE COMMISSIONER TAN *accepts it.*

ASSISTANT: Once more!
VICE COMMISSIONER TAN *and* WANG DEYONG *sit down doltishly*:
Just like old times, like old times. (*They make gestures.*)
WANG DEYONG: I have just arrived and I know nothing of the local
sights.
VICE COMMISSIONER TAN:

When asked I answer,
no question requires no reply.

We are now located on the main thoroughfare of the city, but all
over Zizhou there are thousands of exquisite households and
miles of elaborate buildings. There is, however, one thing you
must know: there are notices posted announcing that drinking
is strictly forbidden on pain of beating.[4] A few days ago, two
commoners fought over a debt. One said the other owed him
money, but the other said that he did not. Since they did not
know any of the eighteen military techniques, they just beat
each other. This one punched and the other one punched, this
one kicked . . .
WANG DEYONG: . . . and the other one kicked.

VICE COMMISSIONER TAN *and* WANG DEYONG *kick each other and fall over.*

ASSISTANT: You still aren't behaving yourselves properly. Here, drink up your soup.

VICE COMMISSIONER TAN *accepts it.*

ASSISTANT: You again!

VICE COMMISSIONER TAN: I must leave now.

WANG DEYONG: Allow me to see you off.

VICE COMMISSIONER TAN: No, no, don't bother.

VICE COMMISSIONER TAN *exits.*

ZHANG XIE *enters and sings:*
(*Sheng chazi*)
I haven't seen last year's friends,
so who is there to know what troubles me?

*The* ASSISTANT *speaks:* Please, come in.

WANG DEYONG: Who is it?

ASSISTANT: The Notary to the Administrative Assistant, Graduate Zhang.

WANG DEYONG: Where is he?

ASSISTANT: He is in the reception room.

WANG DEYONG *shouts:* Drive him out!

ASSISTANT: He is one of the court officials. I don't dare.

WANG DEYONG: Well, then, tell him I am resting, and if he wants to see me, he'll have to wait three years.

ASSISTANT: You're not Chen the recluse.[5]

WANG DEYONG *looks at* ZHANG XIE: He's the one who jilted my daughter.

ASSISTANT: Sir, be polite!

WANG DEYONG: Ask him to come back tomorrow.

ASSISTANT: Subordinates come to the *yamen* to pay their respects after three days. That's the proper etiquette.

WANG DEYONG: How about you let him stand there until his shoes wear out. Then I'll see him.

ASSISTANT: Eight years could pass and you still wouldn't see him.

WANG DEYONG: Invite him in, invite him in. I know what to do.

ASSISTANT: Yes, sir. Please come in.


WANG DEYONG *sings*:
(*Chan zhihua*)
Zhang Xie is someone that I won't receive.


ASSISTANT:
Then, by your orders, I will chase him away.


ZHANG XIE *bows*:
Sir,
I have been favored by the emperor,
and I was hoping you would put in a word for me.[6]


ASSISTANT:
Please sir, try not to rebuke him.


WANG DEYONG:
Then I'll ride the donkey backward,
so I'll never see the brute's face.


ZHANG XIE:
(*Same tune*)
I have committed no offense,
But I am afraid I have yet to learn the proper etiquette.

WANG DEYONG:

When you didn't take the silk whip,

I cried so much that I ruined my eyesight.


ZHANG XIE:

But when I realized my mistake, it was too late to repent.


WANG DEYONG:

My daughter's state of mind was so unhinged,

she never ate again.


ASSISTANT: Clearly.

WANG DEYONG: You were not fated to be my son-in-law, and from now on you are no longer welcome here.

ASSISTANT: Understood, sir.


WANG DEYONG: As a bride, my daughter was worth a fortune.

ZHANG XIE: Clearly, I was so out of touch.

ASSISTANT: I knew early on that you would be constrained.

*Together*: He regrets he was not more careful earlier on.


*All exit.*


# ACT 49


LADY WANG *enters and sings*:

(*Yizhi hua*)

Daughter, come here,

try to come out of your boudoir

to stroll along the flowered paths.

POORLASS *enters*:

I am so happy today, I must enjoy myself;
among flowers like brocade
and drooping willow branches.

LADY WANG'S MAID *and* SHENGHUA'S MAID *(now* POORLASS'S
   MAID*) enter and sing together*:
Through the vivid reds and greens we go,
snapping some enchanting blossoms to wear,
lovely blossoms to wear.

LADY WANG'S MAID:

(*Same tune*)
In the renowned garden of the district *yamen*,
there are swings everywhere,
and we all vie for the ornamented seats.

POORLASS'S MAID:

Playing the "Flower Contest" and singing songs.

LADY WANG:

Frolicking bees chase one another,
and white butterflies dance.

*Together*:
In the flowery paths beyond the city,
gracefully, tiny feet pace,
tiny feet pace.

*The* ASSISTANT *enters*:
(*Same tune*)
I, the assistant,

have specially been sent by His Honor
to summon you, Madam.

WANG DEYONG *enters*:
Top graduate Zhang Xie came to the stairs of the courtyard,
but I did not grant him audience;
I shall not receive him.

*Together*:
Could we forget that because of him,
our daughter's life was lost,
our daughter's life was lost?

WANG DEYONG:
(*Same tune*)
Tomorrow, when I sit in the audience hall
and the top graduate comes,
I shall ask him to stand there until daybreak.

ASSISTANT:
You are shockingly cruel.

LADY WANG:
If he requests to be seen again,
I will still not invite him.

*Together*:
Let him reflect,
on the damage he did by refusing to accept the silk whip,
the silk whip.

LADY WANG *speaks*: Husband, when he comes, as before, do not to receive him.

WANG DEYONG: I'll make him stand there until the third watch—

POORLASS'S MAID:—and from the third watch until daybreak.

ASSISTANT: A goodhearted pair.

WANG DEYONG: I do not want to see him under any circumstances.

ASSISTANT: Sir, you need not consume yourself with worry.

LADY WANG: We must torment this top graduate Zhang.

WANG DEYONG: Until he's thought about this a thousand times.

*Together*: Then, he will recognize the need for an official's support.

*All exit.*

# ACT 50

ZHANG XIE *enters and sings*:

(*Taoliu zhengfang*)

The silk whip was thrust to me, the greatest talent,

but alas, I paid no heed,

and this morning I've received my punishment.

To make the acquaintance of the prefectural magistrate,

who is there to mediate for me?

I will call my assistant.

*The* ASSISTANT *enters and speaks*: Because you did not give it enough thought you now face all sorts of problems. Sir, the Crimson Prince asked to come to Zizhou as governor solely because of you. Generally, illnesses should be treated early, and you must find a solution.

ZHANG XIE: My misery is like the flow of the Yangzi, continual without abating.

ASSISTANT: Vice Commissioner Tan might be able to speak to him on your behalf.

ZHANG XIE: Give me some notepaper; I will write a message to invite him over.

ASSISTANT: I will go over now and invite him.

ZHANG XIE: I must find a person to mediate for me.

ASSISTANT: And now is the right time for action.

> ZHANG XIE: If you measure the water with a stick, you will know its depth.
> *Together*: You can judge from someone's words whether he is wise or stupid.

ZHANG XIE *exits*.

ASSISTANT: There is an old saying that runs:

> Those who succeed are not at ease,
> and those who have ease don't succeed.

That official is a jolly fellow, but he has been so tormented by Crimson Prince that he has asked me to invite Vice Commissioner Tan to intercede. I can see the lofty gates of the *yamen* and the servants running back and forth. But I dare not go straight into the hall. I'll just wait by the central foyer.

VICE COMMISSIONER TAN *shouts from backstage*: Put the chair down.

*Inside they assent.*

ASSISTANT: The Vice Commissioner has just returned. They just put the chair down inside the hall.

VICE COMMISSIONER TAN *enters*: Who is this who has come straight inside the hall?

ASSISTANT: I am here with a letter for you from Notary Zhang.

VICE COMMISSIONER TAN: Where is it?

ASSISTANT: Here.

> VICE COMMISSIONER TAN *takes the letter and sings*:
> (*Shanpo yang*)
> I, Zhang Xie, anxiously prostrate myself repeatedly before you:
> So that you may regard me with affection,
> employ your great talents on my grievance
> and provide some sympathy to bring about my intentions.
> Without your kindness and mediation,
> disaster will surely strike;
> I anxiously await my assistant's return.
> Without further ado,
> I, Zhang Xie, anxiously prostrate myself repeatedly before you.

VICE COMMISSIONER TAN *speaks*: Since you've come to the official residence, I'd better go. This young man will certainly go far.

ASSISTANT: When did you learn physiognomy?

VICE COMMISSIONER TAN: I am a man of war, I'll just walk over.

ASSISTANT: There is no one to carry the chair anyway, so let's go along the main streets.

VICE COMMISSIONER TAN: Cutting across short alleys.

ASSISTANT: Past teahouses.

VICE COMMISSIONER TAN: By wine shops.

ASSISTANT: And here is the government office.

VICE COMMISSIONER TAN: Take this string of cash as a tip.

ASSISTANT: There is no need.

VICE COMMISSIONER TAN: You've served me diligently.

ASSISTANT: Not at all, please, please come in.

ZHANG XIE *enters and bows*:

VICE COMMISSIONER TAN *sings*:

(*Hongna ao*)

I bow with embarrassment at your heaven-sent letter.

ZHANG XIE:

I am honored that you walked here.

VICE COMMISSIONER TAN:

I came immediately to pay my respects to Your Excellency.

Blessings!

ZHANG XIE:

I have some small business to bother you with.

VICE COMMISSIONER TAN:

Tell me,

Tell me.

If it is within my power,

I will manage it for you.

ZHANG XIE:

(*Same tune*)

His Honor and I are old acquaintances,

but when I passed the exams I did not consider his marriage offer.

So he has especially come to administer this prefecture,

and when he saw me today he was still so angry.

I have called you,

I have called you.

Because I wish to find a way for reconciliation,

but I don't have the means.

VICE COMMISSIONER TAN:

(*Same tune*)

He helped me at the start of my career,

and we have always been on splendid amicable terms.

I have heard that his only daughter passed away,

but people say that he has one more.

If that is so,

If that is so,

then I will

find a solution for you.

ASSISTANT:

(*Same tune*)

That whip was handed to you in front of your horse,

and they repeatedly asked you to take it, but you refused.

Miss Shenghua soon departed for the Yellow Springs.

If you manage to restore friendly relations, it will be the work of a
    worthy person.

*Together*:

The mistake will be set right,

the mistake will be set right,

and this will be passed on

as a tale for later generations.

VICE COMMISSIONER TAN *speaks*: Destiny, destiny, things never
    happen randomly. Allow me to report to His Honor. I expect
    I'll succeed.

ZHANG XIE: If you can kindly assist me, I shall be extremely grateful.

ASSISTANT: And Madam and His Honor will cease their
resentment.

VICE COMMISSIONER TAN: This time he will succeed in marrying
his daughter to the top graduate.

ZHANG XIE: If flowers had feelings, they wouldn't fade.

*Together*: If the moon had no regrets, it would be full again.[1]

*All exit.*

# ACT 51

WANG DEYONG *enters and speaks*:

I have acquaintances everywhere,
yet those who know me are few.

Among the officials in Zizhou, the only one I respect is Vice
Commissioner Tan.

*The* ASSISTANT *enters*: What is the Military Affairs Commissioner
talking about?

WANG DEYONG: I am talking about Vice Commissioner Tan.

ASSISTANT: What about him?

WANG DEYONG: Those Guanxi men are the most honest and
forthright.

VICE COMMISSIONER TAN *enters.*

ASSISTANT: Please come in.

WANG DEYONG: Who is it?

ASSISTANT: It's Vice Commissioner Tan.

WANG DEYONG: Please come in.

VICE COMMISSIONER TAN *sings*:

(*Yin fanzi*)

I hurried to pay my respects

to Your Honor, Commissioner of the Prefecture.

I have a small matter

I've especially come to discuss with you

and with your wife. But I'm afraid this may be impolite.

WANG DEYONG:

Ask my daughter and my wife

to come out.

Tell them not to delay.

*Refrain*:

Since we are relatives,

There is no harm in sitting opposite each other.

LADY WANG *enters*:

(*Same tune*)

I have heard it is the Vice Commissioner, the old general

from Guanxi.

VICE COMMISSIONER TAN:

At first I did not dare

to come straight in for an audience.

But by reason of the fact that we served together,

and that we are relatives, I ventured anyway.

Please ask Her Ladyship to come out,

and allow me to pay my respects to her.

Do not hesitate.

*Repeat the refrain.*

POORLASS *enters*:
(*Same tune*)
Mincing along with tiny feet,
slowly stepping on the tiles.

LADY WANG *and* WANG DEYONG:
The old general,
is our relative.

POORLASS:
Greetings, and please forgive me,
I've not had time to pay my respects.

VICE COMMISSIONER TAN:
I have not met the young lady before,
she looks so remarkable.
But please, do not hesitate.

*Repeat the refrain.*

VICE COMMISSIONER TAN *speaks*: In the three passes there are
four military camps with eighteen forts along the borders.
There we shed each other's blood and lay down our lives, and
that is the trade I know. So the following matter may not be
for me to discuss, but we are relatives, and I'll have to be blunt
with you.

WANG DEYONG: Please sit down.

VICE COMMISSIONER TAN: There is no need.

WANG DEYONG: What do you want to discuss?

VICE COMMISSIONER TAN: Just that Zhang Xie has committed a
serious offense against you and has asked me to intercede for
him.

LADY WANG *sings*:
(*Jiangshui ling*)
Please don't mention top graduate Zhang Xie;
when you speak of him, I cannot stop weeping.

WANG DEYONG:
From ancient times to this day sons-in-law have been chosen.

*Together*:
He had no wife,
so he surely could have taken the silk whip.

WANG DEYONG:
Yet he found my daughter not to his taste,
and caused her to fall sick in half a year.

*Together*:
Her fortune too poor,
her fate too meager.

LADY WANG:
Who would have believed that our daughter's mental state would
    change;
that day and night, day and night, her melancholy would grow,
and then, all of a sudden, all of a sudden, she was consigned to the
    Yellow Springs.

VICE COMMISSIONER TAN:

(*Same tune*)

I have especially come to pay a courtesy call.

LADY WANG *and* WANG DEYONG:

We realize you consider us worthy.

VICE COMMISSIONER TAN:

In the hope that you will cease your terrible wrath.

LADY WANG *and* WANG DEYONG:

You might as well,

go ahead and tell us.

VICE COMMISSIONER TAN:

Top graduate Zhang Xie hopes for your protection;

please forgive me for being so blunt.

LADY WANG *and* WANG DEYONG:

If these are your demands, sir,

we will not go against them.

VICE COMMISSIONER TAN:

I never realized you had another daughter.

And I would be willing, be willing, to act as go-between.

LADY WANG *and* WANG DEYONG:

Your intention, your intention, is to make peace between us.

WANG DEYONG:

(*Same tune*)

When I think about it, it always makes me angry.

*Together:*

Because they lost their offspring, a daughter.


LADY WANG *and* WANG DEYONG:

But this daughter is most beloved;

in her gentle way

she is even more beautiful.


WANG DEYONG:

If top graduate Zhang Xie makes up for his previous fault,

I will give this daughter in marriage to him.


VICE COMMISSIONER TAN:

Thank you for your gracious permission.


LADY WANG *and* WANG DEYONG:

We dare not go against your wishes.


VICE COMMISSIONER TAN:

This match will not be in vain.


WANG DEYONG:

Daughter, daughter, what do you think?

What is your opinion, your opinion; what do you have to say?


POORLASS:

(*Same tune*)

I am afraid that my destiny is poor.


*Together:*

Matters of marriage are determined in a former life.

POORLASS:

I will abide by father and mother's wishes.


*Together*:

These are wise words.


POORLASS:

I am grateful for your guidance and matching me with a young
     talent;

it was determined that I should marry the top graduate.

I thank you for the love and kindness you've given me;

in a former life we were already a family.

I am grateful, grateful for Your Honor's firm intention.


*Together*:

We must decide a day, decide a day, to match this pair of love birds.


WANG DEYONG *speaks*: With three cups they will unite with the
     Way and be one with nature. In the private residence, we will
     soon discuss the details.


   VICE COMMISSIONER TAN: I have inconvenienced Your Highness
        and Her Ladyship.

   WANG DEYONG: Let's enjoy ourselves; why bother to rush.

   LADY WANG: Keep on dancing until the moon sinks behind the
        courtesans' quarters.

   *Together*: Until the song ends and the peach-blossom fans stop
        their waving.


*All exit*.

# ACT 52

ZHANG XIE *enters and sings*:

(*Hong shaoyao*)

When the feast for the candidates in the Qionglin Garden ended,

I left through the Donghua Gate.

Just beneath the decorated tower the silk whip was handed to me,

and they all thought that I would gladly take it.

But my heart was not set on marriage,

I wanted only to honor my parents.

How was I to know I would incur the Military Affairs

 Commissioner's enmity,

undiminished to this day?

*The* ASSISTANT *enters and speaks*:

You cannot clap with one hand,

but two hands clap very loudly.

Sir, today Vice Commissioner Tan . . .

ZHANG XIE: What did the Vice Commissioner say?

ASSISTANT: He has finished his third cup. Here he comes.

VICE COMMISSIONER TAN *makes the sound of a neighing horse from*

 *backstage.*

VICE COMMISSIONER TAN *enters*: Guards, each of you take two

 strings of cash as a tip. Here, it's a gift, here, take it.

ASSISTANT: It's always you. Please, please come in.[1]

VICE COMMISSIONER TAN: I've come to pay my respects. Greetings,

 sir.

ASSISTANT: What pleasantries shall we exchange?

ZHANG XIE: No need for formalities. In all matters, I have been greatly favored by you.

VICE COMMISSIONER TAN: A fine mirror—but you clearly didn't know how to polish it!

ASSISTANT: That is *your* specialty.[2]

VICE COMMISSIONER TAN: Why did you reject His Honor's daughter? I have just seen his other daughter and she is very pretty! Very pretty indeed!

ZHANG XIE: He has another daughter! What does she look like?

VICE COMMISSIONER TAN: She has feet and hands, she can walk and run, and she has a nose and a mouth.

ASSISTANT: Without those she wouldn't be human.

VICE COMMISSIONER TAN: Well, this marriage matter is all settled, so choose an auspicious day for the wedding.

ASSISTANT: Yes, sir!

> VICE COMMISSIONER TAN: The selection of an auspicious day will be attended to.
>
> ASSISTANT: And the lady, same as before, will marry the top graduate.
>
> ZHANG XIE: Truly, in wine one finds a way.
>
> *Together*: Just like encountering a fairy inside a flower.

*The* ASSISTANT *exits.*

> VICE COMMISSIONER TAN *sings*:
> (*Sheng jiang ya*)
> I have seen her in person,
> so don't be rude and make them uneasy.
> Now see you don't look down on her,
> and to begin with don't say a word.
> Their daughter in all respects
> is exquisite.

*Refrain*:
It was determined five hundred years ago,
and today you made the match.

ZHANG XIE:
(*Same tune*)
At the beginning I never expected
things would turn out like this.
I was committed to honor my family;
and devoted to finding special beauties.
How would I know that the Military Affairs Commissioner
would get so angry and avoid all mention of the matter?

*Repeat the refrain.*

VICE COMMISSIONER TAN:
(*Same tune*)
Their daughter came out,
walking so slowly.
A heavenly creature of delicate snow-white skin,
a heavenly creature who will have you as her husband.
This time do avoid
stirring up his anger.

*Repeat the refrain.*

ZHANG XIE:
(*Same tune*)
Were it not for you,
how would things have turned out?
This time, I will certainly become a handsome husband,
and not upset the mandarin ducks.

So select a day
to make the match.

*Repeat the refrain.*

VICE COMMISSIONER TAN *speaks*: Today, the Military Affairs
    Commissioner was smiling from ear to ear.
ZHANG XIE: If it were not for you, matters would not have been
    settled.
VICE COMMISSIONER TAN: All things are beyond human design.
*Together*: In the end they are determined by fate.

*All exit.*

# ACT 53

*The* MO *acting as a public administrator holding a parasol enters and
speaks:*[1]

If you set a fire, you will get the smoke too.
but if you carry water from a spring, you'll bring away the moon.

I never realized that the Crimson Prince had yet another daughter.
    Today is an auspicious day and the Military Affairs Commis-
    sioner has granted her a dowry of one hundred thousand strings
    of cash to marry top graduate Zhang Xie. It must be that they
    were destined to meet.

Truly,
    silk-gowned folk go with silk-gowned folk,
    and the cotton clad go with the cotton clad.

*The* CHOU (*unspecified character*) *enters carrying a flower cap:*[2] Clear the way! The flower cap is arriving.

ADMINISTRATOR: And a fine flower cap too! With clusters of pink peonies, and some *Wei* purple peonies; blooming *Yao* yellow peonies and *Heaven's Fragrance* white peonies. These last ones, white as snow, draw pairs of bees and white butterflies from over the wall.

CHOU: You are the administrator; you shouldn't be carrying the parasol. Take the flower hat and I will take the parasol.

ADMINISTRATOR: I have a brother at last.

*The* ADMINISTRATOR *takes the hat and the* CHOU *takes the parasol.*

ADMINISTRATOR: Indeed, they beat the drums and play the lutes to unite both families.

*The* CHOU *dances with the parasol and sings:*
(*Dou shuangji*)
Flower cap,
flower cap,
perfect in all respects.
So many designs,
so many designs,
so skillfully woven.
The flower clusters in the parasol are superbly assembled,
and when I thrust it this high,
it flutters in the wind.

ADMINISTRATOR:
You look just like a *Baolao*,
in the marionette theater.[3]

*The* ADMINISTRATOR *speaks:* The hat with its clusters of exotic flowers enhances the face.

CHOU: Once he tries on the official gown, he will look even more elegant.

ADMINISTRATOR: Among the myriad green branches a speck of red.

*Together:* We need just a little spring color to move us.

*All exit.*

*The* JING *(unspecified character) enters holding a lantern and a musical instrument:*

In the distance I can see the peacock screen open; constant, Chang E cares for all great talents.

The sound of pipes and flutes is loud and clear, as if the immortals have mistakenly entered a little Penglai. *Shouts:* Make way! Make way! The top graduate is coming. Both sides of the crimson gates are lined with red sleeves; not even the immortals could compare with this. Colored silks woven together make a flowery world, and fragrant flowers wafting across a land of brocade.

*The* JING *exits.*

ZHANG XIE, *his head wrapped in a scarf, enters and sings:*
(*Zisu wan*)
The road to Penglai is not far away;
lovers do not complain that this is one shallow step up.[4]
Listening only to the sound of strings and pipes;
you can imagine tonight's fulfillment of the love birds' desire.

*The* ASSISTANT *(to* WANG DEYONG*) enters and speaks*: Please, come in. The Crimson Prince has invited the top graduate to present himself.

WANG DEYONG *enters*.

ZHANG XIE *sings*:
(*Ying xianke*)
Who would have thought
that it was my destiny
to be granted your favor this day and be rewarded with your help.

WANG DEYONG:
I remember the time
when you refused that whip.
how could I have anticipated
that you would become my kin?

ZHANG XIE:
(*Same tune*)
I made so bold,
as to seek your help
for who was to know the moon would now be full once more.

LADY WANG *enters*:
My daughter is once again marrying top graduate Zhang,
and this time they will come together;
the lovers' fortunes are great indeed!

LADY WANG'S MAID *enters and sings*:
(*Same tune*)
. . .[5]

POORLASS *enters dressed up as a bride.*

LADY WANG *sings*:
(*You huazi*)
Her veil will soon be lifted.


LADY WANG'S MAID:
And the colored silk tassels will be no longer needed.


*Together*:
A match made in heaven;
what a fine couple they make!


POORLASS:
Zhang Xie, do you remember when you slashed my arm?
How can we become husband and wife today!

WANG DEYONG *grabs* ZHANG XIE.


LADY WANG:
Father, don't get angry,
and listen to what our daughter has to say.


ZHANG XIE:
(*Same tune, new opening*)
Hold back your fury for a while,
and listen to me,
let me explain.


LADY WANG:
Daughter, speak up and tell us how he wronged you.

POORLASS:

When a thief robbed him of all his possessions,

he came to the temple to sleep.

He was injured,

so I provided him with clothing and food.

We then forged a marriage bond,

so when he passed the exam, how could he accept the silk whip and
     marry someone else?

*Together:*

(*Same tune*)

You were already husband and wife,

and today Heaven has brought you together again.

Don't speak like this;

at present things are not the same.

POORLASS:

I sold my hair to help him reach the capital,

and he passed as first candidate.

But then he told his gatekeepers to drive me out,

and finally slashed my arm.

LADY WANG *sings*:

(*Hefo'er*)

A good man with an education should not act like that.

*Together:*

Unprincipled!

WANG DEYONG:

She was your wife, how could you reject her?

*Together*:
To marry another.

ZHANG XIE:
Originally, I didn't intend to marry you,
but in my desperate situation, I had no choice.
Moreover, the weather was cold and I had no family there,
so I married you without thinking.

*Together*:
From the things you say,
these are not the manners of an educated man!

*The* JING *acting as* GRANDMA LI *enters and sings*:
(*Hong xiuxie*)
Top graduate, greet Grandma Li.
*Together*:
Not easy.

ZHANG XIE:
Grandma. I'd forgotten what you look like.

*Together*:
Who are you?

GRANDMA LI:
The wife
of Grandpa Li.
I came with the young lady,
leaving my child behind.
I put on some makeup
and came over here;
how can you not recognize me?

POORLASS *sings*:

(*Yue ren hao*)

Grandpa's house

has been very kind and generous.

*Together*:

You all must stop this kind of talk;

it is a festive occasion, so let's drink three cups.

WANG DEYONG:

From today on they will be like fish in water,

and as for those earlier words of resentment,

*Together*:

Throw them into the river running East,

throw them into the river running East.

LADY WANG:

(*Same tune*)

Good son, good daughter,

you are now bound together as lovers.

*Together*:

Like phoenix and simurgh you will now fly side by side,

and boast that you are sweet as Zhengzhou pears.

GRANDMA LI:

At the beginning you promised me a mirror,

and now I shall definitely have one.

I will buy one to take home,

and will take home too, my many expressions.

ZHANG XIE *and* POORLASS *speak*: We met in the old temple and were married.

WANG DEYONG *and* LADY WANG:[6] You passed the exams but had no future.

GRANDMA LI *and* LADY WANG'S MAID: But in Zizhou the phoenix and simurgh came to mate once more.

ASSISTANT *and* ALL: A marriage destiny to top all others past and present.

# End

# Appendix I

## DRAMATIS PERSONAE

| Role and Function | Name and Family, Institutional, or Social Role (acts in which they appear) |
|---|---|
| *Sheng* (male lead) | Zhang Xie |
| *Moni* (leader of the troupe) | Leader of the troupe |
| *Dan* (female lead) | Poorlass* |
| *Mo* (additional male role) | Leader of the troupe (1) |
| | Friend of Zhang Xie (1, 2) |
| | Zhang family servant (4, 5) |
| | Mr. He (6) |
| | Traveler *mo* (8) |
| | Local god (9) |
| | Divine judge (10) |
| | Grandpa Li (11, 12, 14, 16, 19, 23, 30, 33, 38, 39, 41) |
| | Assistant to the Wang family (21, 25, 27, 32, 42, 44, 45, 47, 48) |
| | Student (24) |
| | Customer (28) |
| | Clerk in the *yamen* (34) |
| | Gatekeeper (35) |
| | Assistant to Zhang Xie (40, 50, 52) |
| | Steward (53) |
| *Fumo* (secondary additional male role) | Zhang Xie's house servant (2, 5) |

(*continued*)

| Role and Function | Name and Family, Institutional, or Social Role (acts in which they appear) |
|---|---|
| *Jing* (comic male or female) | Friend of Zhang Xie (1, 2) |
| | Mother of Zhang Xie* (5) |
| | Traveler *jing* (8) |
| | Mountain god (10, 16, 33) |
| | Grandma Li* (11, 14, 16, 19, 23, 30, 33, 38, 39, 41, 45, 53) |
| | Innkeeper's wife* (24) |
| | Bookseller (28) |
| | Maid *jing* to Shenghua* (32, 42, 49) |
| | Gatekeeper (35) |
| | Porter Chen Ji (40) |
| | Liu Tuntian (48) |
| | Commissioner Tan (48, 50, 52) |
| | Assistant *jing* (53) |
| *Chou* (clown male or female) | Sister of Zhang Xie* (5) |
| | Diviner (4) |
| | Robber (8) |
| | Small demon (10) |
| | Xiao'er (11, 12, 16, 26, 28) |
| | Prime Minister Wang Deyong (21, 32, 44, 45, 48) |
| | Student (24) |
| | Porter Li Sheng (40) |
| | Assistant Chou (53) |
| *Tie* (additional female role) | Shenghua, Prime Minister's daughter* (13, 17, 21, 25, 27, 29, 32) |
| | Maid *tie* to Lady Wang (42, 45, 47, 49, 53) |
| *Wai* (extra male or female role) | Father of Zhang Xie (2, 5) |
| | Lady Wang, Mother of Shenghua* (15, 17, 21, 25, 27, 29, 32, 42, 45, 47, 49, 53) |

*These are female characters.

# Appendix II

## SYNOPSIS OF ACTS

Originally, Zhang Xie was not divided into acts, and the current division is the result of Qian Nanyang's edition of this play. Qian's division was based both on the musical structure and the entry and exit of roles and characters. I have further divided some of the acts into scenes to show the smallest units of composition and to further clarify the structure of the play.

### ACT 1. INTRODUCTION AND ALL KEYS

This is the introductory scene. The *mo* role enters and in two songs makes a general statement about the passing of time and the brevity of life, urging the public to enjoy the moment. At the end of the second tune, the *mo* sings and narrates a so-called southern *All Keys* (*Zhugongdiao*), a type of medley that alternates song and narrative on the story of Zhang Xie. Zhang Xie informs his parents that he is ready to go to the capital to take the civil service examination.

## ACT 2. SECOND INTRODUCTION
## (SHENG AND TROUPE)

The *sheng* as actor enters and asks the troupe to lead him into the character he will impersonate, the scholar Zhang Xie. The *sheng* role steps into the character of Zhang Xie, introduces the play once more and then leaves to look for friends to discuss a dream.

**Scene 1:** Zhang Xie and his two friends joke around trying to compose rhymes.

**Scene 2:** Zhang Xie returns home and asks permission from his father to go to the capital to take the imperial exams.

## ACT 3

**Scene 1:** Poorlass introduces herself. She describes how she comes from a good family but was orphaned at a young age and lost all her property. She has been living alone in the village temple for some years.

## ACT 4

**Scene 1:** Zhang Xie's servant goes to look for the dream diviner. The diviner interprets Zhang Xie's dream, and then follows the same routine with Zhang Xie servant's dream.

## ACT 5

**Scene 1:** Zhang Xie's father, mother, and servant enter worried at Zhang Xie's imminent departure. Zhang Xie enters the stage to bid farewell to his parents as he is about to depart. Zhang Xie's sister is the last to come in to see her brother depart. Zhang Xie's parents give him some money for the road and impart words of caution to their son.

## ACT 6

**Scene 1:** The main female role appears again explaining her misfortune. She introduces her benefactors: Grandma and Grandpa Li. A villager comes to call on her with a request.

## ACT 7

**Scene 1:** Zhang Xie is on the way to the capital city and describes the hardships of the road.

## ACT 8

**Scene 1:** A bandit appears and introduces himself.
**Scene 2:** Two merchants are about to cross the mountain. They are robbed by the bandit. This is a comic scene with much acrobatic display.
**Scene 3:** Because the merchants have lost all their wares, they are forced to go down the mountain.

## ACT 9

**Scene 1:** Zhang Xie enters singing of the hardships of the road. The robber enters and attacks Zhang Xie, taking all his possessions and clothes.
**Scene 2:** The mountain god appears disguised as an old man, wakes up Zhang Xie, and sets him on the path to the old

temple where Poorlass lives. The god disappears suddenly, and then Zhang Xie exits.

## ACT 10

**Scene 1:** The three gods of the temple are waiting for Zhang Xie to arrive. The mountain god calls in a judge god and an imp to assist him in making Zhang Xie's arrival more comfortable. The mountain god, ashamed of the dilapidated state of his temple, asks them to pose as doors. Zhang Xie arrives, enters the temple, bolts the doors, and exits the stage.

**Scene 2:** A little later, Poorlass arrives and bangs on the door asking to be let in. Because she is in fact banging the back of one of the gods posing as doors, a comic scene ensues.

**Scene 3:** In the last scene, Poorlass thoroughly questions Zhang Xie and then explains her background and plight.

## ACT 11

**Scene 1:** This act introduces Grandpa and Grandma Li, and their middle-aged son Li Xiao'er. They briefly describe themselves as well-to-do, landholding villagers and discuss Poorlass's plight. They order Xiao'er to bring her some food, but Xiao'er refuses. He agrees to take her food when Grandma Li consents to his proposal to marry Poorlass.

## ACT 12

**Scene 1:** Zhang Xie and Poorlass discuss their predicament in a song. While trying to find a solution, Xiao'er arrives with some food. He meets Zhang Xie.

**Scene 2:** Xiao'er mentions to Poorlass that his parents have agreed to their marriage and Poorlass, enraged and somewhat out of character, insults Xiao'er. Grandpa Li arrives and explains to Poorlass that the only way to convince Xiao'er to bring her food was to deceive him.

**Scene 3:** In a final scene, Grandpa Li meets Zhang Xie and agrees to bring him clothes.

## ACT 13

**Scene 1:** This act introduces the family of the Military Affairs Commissioner Wang Deyong. The daughter Shenghua enters, introduces herself and her surroundings, and explains her family background and her parent's lineage.

## ACT 14

**Scene 1:** Zhang Xie and Poorlass note the tranquility of the days after Zhang Xie's arrival and his gradual recovery. Zhang Xie asks Poorlass to marry him, but Poorlass takes offence and leaves.

**Scene 2:** Grandma and Grandpa Li enter and find out that Zhang Xie has asked Poorlass to marry him. Grandma Li acts as go-between and convinces Poorlass that marriage to Zhang Xie is a good idea. Poorlass agrees, but only on the condition that they first cast the divination blocks and ask the gods.

## ACT 15

**Scene 1:** Lady Wang enters and explains that her daughter has come of age and they must find a suitable match for her. Their ideal candidate would be the top graduate.

## ACT 16

**Scene 1:** Marriage scene. The mountain god enters and introduces himself, followed by Grandpa Li and Xiao'er, who prepare to officiate the marriage ceremony. Zhang Xie and Poorlass follow shortly and make their vows. The ceremony is peppered with buffoonery from the gluttonous god concerned only with food offerings of meat and wine.

**Scene 2:** Zhang Xie and Poorlass, alone on stage, sing a tune in which they alternate songs promising to honor each other forever.

**Scene 3:** Grandma Li enters with Grandpa and Xiao'er to celebrate the marriage feast. The scene concludes with a mime by the gluttonous Xiao'er posing as a table while stealing the food.

## ACT 17

**Scene 1:** Lady Wang and Shenghua describe the scene in the Military Affairs Commissioner's mansion. Shenghua worries that her youthful years will pass, and her mother reassures her that she will find a suitable match for her to marry.

## ACT 18

**Scene 1:** Zhang Xie enters and reveals that marrying Poorlass was not in his plans. Poorlass enters and discloses her love for Zhang Xie. Zhang Xie expresses his desire to travel to the capital to take the exams, and they discuss how to subsidize the trip. Poorlass proposes to sell her hair to Grandma Li.

# ACT 19

**Scene 1:** Poorlass goes to the Lis to borrow money for Zhang Xie. Grandma Li is reluctant to part with her money, but Grandpa Li convinces her. Once Grandma agrees, they all drink a cup of wine to celebrate and seal the agreement, and Poorlass returns to the temple.

# ACT 20

**Scene 1:** Zhang Xie is impatient and angry waiting for Poorlass to find out whether she has managed to raise some money for him for the road. Having drunk one cup of wine, she comes back flushed and Zhang Xie beats her thinking she has been drinking. Grandpa Li enters and explains everything to Zhang Xie.

**Scene 2:** Poorlass chastises Zhang Xie for his conduct and he apologizes, promising once more to never abandon her. Grandma Li enters to bid farewell to Zhang Xie.

**Scene 3:** Poorlass and Zhang Xie sing a parting song in which she expresses doubts about the sincerity of his pledge to her, and he reassures her of his commitment.

# ACT 21

**Scene 1.** The Military Affairs Commissioner, Wang Deyong (father of Shenghua and husband of Lady Wang), is introduced for the first time by his assistant. Shenghua and Lady Wang enter to discuss Shenghua's betrothal to the top graduate.

## ACT 22

**Scene 1:** Zhang Xie reminisces about his hometown and his parents. He recalls Poorlass back in the old temple with some disdain, intimating he has renounced his pledge to her.

## ACT 23

**Scene 1:** Poorlass, sad and dejected, enters on her way to visit the Lis. Grandma and Grandpa Li make jokes about love and desire, and they all reassure her that one day Zhang Xie will become an official.

## ACT 24

**Scene 1:** Zhang Xie reaches the capital and meets two students—the wit and the dull-witted—also waiting to take the exams. They introduce him to the city and show him an inn where he can settle until the examinations begin. Much buffoonery ensues when the innkeeper comes to chase after one of the students because he owes her money.

## ACT 25

**Scene 1:** Lady Wang enters with her daughter. They are all waiting for the examination results and are making preparations to select and persuade the top graduate to marry Shenghua.

## ACT 26

**Scene 1:** Poorlass enters worried about Zhang Xie's silence and ignorant of his outcome in the examinations. Xiao'er enters singing a tune hinting at Poorlass's circumstances. She listens knowingly. Poorlass asks Xiao'er to buy a booklet with the names of the successful examinees the next time he goes to the village.

## ACT 27

**Scene 1:** Lady Wang, Shenghua, and the assistant enter and describe the bustling scene in the capital. They learn the name and locality of the top graduate, and prepare to hand him the silk whip, which, if he accepts, would signal that he would marry her.

**Scene 2:** Zhang Xie, dressed as the top graduate, enters singing. A joyful Shenghua follows and hands him the silk whip, which he seems to accept. But he soon rejects it, refusing to marry Shenghua.

**Scene 3:** In a third scene, Zhang Xie meets Wang Deyong who tries to convince him to marry his daughter, but Zhang Xie refuses and leaves.

**Scene 4:** Angry, Wang Deyong makes a series of comic vicious remarks about Zhang Xie to his assistant. He calls Lady Wang and Shenghua to discuss the matter with them.

## ACT 28

**Scene 1:** Xiao'er goes to town on an errand and buys the list of the successful examinees from a bookseller.

## ACT 29

**Scene 1:** Lady Wang and Shenghua enter and express their disappointment with Zhang Xie. They feel humiliated and disconsolate that Zhang Xie did not take the silk whip.

## ACT 30

**Scene 1:** Poorlass comes in worried because she had heard nothing from Zhang Xie, but the Lis arrive to offer their congratulations and inform her that Zhang Xie has passed as top graduate. Poorlass explains to the Lis her resolve to go to the capital to look for Zhang Xie and asks for their opinion.

## ACT 31

**Scene 1:** Zhang Xie announces that he has passed the examination as top graduate. He is grateful to his emperor and his parents. As a filial son, he sends a note to his parents to inform them of his success.

## ACT 32

**Scene 1:** Lady Wang enters and explains that the humiliation of Zhang Xie refusing the silk whip has made her daughter sick. Shenghua enters supported by her maid and is very sick, and she describes her humiliation.
**Scene 2:** Lady Wang berates her husband for mentioning Zhang Xie in front of their daughter. Wang Deyong asks for a doctor

again, but none dare treat her. The maid enters, preoccupied, and explains that Shenghua is on her last breath.

**Scene 3:** Wang Deyong's assistant enters, reflecting on the actions of Zhang Xie. Shenghua dies, and Wang Deyong swears he will avenge his daughter by requesting to be assigned to a superior post in the same district as Zhang Xie.

## ACT 33

**Scene 1:** Poorlass is about to leave for the capital and goes to the temple to ask for the protection of the mountain god. Grandpa Li comes to send her off. The mountain god gives his blessing, and then Grandma Li, played by the same role, gives her blessing.

## ACT 34

**Scene 1:** Zhang Xie is now in the *yamen* preparing to go and take up his post in Zizhou. He orders the *yamen* guards not to let peasants or women through the gates.

## ACT 35

**Scene 1:** Poorlass arrives in the *yamen*, but the gatekeepers have strict orders from Zhang Xie to keep out all women and peasants. The gatekeepers suggest she shout to draw the attention of Zhang Xie, and when he finally comes out, he rejects her.

**Scene 2:** Poorlass expresses her disappointment in Zhang Xie and begs her way back to her village.

## ACT 36

**Scene 1:** Zhang Xie officially rejects Poorlass. He accuses her of forcing him to marry her and resolves to kill her when he passes through Mount Wuji.

## ACT 37

**Scene 1:** Poorlass returns home.

## ACT 38

**Scene 1:** The Lis see Poorlass arriving in the distance and speculate as to why she is alone.

## ACT 39

**Scene 1:** Poorlass greets the Lis, but dares not tell them that she has been rejected. She is welcomed by the Lis who ask her to stay.

## ACT 40

**Scene 1:** After having spent some time in the city, Zhang Xie prepares to leave to take up his post. He hires some porters to carry his luggage. They reach Mount Wuji.
**Scene 2:** Zhang Xie, humiliated by Poorlass's trip to the capital, reflects on what to do with her.

# ACT 41

**Scene 1:** Poorlass goes over to the Lis to ask Grandma Li to help her pick tea, but Grandma Li is busy.

**Scene 2:** Zhang Xie reaches the village and finds Poorlass picking tea. They greet each other, and Zhang Xie attempts to kill her, hacking at her arm with a sword. Poorlass falls to the ground but is not dead.

**Scene 3:** Grandma Li finds Poorlass soaked in blood and calls Grandpa Li. Poorlass claims she tripped and fell, and she is unwilling to denounce Zhang Xie. The Lis take her back to the temple.

# ACT 42

**Scene 1:** The Wangs, accompanied by their entourage, leave the capital for Zizhou. They reminisce about their daughter Shenghua and regret her fate.

# ACT 43

**Scene 1:** Poorlass is in the temple recovering from her wounds. She complains of her bitter fate and laments Zhang Xie's ungratefulness.

# ACT 44

**Scene 1:** The Wangs and their retinue arrive at the temple in Mount Wuji where they are planning to stop for the night.

## ACT 45

**Scene 1:** After the Wangs reach the temple, the servants go in to inspect the place and find Poorlass. The maid runs out to inform the Wangs.

**Scene 2:** Poorlass comes out to greet the Wangs. The Wangs, surprised at her likeness to their daughter, decide to adopt her.

**Scene 3:** Grandma Li comes to meet the Wangs, and they employ her to take care of Poorlass on the road.

## ACT 46

**Scene 1:** Zhang Xie has arrived in Zizhou and will select an auspicious day to take up his post.

## ACT 47

**Scene 1:** Poorlass is now the adopted daughter of Lady Wang and Wang Deyong. She is described here according to her new status, as the daughter of a noble household.

## ACT 48

**Scene 1:** Wang Deyong has arrived in Zizhou and old acquaintances come to meet him. Among them are Liu Yong (or Liu Tuntian), the famous poet. They exchange pleasantries.

**Scene 2:** Next comes his old friend the Military Vice Commissioner Tan. They joke around and perform some gestures.

**Scene 3:** Zhang Xie comes to present himself to Wang Deyong, but Wang Deyong refuses to see him. When he eventually agrees, Wang Deyong blames Zhang Xie for his daughter's death.

## ACT 49

**Scene 1:** Poorlass comes out with Lady Wang and the two maids. The assistant and Wang Deyong come out and inform Lady Wang that Zhang Xie paid a courtesy visit, but Wang Deyong refused to see him.

## ACT 50

**Scene 1:** Zhang Xie is now aware of his mistake and tries to find a solution. His assistant suggests he write to Vice Commissioner Tan asking him to intercede.

**Scene 2:** The assistant brings the letter to Vice Commissioner Tan's official residence, and the Vice Commissioner agrees to mediate.

## ACT 51

**Scene 1:** Vice Commissioner Tan goes to see Wang Deyong and Lady Wang and suggests that they marry their new daughter to the newly arrived Zhang Xie. After some reluctance, Wang Deyong agrees to his friend's wishes.

## ACT 52

**Scene 1:** Vice Commissioner Tan tells Zhang Xie that Wang Deyong has agreed to marry his adopted daughter to him. Zhang Xie expresses his gratitude.

**Scene 2:** Vice Commissioner Tan berates Zhang Xie and warns him not to make the same mistake twice.

## ACT 53

**Scene 1:** A steward and an assistant enter the stage with a parasol and a hat while singing and dancing.

**Scene 2:** An assistant enters holding a lantern and a musical instrument announcing the marriage cortège and making way for the married couple.

**Scene 3:** When Poorlass sees Zhang Xie, she accuses him of being ungrateful and unprincipled and of having abandoned her. Poorlass and Zhang Xie are married once more.

# Appendix III

## ROLES IN ACTS

| Act | Scene 1 | Scene 2 | Scene 3 | Scene 4 |
|---|---|---|---|---|
| 1 | *mo* | | | |
| 2 | *sheng, troupe* | *sheng, mo, jing* | *sheng, wai* | |
| 3 | *dan* | | | |
| 4 | *sheng, mo, chou* | | | |
| 5 | *wai, jing, sheng, mo, chou* | | | |
| 6 | *dan, mo* | | | |
| 7 | *sheng* | | | |
| 8 | *chou* | *mo, jing, chou* | *mo, jing* | |
| 9 | *sheng, chou* | *sheng, jing* | | |
| 10 | *jing, mo, chou, sheng* | *jing, mo, chou, dan* | | |
| 11 | *mo, jing, chou* | | | |
| 12 | *sheng, dan* | *chou, dan, sheng, mo* | *dan, sheng, mo* | |
| 13 | *tie* | | | |
| 14 | *sheng, dan* | *mo, jing, sheng, dan* | | |

*(continued)*

| Act | Scene 1 | Scene 2 | Scene 3 | Scene 4 |
|---|---|---|---|---|
| 15 | *wai* | | | |
| 16 | *jing, mo, chou, sheng, dan* | *sheng, dan* | *mo, jing, chou, sheng, dan* | |
| 17 | *wai, tie* | | | |
| 18 | *sheng, dan* | | | |
| 19 | *mo, jing, dan* | | | |
| 20 | *sheng, dan, mo* | *dan, sheng, mo, jing* | *dan, sheng* | |
| 21 | *mo, chou, wai, tie* | | | |
| 22 | *sheng* | | | |
| 23 | *dan, jing, mo* | | | |
| 24 | *sheng, mo, chou, jing* | | | |
| 25 | *wai, tie, mo* | | | |
| 26 | *dan, chou* | | | |
| 27 | *wai, tie, mo* | *mo, sheng, tie* | *chou, mo, sheng* | *chou, mo* |
| 18 | *jing, mo, chou* | | | |
| 29 | *wai, tie* | | | |
| 30 | *dan, jing, mo* | | | |
| 31 | *sheng* | | | |
| 32 | *wai, jing, tie, chou* | *wai, chou, mo, jing* | *mo, chou* | |
| 33 | *jing, mo, dan,* | | | |
| 34 | *sheng, mo* | | | |
| 35 | *mo, jing, dan, sheng* | *dan* | | |
| 36 | *sheng* | | | |
| 37 | *dan* | | | |
| 38 | *mo, jing* | | | |

| Act | Scene 1 | Scene 2 | Scene 3 | Scene 4 |
|-----|---------|---------|---------|---------|
| 39 | *dan, jing, mo* | | | |
| 40 | *sheng, mo, chou, jing* | *sheng* | | |
| 41 | *dan, jing* | *dan, sheng* | *jing, dan, mo* | |
| 42 | *wai, mo, chou, jing, tie,* | | | |
| 43 | *dan* | | | |
| 44 | *mo, chou* | | | |
| 45 | *wai, mo, chou, tie* | *chou, dan, tie* | *chou, dan, jing, mo* | |
| 46 | *sheng* | | | |
| 47 | *mo, wai, tie, dan, chou* | | | |
| 48 | *mo, chou, jing* | *mo, chou, jing* | *sheng, chou, mo* | |
| 49 | *wai, dan, jing, tie, mo, chou* | | | |
| 50 | *sheng, mo* | *mo, jing, sheng* | | |
| 51 | *chou, mo, jing, wai, dan* | | | |
| 52 | *sheng, mo, jing* | *jing, sheng* | | |
| 53 | *mo, chou* | *mo* | *sheng, mo, chou, dan, wai, tie, jing* | |

# NOTES

## PREFACE

1. Ye Gongchuo was minister of communications of the Republic of China. In 1920, he was asked to serve as principal of the Railway College, but he resigned shortly after.

2. Ye Gongchuo discovered the books in 2009. See Wang Tiancheng 汪天成, "*Yongle dadian xiwen sanzhong* de zai faxian yu *Zhang Ye zhuangyuan* de liuchuan"《永樂大典戲文三種》的再發現與《張葉狀元》的流傳, *Journal of the National Academy of Chinese Theater Arts* 31, no. 1 (2010): 1–7; Yu Weimin 俞為民, "*Yongle dadian* ben *Zhang Xie zhuangyuan* kaoshu"《永樂大典》本《張協狀元》考述, *Journal of the National Academy of Chinese Theater Arts* 31, no. 1 (2010): 8–12; and Kang Baocheng 康保成, "*Yongle dadian xiwen sanzhong* de zai faxian yu haixia lianan xueshu jiaoliu"《永樂大典戲文三種》的再發現與海峽兩岸學術交流, *Wenyi yanjiu* 1 (2014): 90–102.

3. *Playboy* was first translated by William Dolby as *Grandee's Son Takes the Wrong Career* in *Eight Chinese Plays: From the Thirteenth Century to the Present* (London: Paul Elek, 1978), 30–52. It was later translated by Wilt Idema and Stephen H. West in *Chinese Theater, 1100–1450: A Sourcebook* (Wiesbaden: Verlag, 1982), 205–211. *Little Butcher Sun* has been translated by West and Idema in *Monks, Bandits, Lovers and Immortals: Eleven Early Chinese Plays* (Cambridge: Hackett, 2010), 389–454. There is an earlier translation of *Top Graduate Zhang Xie* by Tadeusz Żbikowski (1930–1989) published in *Early Nan-hsi Plays of the Southern Song Period*,

but it contains many errors of translation (Warsaw: Wydawnictwa Uniwersytetu Warszawskiego, 1974). For the dates of these plays, see Aoki Masaru 青木正兒 (1887–1964), *Zhongguo jinshi xiqu shi* 中國近世戲曲史, trans. Wang Gulu 王古魯 (Beijing: Zuojia chubanshe, 1958), 91. *Playboy* and *Little Butcher* are also mentioned in Zhong Sicheng's 鍾嗣成 (ca. 1279–1360) *Register of Ghosts* (*Lugui bu* 錄鬼簿, preface 1360) in *Zhongguo xiqu lunzhu jicheng* (hereafter LZJC) 中國戲曲論著集成, vol. 2 (Beijing: Xinhua shudian, 1959). Zhong notes that *Little Butcher Sun* was composed by a Hangzhou doctor called Xiao Dexiang 蕭德祥, a contemporary of his who also composed other southern *nanxi* drama (134–135). It is possible that this play was originally composed as a southern drama. In the *Register*, the play *Playboy* is attributed to two thirteenth-century Yuan authors: to the Jurchen Li Zhifu 李直夫 (109) and to the Music Academy troupe leader (*Jiaofang sezhang* 教方色長) Zhao Wenyin 趙文殷 (113). Scholars believe these to be earlier versions of this play, but no texts are available that can corroborate it. See *Register*, LZJC, vol. 2, 109, 113, and 134–135. See also Idema and West, *Chinese Theater*, 205–208.

4. Qian Nanyang 錢南揚 (1899–1987), *Yongle dadian xiwen sanzhong jiaozhu* 永樂大典戲文三種校注 (Taipei: Huazheng shuju, 1985), 1–217; Wang Jisi 王季思 (1906–1996), *Quan Yuan xiqu* 全元戲曲, vol. 9 (Beijing: Renmin chubanshi, 1990); and Hu Xuegang (1925–), *Zhang Xie zhuangyuan jiaoshi* 張協狀元校釋, Wenzhou wenxian congshu (Shanghai: Shehui kexue chubanshe, 2006).

## INTRODUCTION

1. The term *zaju* (literally, "variety show" or "miscellaneous shows") has been used since at least the late-Tang dynasty in relation to forms of performance. In the mid-Ming dynasty it clearly referred to a style of northern drama, but occasionally it designated southern drama, as in the term "Wenzhou *zaju*." The northern *zaju* is generally a four-act play in which a wedge can be inserted and in which only one character can sing throughout the play. Each act can include a number of songs that can vary between four and twenty, and all songs must belong to the same key or mode.

2. This play between role and character is taken to an extreme in the Qing dynasty by the playwright Li Yu 李漁 (1610–1680) in his play

*What Can You Do About Fate?* (*Naihetian* 奈何天), included in *Li Weng chuanqi shizhong jiaozhu* 笠翁傳奇十種校注, ed. Wang Xueqi 王學奇 (Tianjin: Guji chubanshe, 2009), 565–665.

3. *Xiqu* is the term we now commonly use to designate Chinese theater as a musical form. The term modern scholars used in the West for the early Yuan and Ming theater is "classical theater" (A. C. Scott), and more recently "autochthonous theater" as opposed to spoken Chinese theater (*huaju*). Because my discussion is not related to modern spoken forms of theater, I will keep the term "Chinese theater" for classical Chinese theater and will use "southern drama" for *xiwen* and *nanxi*.

4. See Liu Xun 劉壎, *Shuiyun cungao* 水雲村稿, "Ci ren Wu Yongzhang zhuan" 詞人吳用章傳, in *Lidai quhua huibian: Xinbian Zhongguo gudian xiqu lunzhu jicheng, Tang Song Yuan bian* (歷代曲話彙編: 新編中國古典戲曲論著集成, 唐宋元編), ed. Yu Weimin 俞為民 and Sun Rongrong 孫容容 (Hefei: Huangshan shushe, 2005), 1:185–186. Liu notes that Wu was born during the Song dynasty, in the Shaoxing reign (1131–1162).

5. See Zhou Mi, *Guixin zazhi bieji shang* 癸辛雜識別集上, Tang Song shiliao biji congkan (Beijing: Zhonghua shuju, 1997), 261–263.

6. See Zhou Deqing, *Zhongyuan yinyun, Zhongguo xiqu lunzhu jicheng* (hereafter LZJC) 中國戲曲論著集成 (Beijing: Xinhua shudian, 1959), 1:173.

7. See also, for example, the section entitled "Southern Drama's Lure of Lewdness" (*Xiwen huiyin* 戲文誨淫) by the Lin'an (Hangzhou) Yuan scholar Liu Yiqing 劉一清, in his text *Qiantang yishi* 錢塘遺事, *juan* 6, in *Yingyin Wenyuange siku quanshu* (Taiwan: Shangwu yinshu guan, 1983), 408:1000. See also Yu and Sun, *Lidai quhua huibian*, 458. And the early Ming scholar collection of Random Notes (*biji* 筆記), Ye Ziqi 葉子奇, *Caomuzi* (1378) 草木子 (Beijing: Zhonghua shuju, 1959), 83. Both scholars, Liu and Ye, use the term *xiwen* to describe some form of performed story and the actor's art. But both already are far removed from the early Southern Song.

8. Zhu Yunming, "*Gequ*" 歌曲, in *Wei Tan* 猥談, in *Guang baichuan xuehai* 廣百川學海, compiled by Feng Kebin 馮可賓 (*Jinshi*, 1622) (ca. 1642; repr., Taibei: Xinxin shuju, 1970), 1353–1354. Zhao Hongfu was Emperor Guangzong's (r. 1190–1994) cousin on his father's side. See Xu Fuzuo 徐復祚 (1560–1630), *Qu lun* 曲論, LZJC, 4:243. See also Qian Nanyang, *Xiwen gailun* 戲文概論 (Taipei: Muduo chubanshe, 1989), 21–25.

9. The term "song-lyric" here refers to song-drama (or dramatic song) rather that the earlier Song dynasty lyric.

10. The attribution of authorship to Xu Wei has been questioned by Luo Yuming 駱玉明 and Dong Rulong 董如龍 in their article "*Nanci xulu fei Xu Wei*" 南詞敘錄非徐渭, *Fudan xuebao* (shehui kexue ban) 6 (1987): 71–78. Luo and Dong note that neither Xu himself nor any of his close friends ever mentioned the work, and that the period mentioned in his preface during which he was supposed to have been in Fujian does not correspond to those given in his autobiography. For the sake of convention, I will retain Xu's authorship.

11. The dates for this reign are 1119 to 1125.

12. The term *gulin shengsou* or "scamps' song" first appears in Xu and Zhu's writings, and in both cases, it is associated with urban slang and is believed to be a term in local dialect (probably Minnan 閩南) used in city markets that, according to Qian Nanyang, described the singing style of *xiwen* and not a type of drama. See Qian, *Xiwen gailun*, 4–5. Zeng Yongyi 曾永義 has a different interpretation, and believes that *gu* 鶻 stems from *canggu* 參鶻, one of the two actors of the Tang dynasty adjutant play (*Canju xi* 參軍戲) explained in the section on "Origin and Role Formation." *Shengsou* is a term still used in the contemporary *Minnan* dialect to refer to the performance of comedians. Zeng Yongyi 曾永義, "Ye tan nanxi de mingcheng, yuanliu yu liubo" (也谈"南戏"的 名称、渊源、形成与流播), *Xiqu yuanliu xinlun* (Taibei: Li Xu wenhua shiye, 2000), 130–133. See Xu Wei, *Nanci xulu* 南詞敘錄, LZJC, 3:239. See also Li Fupo 李复波 and Xiong Chengyu 熊澄宇, eds., *Nanci xulu zhushi* 南詞敘錄注釋 (Beijing: Zhongguo xiju chubanshe, 1989), 5–14. Xu Wei's *Nanci xulu* has been translated and annotated by K. C. Leung, *Hsü Wei as Drama Critic: An Annotated Translation of the "Nan-tz'u hsü-lu"* (Eugene: University of Oregon Asian Studies Program, 1988).

13. We have thirty-two extant texts of *The Lute*, but all of them were printed in the mid-Ming, and none earlier than *Zhang Xie*; the closest text we have to a Yuan original is a Qing edition published in 1674. *The Lute* remained enormously popular not just as a love story, but also as *the* dramatic model, particularly with regard to the linguistic register of drama and for its musico-phonetic composition, and a favorite on the stage. In *The Lute*, the scholar is forced to abandon his wife and parents not because of personal ambition, but rather because of the pressure

exerted on him by familial aspirations for social status and the government's needs for men of talent to fill in the ranks of the national bureaucracy, underlining the tragic incompatibility of the personal and public demands placed on the scholar.

14. For *Zhao the Chaste Maid*, Xu Wei mentions two lines from a poem by Lu You 陸游 (1125–210), which he mistakenly attributes to the poet Liu Houcun: "After he died, who could control the truth [i.e., his reputation]? The whole village listened to the song 'Cai the Second Son' [from *Zhao the Chaste Maid*]" (死後是非誰管得, 滿村聽唱蔡中郎). See Li and Xiong, ed., *Nanci xulu zhushi*, 5–14. The catalog of performances in Tao Zongyi's (1316–1403) *Nancun Chuogenglu* already mentions the play *Cai Bojie*. See Tao Zongyi 陶宗儀, *Nancun Chuogenglu* 南村輟耕錄, Yuan Ming shiliao biji congkan, juan 15 (1959; repr., Beijing: Zhonghua shuju, 2004), 306–316.

15. Two other early plays were discovered in 1975 and 1967 that were buried in tombs. One, *The Golden Hairpin* (*Xuande liunian chaoben Liu Xibi Jinchai ji* 宣德六年抄本《劉希必金釵記》), discovered in 1975 and dating from 1431–1432, shows that by comparison the changes in *Top Graduate* may not have been so comprehensive. The other, *The White Rabbit* (*Chenghua nianjian yongshuntang kanben xinbian Liu Zhiyuan huanxiang Baitu ji* 成化年間永順堂刊本新編《劉知遠還鄉白兔記》), was discovered in 1967 and dates from the Chenghua period (1465–1487). There is, to my knowledge, no other printed southern play that dates to the fifteenth century. See Liu Nianzi 劉念茲, ed., *Xuande xieben Jinchai ji* 宣德寫本 《金釵記》 (Guangzhou: Guangdong renmin chubanshe, 1985), and his "*Jinchai ji* jiaozhu houji" 《金釵記》校注後記. See also Wu Guoqin 吳國欽, "Lun Ming ben Chaozhou xiwen *Liu Xibi Jinchai ji*" 論明代本潮州戲文 (《劉希必金釵記》), in *Zhongshan daxue xuebao* (1997), 5:113–123.

16. This is tied to the much more complicated and pressing question of how we define Chinese theater. Wang Guowei (1877–1927), considered the father of modern dramatic scholarship, established the genesis of Chinese theater in the Yuan dynasty, grounding his findings on textual evidence, mostly dramatic texts. But he was soon criticized for focusing only on materials at hand. Ren Zhongmin 任中敏 (1897–1991), in a series of strongly remonstrative articles, argued that a much earlier theater began to form in the Spring and Autumn period and was fully

formed as a "story told on-stage" by the Tang dynasty. The main problem with both approaches is one of definition. Although modern scholars of Chinese drama now include Tang and early Song performances in the historical formative process of drama as proto-theatrical forms, most scholars also tacitly adhere to Wang Guowei's understanding of theater as a sung, danced, and dialogical synthesis that congealed in the late Yuan. See Regina Llamas, "Wang Guowei and the Establishment of Chinese Drama in the Modern Canon of Classical Literature," *T'oung Pao* 1–3 (2010): 1–37.

17. This, of course, is a simple and inadequate way of looking at the evolution of music and form, not the least because, as the late Qing scholar Wang Li has noted, the process of change from earlier musical forms and later Yuan and Ming drama was extremely slow and not entirely musical. The evolution from one form to another was not because a genre lost its music, or because its prosody became increasingly complex and its language obscure and difficult to understand or simply because it did not harmonize or suit regional tastes, but it was gradual and, in its trajectory, it met with extant and new popular and palace entertainment forms that mixed narrative and musical components. For a detailed explanation of these differences, see Wang Li (1889–1956), *Ci Qu shi* 詞曲史 (Nanjing: Jiangsu jiaoyu chubanshe, 2005), 184–195.

18. See Wang Shizhen, *Quzao* 曲藻, LZJC, 4:27. Wang notes that "dramatic song evolves from *ci* lyrics. Ever since the Jin and Yuan dynasties governed China, the foreign music used was clamorous and cold. Amidst the urgency [of pace], *ci* [prosody] could not be employed, so new sounds were introduced to make it more pleasing." (曲者, 詞之變. 自金, 元入主中國, 所用胡樂, 嘈雜淒緊, 緩急之間, 詞不能接, 乃更為新聲以媚之) (25). Wang praised the first, and seemingly canonized a generation of northern *qu* writers as men of extraordinary talent (*caiqing* 才情) with a knack for musical norms (*shenglu* 聲律) (25). But like Xu Wei, he regretted the absorption of northern barbarian words (染胡語) and the changes these wrought in phonology. For the evolutionary view of drama as the transformation of music, prosody, and language, see also Shen Chongsui 沈寵綏 (d. 1645), *Duqu xuzhi* 度曲須知, LZJC, 5:197–199; and Wang Jide 王驥德 (d. 1623), *Qulü* 曲律, LZJC, 4:55–56. This has carried on to the early Republican period, in which Wu Mei

吳梅 (1884–1939), for example, also has noted that "drama-song is a variant of the Jin and Song song-lyric tunes" (曲也者，為宋金詞調之別體). See Wu Mei, *Guqu zhutan* 古曲塵談, *Yuanqu* 原曲 (Taiwan: Shangwu Yinshuguan, 1989), 1.

19. Xu Wei, *Nanci xulu*, LZJC, 4: 239. For the *gong* and *diao*, see note 32.

20. See Xu Wei, *Nanci xulu*, LZJC, 3:240.

21. For the earliest guess on a Yuan date, see Aoki Masaru 青木正兒 (1887–1964), *Zhongguo jinshi xiqu shi* 中國近世戲曲史, trans. Wang Gulu 王古魯 (Beijing: Zuojia chubanshe, 1958), 90–92. Aoki Masaru concedes that this may be a Song play rewritten in the Yuan, but then cites Ming formularies in which arias of the play are included to argue for a Yuan date. Zhou Yibai 周貽白 believes it could be a Yuan evolution of an earlier play, but argues it is impossible to know. See Zhou, *Zhongguo xijushi changbian* 中國戲劇史長編 (Shanghai: Shiji chuban jituan, 2004), 138–139.

22. See Wang Guowei, *Song Yuan xiqu kao* (hereafter SYXQK), in *Wang Guowei Xiqu lunwenji* 王國維戲曲論文集： 宋元戲曲考及其它 (Taipei: Liren, 1998), 137, 144–145.

23. Qian Nanyang 錢南揚, "*Zhang Xie xiwen zhong de liangge zhongyao ziliao*" 張協戲文中的兩個重要資料, *Wuhan daxue wenzhe jikan* 武漢大學 文哲季刊 2, no. 1 (1931): 137–144; Qian Nanyang, *Yongle dadian xiwen sanzhong jiaozhu* 永樂大典戲文三種校注 (Beijing: Zhonghua shuju, 1981), 1; and Qian, *Xiwen gailun*, 25. Yu Weimin also proposes a northern Song date based on characters and institutions in the play, but argues that Cao Bin's poem is spoken, so it has nothing to do with Cao Bin. See Yu Weimin 俞為民 and Liu Shuiyun 劉水雲, *Song Yuan nanxi shi* 宋元南戲史 (Nanjing: Fenghuang chubanshe, 2009), 207–209; and Yu Weimin, *Song Yuan nanxi kaolun xubian* 宋元南戲考論續編 (Beijing: Zhonghua shuju, 2004), 128.

24. The Crimson and Green is mentioned in Zhou Mi's 周密 *Wulin jiushi* 武林舊事 (c. 1280). See *Wulin jiushi*, in WSZ, 377. The Music Bureau was established between 1127 and 1130 and was reestablished in 1144. But because it was not used that often and was very expensive to upkeep, it was permanently dismantled in 1164. Thereafter, musicians were drawn from the city register. See Ch'en Li-li, "Some Background Information on the Development of the Chu-kung-tiao," *Harvard Journal of Asiatic Studies* 33 (1973): 224–237; especially 227n11.

25. For example, Cheng Qianfan 程千帆 (1913–2000) and Wu Xinlei's 吳新雷, *Liang Song wenxue shi* 兩宋文學史 (Shanghai: Shanghai guji chubanshe, 1998), 675; Hu Ji 胡忌, *Song Yuan zaju kao* 宋元雜劇 考 (Beijing: Gudian wenxue chubanshe, 1957), 61; Sun Chongtao 孫崇 濤, "*Zhang Xie Zhuangyuan* yu Yongjia zaju" 《張協狀元》 與永嘉 雜劇, *Wenyi yanjiu* 文藝研究 6 (1992): 105–114, especially 107–108; Hu Xuegang 胡雪岡, "Wenzhou nanxi *Zhang Xie zhuangyuan* de chuang-zuo niandai" 溫州南戲 《張協狀元》 的創作年代, in *Wenzhou nanxi kaoshu* 溫州南戲考述 (Taipei: Guojia chubanshe, 2006), 47–63 (repr., "Dui *Zhang Xie zhuangyuan* xieding yu Yuandai zhongqi yihou" 對 (《張協狀元》) 寫定於元代中期以後, *Yishu baijia* 2 (2003): 36–45; and Liao Ben 廖奔 and Liu Yanjun 劉彥君, *Zhongguo xiqu fazhan shi* 中國戲曲發展史 (Shanxi: Shanxi jiaoyu chubanshe, 2003), 1:335.

26. See, for example, Feng Qiyong 馮其庸 (1924–2017), "Lun nanxi *Zhang Xie zhuangyuan* dao *Pipa Ji* de guanxi jian lun qi chansheng nian-dai" 論南戲 《張協狀元》 與 《琵琶記》 的關係兼論其產生年代, *Social Sciences Front Bimonthly* 2 (1984): 321–327. The evolution of the scholar is based on the comparison of two lines from a poem by Lu You(see note 14).

27. Sun also pointed out that some expressions in the play are typical of the Wenzhou dialect and prevail to this day. But these are few and insufficient to consider it an original Wenzhou composition. See Sun Chongtao, "*Zhang Xie Zhuangyuan* yu Yongjia zaju," 106–107. See also Liao and Liu, *Zhongguo xiqu fazhanshi*, 322–336.

28. See Yu, *Song Yuan nanxi kaolun xubian*, 119–120. Xu also adds the songs contained in the formularies, but these are clearly drawn from the *Yongle* texts. The All Keys is also not a play. Zhou Yibai, *Zhongguo xiju shi changbian*, 148.

29. See Aoki, *Zhongguo jinshi xiqu shi*, 92. See also Yang Hoi-seok 梁會錫, who follows the work initiated by Aoki Masaru, looking into tune titles. Yang Hoi-seok, "*Zhang Xie zhuangyuan* xieding yu Yuandai zhongqi yihou" 《張協狀元》 寫定於元代中期以後, *Yishu baijia* 1 (2000): 48–49. Yang also adds that the allusion in scene twenty-four of *Zhang Xie* to the early Tang general Yuchi Jingde 尉遲敬德 is possibly a refer-ence to a play on the popular subject on General Yuchi Gong 尉遲恭 and the peasant leader and warrior, General Shan Xiongxin 單雄信.

There are a number of extant plays, authored and anonymous on this subject matter, but no southern play.

30. See Qian, *Yongle dadian xiwen sanzhong*, 231–232. The song is "Paige" 排歌, and the actress Wang Jinbang calls the play a *chuanqi* 傳奇, a term later used to designate all southern drama. Qian believes this text may have existed as a play-book or *zhangji* 掌記 (acts 5 and 10 of this play), which is a kind of promptbook that troupes carried with them. See also Yu Weimin, "*Yongle dadian* ben *Zhang Xie zhuangyuan* kaoshu" 《永樂大典》 本 《張協狀元》 考述, *Journal of the National Academy of Chinese Theater Arts* 31, no. 1 (2010): 9.

31. For an extended explanation of the early southern formularies see the section on "Music." See Jiang Xiao's preface to *Jiugong shisan diao* 九宮十三調, in *Zhongguo gudian xiqu xuba huibian* 中國古典戲曲序跋彙編 (Shandong: Qilu shushe, 1989), 1:28–29.

32. Rulan Chao Pian defines mode as follows: "A mode is defined by the pitch on which the basic scale is constructed and by the choice of the candencing note." A mode is a musical term that indicates the pitch on which a basic scale is constructed. Modes were formed through a mathematical system, which combined the twelve tones or pitches (*shi'er lü* 十二律) with seven basic notes creating a total of eighty-four *gong* and *diao* modes. The combination of the twelve pitches (*lülü*) and the first note or *gong* are all called *gong* modes, and the combination of the twelve pitches and any of the other six notes are called *diao* modes, thus the term *gongdiao* for *keys or modes*. Pian, however calls the All Keys and Modes, just the "All Keys." I will use the term key/modes or simply All Keys for the sake of simplification. See Rulan Chao Pian, *Sonq Dynasty Musical Sources and Their Interpretation* (Hong Kong: Chinese University Press, 2003), 43–58, esp. 43–50; Yu Weimin, *Zhongguo gudai quti wenxue gelü yanjiu* 中國古代曲體文學格律研究 (Beijing: Zhonghua shuju, 2012), 35; and Yang Yinliu 楊蔭瀏, *Zhongguo gudai yinyue shigao* 中國古代音樂史稿 (Taibei: Dahong, 1997), 3:115–128.

33. Shen Jing's is the *Zengding chabu nan jiugong shisandiao qupu* 增定查補 《南九宮十三調曲譜》 abbreviated as *Nan jiugong shisandiao qupu* (Beijing: Beijing daxue chuban pu, 1921?), and Xu and Niu's is the *Huizuan Yuan pu nanqu jiugong zhengshi* 彙纂元譜南曲九宮正始, in *Xuxiu Siku quanshu*, vols. 1748–1749 (Shanghai: Shanghai guji

Chubanshe, 2002). These formularies are large collections of songs intended as models for song composition and, sometimes, pronunciation and singing. Their degree of detail is uneven, with some including only the title of the song, the key, and the song proper, whereas others included, in addition to the keys, songs, and song structure (lines to a song and words to a line as well as some variants of the song), the tones of each word, the rhyme, the beat, and, at times, glossaries of the words.

34. In fact, forty years later, Shen Jing's formulary was, on the request of Feng Menglong (1574–1645) and Niu Shaoya, corrected and expanded by Shen's nephew, Shen Zijin 沈自晉 (1583–1665). Zijin edited and increased his uncle's formulary, addressing new arising problems of composition and adding a detailed set of criteria, in which he discussed the selection of songs. But he did not merge both texts and did not change the names or structure of his uncle's text. Shen Zijin's text, unlike the other two enormously influential texts by Feng and Niu, included many new songs and song forms. For Shen Zijing's work see *Guangji Ciyin xiansheng zengding nanjiugong cipu* 廣輯詞隱先生增定 《南九宮詞譜》, in *Xuxiu Siku quanshu*, vols. 1747–1748 (Shanghai: Shanghai guji chubanshe, 1995–2002); and Shen Zijin, *Chongding nanci quanpu fanli* 重定南詞全譜凡例, in *Zhongguo gudian xiqu xuba huibian* 中國古典戲曲序跋彙編, ed. Cai Yi 蔡毅 (Jinan: Qilu shushe, 1989), 1:37–42. See also Yu, *Zhongguo gudai quti wenxue gelü yanjiu*, 447–448.

35. *Zhang Xie* is alternatively written 張叶, pronounced the same (*xie*), which is a variant character of 協. Xu and Niu's collections use the name Zhang Xie 張協, as opposed to the often written alternative *Zhang Xie* 張叶. Yu Weimin notes that wherever *Zhang Xie* is cited, in other songs, or as above, as part of a repertoire, the character used is 協. See Yu, "*Yongle dadian* ben *Zhang Xie zhuangyuan* kaoshu," 8–12.

36. See Yu, *Song Yuan nanxi kaolun xubian*, 119–156, esp. 120, where he places the song "Hongshan'er huantou" from *Zhang Xie* side by side with the song included in Xu and Niu's anthology. The variations are editorial (stylistic and prosodic) but do not change the basic meaning of the song.

37. Wang Guowei noted that *nanxi* and Yuan northern drama (*zaju*) share thirteen songs, but after *Zhang Xie* was found, the number increased. Aoki Masaru found thirty-seven. In a recent study of northern and southern plays with the same name, Du Liuping found 124 shared titles,

of which 54 were adaptations of northern songs. See Du Liuping 都劉平, *Song Yuan nanxi yu beizaju tongming jumu guanxi yanjiu* 宋元南戲與北雜劇同名劇目關係研究 (Hebei: Hebei Shifan University, 2014). See Wang, SYXQK, 137–142.

38. Yang Hoi-seok, "*Zhang Xie zhuangyuan* xieding yu Yuan," 51. In addition to the shared songs in northern and southern theater, Yang notes that there are eighteen songs with no entering tone ending in stop consonants p-t-k-, reflecting a northern origin. He also argues that the play includes many popular sayings, but this is not evidence of an earlier origin.

39. Yang traces the song title *Yingxian ke* back to the Jin 金 (1115–1234) dynasty, but in fact, it also appears in the Tang Extended Melodies (*daqu*). See most notably Hu Xuegang, "Dui '*Zhang Xie zhuangyuan* xieding yu Yuandai zhongqi yihou' yiwen de shangque" 對「《張協狀元》寫定於元代中期以後」一文的商榷, *Yishu baijia* 2 (2003): 36–45; and ten years later: "Nanxi *Zhang Xie zhuangyuan* de bianju shidai: Dui '*Zhang Xie zhuangyuan* xieding yu Yuan dai zhongqi yihou' yiwen de shangque" 南戲《張協狀元》的編劇時代：對「《張協狀元》寫定於元代中期以後」一文的商榷, in *Wenzhou daxue xuebao*, 26 (2013), 35–44; Xu Hongtu 徐宏圖, "Zhongguo xiqu de chengshou biaozhi shi nanxi er bu shi Yuan zaju: Dui *Zhang Xie zhuangyuan* bianju shidai xinzheng yiwen de shangque" 中國戲曲的成熟標誌是南戲而不是元雜劇:對（《張協狀元》編劇時代新証）一文的商榷, *Zhongguo xiqu xueyuan xuebao* 33, no. 1 (2012): 53–58.

40. In a more exhaustive manner, Yang Dong has researched the tune "Hillside Sheep" (Shanbo yang 山坡羊), used both in northern and southern theater (but more popular in the south), to show that the origin of this tune is northern. Yang Dong, "*Shanpo yang* qudiao yualiu shukao" "山坡羊" 曲調源流述考, *Wenxue yichang* 2 (2010): 93–101. The first southern instance of this song appears in *Zhang Xie*, acts 35 and 50.

41. Yang Dong 楊棟, "*Zhang Xie zhuangyuan* bianju shidai xinzheng" 《張協狀元》編劇時代新証, *Wenyi yanjiu* 8 (2010), 90–97. Against this methodology Yang Dong also wrote: "Xueli fangfa yu shishi zhenxiang: Dui '*Zhang Xie zhuangyuan* bianju shidai xinzheng zhiyizhe dabian" 學理, 方法與事實真相：對《張協狀元》編劇時代新証 質疑者答辯, *Zhongguo xiqu xueyuan xuebao* 34 (2013): 40–57, and "Fansi: Nanxi xianshu lun de luoji siwei fangshi: Da Hu Xuegang

jiaoshou" 反思：南戲先熟論的邏輯思維方式–答胡雪岡教授, *Hebei shifan daxue xuebao* 35 (2015): 85–94.

Yet another theory proposes an early Yuan date given the play's inclusion of the taboo words for names of emperors. Thus, for example, the "*lang*" in *fulang* 浮浪 (literally, "to loaf about," here is translated as "wanton bouts") in act 2 in the tune "The Red Sway of the Candle's Shadow" is homophonous with the courtesy name of the first emperor *lang* 朗, and could not have been used. See Liu Huaitang 劉懷堂, "*Yongle dadian zhi Zhang Xie zhuangyuan yingshi yuanchu zuopin*" 《永樂大典》之《張協狀元》應是元初作品, *Xiju* 4 (2008): 101–109.

42. The two imperial entertainment offices were the Court Entertainment Bureau (*Jiaofang si* 教坊司), and the Office of the Bell and Drum (*Zhonggu si* 鐘鼓司). See Wilt Idema, "From Stage Scripts to Closet Drama: Editions of Early Chinese Drama and the Translations of Yuan Zaju," *Journal of Chinese Literature and Culture* 3, no. 1 (2016): 175–202.

43. Idema, "From Stage Scripts to Closet Drama," 183–184. Idema suggests this may have been an attempt to downplay the central male and female roles, and enliven the stage business. See also Stephen H. West, "Text and Ideology," in *Ming Qing xiqu guoji yantaohui lunwenji* 明清戲曲國際研討會論文集, ed. Hua Wei and Wang Ayling (Taipei: Zhongguo wenzhe yanjiusuo, 1998), 251. Idema and West both follow Sun Kaidi who notes that virtually all of the later commercial editions (with the two exceptions of the *Thirty Yuan Plays* and the work of the Ming prince Zhu Youdun) stem from palace editions. West argues that one reason for the changes in textual formats, from the long arias to shorter arias and more dialogue, was a democratization of acting, in which all actors would share equally in performance time. But there can be a number of reasons for this change in textual formats, including their reading value. See also Dale Johnson, "Yuan Dramas: New Notes to Old Texts," *Monument Serica* 30 (1972–1973): 426–438.

44. West argues that this was not just a process of textual configuration, but also a means to "domesticate the content, to rein in any dangerous social or cultural energies that were destabilizing to the Ming court or to the ideological world of the literati" (237). See West, "Text and Ideology," 237–283.

45. Our closest early southern play is a manuscript version of *The Golden Hairpin* (1431–32), which scholars believe is representative of the

dramatic templates that circulated at the time. Of this play, we have twenty-one arias included in later anthologies. It relates the story of Liu Wenlong who leaves his wife and aging parents to go to the capital to take the exams. As he leaves, his wife of three days gives him three objects: half a golden hairpin, one slipper of a pair, and half a flower mirror. Once he passes the exams, the prime minister tries to betroth his daughter to Liu, but he refuses. In retaliation for his refusal, Liu is posted far away in the western regions, where he remains for eighteen years, and is forced to marry the daughter of the local khan.

46. The earliest specimens in this tradition included in the *Thirty Yuan Plays* (*Yuankan sanshi zhong* 元刊雜劇三十種) consist mostly of long song suites, with some stage directions and a bare dialogical framework. These texts, which were printed in Dadu (modern-day Beijing) and Hangzhou, are believed to be mostly very early Ming prints and perhaps some very late-Yuan editions—that is, from the late fourteenth century and early fifteenth century. This was roughly the same time frame in which *Zhang Xie* was selected to be included in the *Yongle* collectanea. See Komatsu Ken and Bunkio Kin, "Shilun *Yuankan zaju sanshizhong* de banben xingzhi" 試論 《元刊雜劇三十種》 的版本性質, trans. Huang Shizhong 黃仕忠, *Wenhua yichan* 2 (2008): 1–10, who argues that among the *Thirty*, there are four (of seven) northern printed texts that may be genuinely Yuan and the rest, including all southern printed ones, are Ming. See also Zhang Jingjing 張倩倩, *Yuankan zaju sanshizhong bingfei kanyu yuandai shuo* 《元刊雜劇三十種》 并非刻於元代說, *Weiyi pinlun* 12 (2015): 122–126, who disagrees, noting that these texts are all early Ming. See also, more recently, Zheng Weini 煒旎, *Yuan kan zaju sanshizhong* yanjiu 《元刊雜劇三十種》 研究 (Shanghai: Shanghai guji chubanshe, 2016), 16–21. West notes that of the thirty extant texts, seven were printed in the northern city of Beijing (Dadu 大都). Four we know from the title and three more are conjectural, whereas the remaining twenty-three probably all were printed in Hangzhou (242–243). See West, "Text and Ideology," 237–283. None of these plays listed authors, showing perhaps a continual process of composition and recomposition in performance.

47. The term *shuhui* 書會 is first used in Guanpu Naideweng 灌圃耐得翁, pseud., *Ducheng jisheng* 都城紀勝 (Preface 1235), "Sanjiao waidi" 三教外地, in *Dongjing menghua lu wai si zhong* 東京夢華錄: 外四種

(Beijing, Wenhua yishu chubanshe, 1998), 101; and Zhou Mi 周密 (1232–1298), *Wulin jiushi* 武林舊事, "Zhuse jiyi ren" 諸色伎藝人, 454, a city memoir of Southern Song Hangzhou. But in the early Ming, the term was still in use. See Xu Shuofang 徐朔方 (1923–2007), *Shuo xiqu* 說戲曲 (Shanghai: Shanghai guji cubanshe, 2000), 43–51, and Xu Shunping 徐順平, "Shuhui de xingzhi jiqi yanbian" 書會的性質 及其演變, *Wenzhou shiyuan xuebao* (*Zhexue shehui kexue ban*), 1 (1993), 16–21. For the *shuhui* as associations of writers and men of education see Liu Nianci 劉念茲, *Nanxi xinzheng* (南戲新證) (Beijing: Zhonghua shuju, 1986), 22 and 36.

48. See Wang Jise 王季思 (1906–1996), ed., *Quan Yuan xiqu* 全元戲曲 (Beijing: Renmin wenxue chubanshe, 1990), 116–129. For the dating, see Stephen H. West and Wilt Idema, *Chinese Theater*, 299–343. West and Idema note that Yan Dunyi dates the play to the first half of the fifteenth century, although they believe it could be the end of the fourteenth century (308). See Yan Dunyi 顏敦易, *Yuanqu zhenyi* 元曲斠疑 (Beijing: Zhonghua shuju, 1960), 439–456. See also Stephen H. West and Wilt L. Idema, *Monks, Bandits, Lovers and Immortals:* ix–xxxvi, 283–314.

49. See Liao Ben 廖奔, *Zhang Xie zhuangyuan de zuozhe, Shuang cairen* 《張協狀元》的作者是雙才人, *Shupin*, 4 (2001), 62.

50. See, for example, Sun Chongtao's explanation of the association of Nine Mountain (*Jiushan*) with Wenzhou. Sun believes Zhang Xie to be a southern Song play. He argues that in addition to the introduction to the troupe provided in the prologue, Nine Mountain is a term that was used for nine hillocks in the Lucheng 鹿城 area of Wenzhou. Most of his evidence, however, comes from Qing gazetteers. See Sun Chongtao, "*Zhang Xie Zhuangyuan* yu Yongjia zaju," 106.

51. This other Nine Mountain Association was first noted by Zhou Yibai, *Zhongguo xiju shi changbian*, 138–139. The table of contents of the Qing formulary by the scholar Zhang Dafu 張大復 (1554–1360) *Hanshantang qupu* 寒山堂曲譜 includes a Yuan play called "Dong Xiuying huayue dongqiang ji" 董秀英花月東牆記 attributed to *jiushan shuhui shijiu jingxian* 九山書會捷機史九敬先. Because Dong Xiuying is a Yuan play, this Nine Mountain Association has to be from the Yuan. Some scholars believe this may be the case, but the logic is not clear. Could

the play not have been composed earlier? Or could Dong Xiuying be a rewriting of an earlier play? See Yang, "*Zhang Xie zhuangyuan* xieding yu Yuandai zhongqi yihou," 46–47. See also Ye Changhai 葉長海, "Yongjia kunqu yu haiyan qiang" 永嘉崑劇與海鹽腔, in 2002 *Liang'an xiqu dazhan xueshu yantaohui lunwenji* 兩岸戲曲大展學術研討會論文集, ed. Zeng Yongyi (Taipei: Chuanyi zhongxin, 2003), 537–547. Also see Hu Xuegang, "Shijiu jingxian he 'Dong Xiuying huayue dongqiang ji'xiaokao" 史九敬先和《董秀英花月東牆記》小考, *Zhejiang Journal* 3 (1987): 51–54. A play by this title also has been attributed to Bai Pu (1226–after 1307). There are various opinions on the meaning of *jieji* 捷機, the most probable of which is that it means comic. But other interpretations argue that it could be a homophone for *jieji* (節級), a term used in the early Song for those playing military officials; or a role in a *yuanben* comedy; or members of the association. Also see Yang Hoi-seok, "Lun zaju zuojia Shijiu jingxian yu nanxi zuojia Shijiu jingxian" 論雜劇作家史九敬先與南戲作家史九敬先," in *Nanxi Guoji xueshu yantaohui lunwenji* (Beijing: Zhonghua shuju, 2001), 258–267.

52. Southern drama normally features two or three songs but at times just one. In many instances, the first song encourages the audience to remember the transience of life and enjoy the moment; in others, this first song is simply a summary of the story.

53. See Qian, *Yongle dadian xiwen sanzhong*, 4; and Qian, *Xiwen gailun*, 164

54. Later, it is also called the introduction to the play or *jiamen* 家門 (literally, "the main door").

55. For a definition of mode see note 32. See also John H. Levis, *Foundations of Chinese Musical Art* (New York: Paragon, 1963), 63–85, esp. 72–73.

56. See Wang Zhuo, *Biji manzhi* 碧雞漫志 (ca. 1149), LZJC, 1:115. Ch'en Li-li argues that the All Keys was an oral form intended for a broader audience (rather than a highly educated public) and possibly for a reading public. See Ch'en Li-li, "Outer and Inner forms of Chukung-tiao with Reference to Pian-Wen, Tz'u and Vernacular Fiction," *Harvard Journal of Asiatic Studies* 32 (1972): 124–149, esp. 137–138; and *Master Tung's Western Chamber Romance* (New York: Columbia University Press, 1994), xi–xxix, esp. xxii. Wilt Idema, in contrast, believes that these All Keys were satires intended for young educated scholars and literate upper-class audiences. He argues that the influence of earlier

Song lyricists in the composition of the *Western Wing* All Keys strongly suggests an urban literate class; the nature of the language (written in a mixture of classical and colloquial language) and the complexity of song composition also point to a literati hand. See Wilt L. Idema, "Performance and Construction of the Chu-kung-tiao," *Journal of Oriental Studies* 16 (1978): 1–2, 63–78; and also Wilt L. Idema, "Data on the Chu-Kung-Tiao: A Reassessment of Conflicting Opinions," *T'oung Pao* 79 (1993): 69–112, esp. 69 and 103.

57. For example, in the first section of the complete All Keys, we have the extant text *Master Dong's Western Wing* (*Dong Jieyuan Xixiang ji* 董解元西廂記), and the modes change a total of thirty-four times. The total All Keys is divided into eight parts, makes use of all seventeen modes, and changes modes 199 times. See Ling Jingyan 凌景埏, ed., *Guben Dong Jieyuan Xixiang ji* 古本董解元西廂記 (Shanghai: Guwen wenxue chubanshe, 1957); and Li-li Chen, *Master Tung's Western Chamber Romance* (New York: Columbia University Press, 1994). The most often used mode is the *xianlü diao* (fifty-two times), followed by the *dashi diao* (twenty-nine times), and the *zhonglü diao* (twenty-five times).

58. A *zaju* (see also note 1) is divided into four acts. Each act makes use of only one suite of songs—an average of eighteen songs—one rhyme and *one mode*. If, however, one suite can use only one rhyme and one mode within each act, this would suggest that contrary to the musical intent of the All Keys, which aspired for change of pitch (or even keys), northern drama's musical and aesthetic intent would be consonance within one act. Conversely, if keys were used, southern theater would provide a more harmonious arrangement of tunes. Arguably, the musical structure of the All Keys is closer in form to southern drama than to the more restrictive northern form in which all songs in one act have to be subsumed under one key. Structurally too, southern drama employs as its basic building block one or two songs and a coda, which also would place it closer to the All Keys than the average eighteen tunes to a suite of northern drama. For the suite structures that are similar in both the All Keys and southern drama, see Hu Xuegang 胡雪岡, "Zaoqi nanxi Wenzhou qiang jiqi yu sida shengqiang de guanxi" 早期南戲溫州腔及其與四大聲腔的關係, originally published in 1982, rept. in *Wenzhou nanxi lungao* 溫州南戲論高 (Taiwan: Guojia chubanshe, 2006), 221–254.

59. See Luo Di 洛地, "Zhugongdiao, Yuanqu zhi suowei 'gongdiao' yiyi" 諸宮調, 元曲之所謂「宮調」疑議, *Journal of Jiangsu Normal University* 39, no. 5 (2013): 31.

60. I am grateful to *Asia Major* for allowing me to use portions of an earlier paper on this subject entitled "Retribution, Revenge and the Ungrateful Scholar in Early Chinese Southern Drama," *Asia Major* 20, no. 2 (2007): 75–101.

61. See Qian, *Xiwen gailun*, 121–125, and Yu Weimin 俞為民, *Song Yuan nanxi kaolun* 宋元南戲考論 (Taipei: Taiwan shangwu yinshuguan, 1994), 39–41. One of the reasons for the popularity of this theme in southern plays may be that the ratio of scholars from the south taking the exams was quite large. See Benjamin A. Elman, *A Cultural History of Civil Examinations in Late Imperial China* (Taipei: SMC, 2000), 88–97. Elman also notes that the examination system during the late Yuan and early Ming was not the chief means of official recruitment.

62. Shen Jing 沈璟 (1553–1610), *Shuazi xu* 刷子序, *Nan jiugong shisan diao* 南九宮十三調, *Shanben xiqu congkan* 善本戲曲叢刊, series 3 (Taipei: Taiwan xuesheng shuju, 1984), 27:191–192. See also Yu, *Song Yuan nanxi kaolun*, 41–42.

    The last sentence refers to the titles of two plays, *Huanxi yuanjia* and *Zha nizi* (also known by the title *Ying yan zhengchun* 鶯燕爭春), which is the last phrase of the quoted poem. *Huanxi yuanjia* is also the name of a Ming collection of love stories, but it more generally refers to the pattern of male–female relationships, which follow the seasonal order. They begin with the warm and tender sentiments of spring love, which proceed unsteadily through separation and betrayal in the cool days of autumn, to resentment followed by death and revenge. In other words, young amorous girls fight over men and never consider that they will be abandoned, thus ignoring the countless accounts of similar past experiences.

63. This is *Zha nizi* 詐妮子.

64. Although Chen Shuwen is still an ungrateful scholar, the story is a little different. The scholar is already married and has passed the exams. On his way to take up his post, he meets a courtesan whom he likes and marries. When faced with his wife's return, he decides to kill the courtesan by drowning her in the river. See Regina Llamas, "Retribution, Revenge and the Ungrateful Scholar in Early Chinese Southern Drama," *Asia Major* 20, no. 2 (2007): 88.

65. Qian, *Yongle dadian xiwen sanzhong*, 2.

66. That is, a moral nature that was common to all. See Peter Bol, "Neo-Confucianism and Local Society, Twelfth to Sixteenth Century: A Case Study," in *The Song-Yuan-Ming Transition in Chinese History*, ed. Paul Jakov Smith and Richard von Glahn (Cambridge, MA: Harvard University Asia Center, 2003), 249. The difficulty of enlisting ethical young men, however, seems to have been a problem throughout the dynasty.

67. Liu, *Xuande xieben Jinchai ji*, 14. Or in an early scene in *Wang Kui*: (Same tune [*Shuang Xichi*] Second opening): "I am wholeheartedly intent on acquiring prestige and profit, / so we will part for a while, but in no time we shall be reunited. / Alas, with all this love and affection / how can I not complain? / I shall become the top graduate, don the green robe and then return; / so what need is there to bitterly long with nostalgia?" [前腔 [雙鸂鶒] 第二換頭] / 一心為利名牽, / 暫別間不久團圓. / 嘆許多恩愛, / 怎不教我埋怨? / 做狀元, 掛綠袍, 那時回轉, / 何須苦苦長憶念? See Qian Nanyang, ed., *Song Yuan xiwen jiyi* 宋元戲文輯佚 (Shanghai: Shanghai gudian wenxue chubanshe, 1956), 38.

68. Liu, *Xuande xieben Jinchai ji*, 15–16. Here it breaks off; characters are missing.

69. See *Zhang Xie, Liu Wenlong, Chen Shuwen*, and *Jinchai ji*. In the case of *Liu Zhiyuan*, he is not a scholar, but the desire for fame is the same.

70. These cautionaries sentences were popular idiomatic expressions. See act 22, the song-lyric *shuidiao getou*: "I remember wearing the brightly colored dress to enter the hall, and at the time of parting, the words of caution my parents gave me; when I think about it, it was all good advice." This shows the connection between the All Keys and the play proper, because these words of caution are not found elsewhere in the play.

71. This characteristic of the female role has prevailed through the ages in two favorite scenes: *The White Rabbit* and act 20 of *The Lute*. In *The White Rabbit*, Li Sanniang 李三娘, although three months pregnant, has been forced to divorce Liu Zhiyuan, who has now gone to a nearby military camp. Brutally treated by her sister-in-law, she is forced to deliver her baby over a pile of grass, severing the umbilical cord with her teeth. Similarly, in *The Lute*, a great famine is devastating the land. Miss Zhao, in order to feed her elderly parents-in-law, threshes the grain to

give to her in-laws while she eats the husks. See *Xinbian Liu Zhiyuan huanxiang baitu ji* 新編劉知遠還鄉白兔記 reprint of the Nuanhong-shi edition (Jiangsu: Jiangsu guling keyinshe, 1997), 56a-b, 57a-b. Also see Gao Ming, *Yuan ben Pipa ji jiaozhu*, ed. Qian Nanyang (Shanghai: Shanghai guji chubanshe, 1980), 112–116.

72. See Lien-sheng Yang, "The Concept of *Pao* as a Basis for Social Relations in China," in *Chinese Thought and Institutions*, ed. John King Fairbank (Chicago: University of Chicago Press, 1957), 291–309; Karl S. Y. Yao, "*Bao* and *Baoying*: Narrative Causality and External Motivations in Chinese Fiction," *Chinese Literature: Essays, Articles and Reviews* 11 (December 1989), 115–137.

73. It can also be read as follows: "I want that guilty conscience of yours to last as long as your honor and glory." But we would have to assume he has a conscience.

74. The earliest specimens believed to be the earliest northern dramatic plays, *The Thirty Miscellaneous Comedies Printed in the Yuan* (*Yuan kan zaju sanshi zhong*) 元刊雜劇三十種, also are not divided into acts. *The Story of the Golden Hairpin*, dated to about thirty years later (1432) is divided into sixty-seven acts. Liu, *Xuande xieben Jinchai ji*, 133. Most of the acts are quite short: two or three songs and some dialogue; see also Qian, *Xiwen gailun*, 170.

75. The first term for act division in theater is probably based on entering (*chu*, literally, "come out into") the stage. This is also common in stage instructions, in which the usual term used when roles enter the stage is also *chu*, as in act 5: "*The chou (acting as Zhang Xie's sister) runs out and sings*" (*chou zouchu chang* 丑走出唱); see Qian, *Xiwen gailun*, 167–169. After the mid-Ming dynasty, the terms used for act division in addition to *chu*, were *zhe* 折, *chu* 齣, and *zhe* 摺.

76. Popular sayings are used throughout, sometimes just as introduction to a short speech, and although they make for a lively reading (especially in act 17), they break the flow of the dialogue.

77. Yu, "*Song Yuan nanxi kaolun xubian*," 140.

78. Out of fifty-three acts, thirty are played by the three comics, a variation of the *mo* and a comic, and the two comics. In almost all early southern *nanxi*, the role with the most number of scenes is the *mo*, possibly because of his "intermediary" nature. Because these are adaptations of

northern plays, a comparison with the other two plays is not useful. If compared with *The Lute*, however, out of the forty-two acts in this play, twenty are performed by some variation of the comic roles (see appendix III). See Yu, "*Song Yuan nanxi kaolun xubian*," 138–144.

79. Sometimes reduced to three: the main male role (*sheng*), the main female role (*dan*), and the comic (*jing*).

80. The story of the *Adjutant Zhou Yan* also appears in the Tang dynasty text by Duan Anjie, *Yuefu zalu* 樂府雜錄, LZJC, 1: 49–50.

81. Duan Anjie, *Yuefu zalu*, 49. In fact, it is unclear what is incorrect: whether he later became an adjutant or that the emperor pardoned him and invested him with the rank of adjutant.

82. See Wang, SYXQK, 18–19. See also Ren Bantang, "Xiqu, xi nong yu xixiang" 戲曲, 戲弄與戲象, *Xiju luncong* 1 (1957): 25–41.

83. Guanpu Nai Deweng 耐得翁, *Ducheng jisheng* 都城紀勝, in *Dongjing menhualu* 東京夢華錄外四種 (Beijing: Zhongghua shuju, 1962), 96.

84. Guanpu Nai Deweng, *Ducheng jisheng*, 96; see also Wu Zimu 吳自牧 and Mengliang Lu 夢梁錄 (ca. 1275), in *Dongjing menhualu* 東京夢華錄外四種 (Beijing: Zhongghua shuju, 1962), 309.

85. Hu Zhiyu, "Preface to the Poem: Presented to Miss Song" 贈宋氏序, in *Zishan daquanji* 紫山大全集, *juan* 8, in *Yingyin Wenyuange siku quanshu*, 1196:171.

86. In one of the introductions to an important text for this period, the *Green Bower Collection* (*Qinglou ji* 青樓集; ca. 1320s), a collection of short biographies on female performers, the author notes that *zaju* discussed stories of human interest that could "enrich people's morals and improve the customs" (皆可以厚人論, 美風化). Xia Tingzhi 夏庭芝 (ca. 1316–1370), *Green Bower Collection, Qinglou ji* 青樓集, LZJC, 2: pp. 7–8.

87. But generally without the word *fu*. What this *fu* as assistant or secondary refers to is no longer clear. We do not know of any main *jing* or *mo* terms at the time. It is possible that the term *fu* here does not refer to the general idea of subsidiary, but rather is being used as a verb, to "fit" into a *jing* or a *mo*.

88. These two comics resonate, especially in later comedy with the White clown and the August clown, or Arlecchino and Pierrot in other traditions.

89. *Top Graduate Zhang Xie* also engages in this critical pursuit with its scathing commentary on the figure of the scholar and the education process, but this is expressed mainly through the song of the main

female role, Poorlass, and Zhang Xie's actions. Yet, if we single out the comic parts and roles, we find that these often are tangentially related to the main story line—they thrive on slapstick, the absurd, and at times crude remarks. The same passage appears in one of the prefaces of the *Green Bower Collection* (*Qinglou ji* 青樓集) and Sun Chongtao suggests that this preface may have preceded Tao Zongyi's. See Sun Chongtao 孫崇濤 and Xu Hongtu 徐宏圖, *Qinglou ji jianzhu* 青樓集箋註 (Beijing: Zhongguo xiqu chubanshe, 1990), 45; see also Tao, *Nancun Chuogenglu*, 306. There are some slight variations in the terms used for the performers. The play leader is called the *yinxi*. The *moni* has no particular function. For a detailed overview of the types, see Ren Bantang 任半塘, *Tang xinong* 唐戲弄 (Shanghai: Shanghai guji chubanshe, 1984), 820–849.

90. Tao, *Nancun Chuogenglu*, 306.

91. Xia Tingzhi, *Qinglou ji*, LZJC, 2:29–30. The complete section is as follows: "Song dynasty southern drama included song, recitation and badinage. In the Jin dynasty, the farce (*yuanben*) and the comedy (*zaju*) were combined into one. It is only in the present dynasty that they split into two. The farce originally had five people: one is called the *fujing*: in ancient times it was called the adjutant. One is called the *fumo*: in ancient times it was called the grey hawk. The *mo* can strike the *jing*, just like the hawk can strike birds. One is called the *yinxi* (troupe leader); one is called the *moni* and one is called *gu* (official)." 宋之戲文, 乃有 唱, 念, 有諢. 金則院本, 雜劇合而為一. 至我朝乃分院本, 雜劇為二. 院本始作凡五人: 一曰副淨, 古謂參軍; 一曰副末, 古謂蒼鶻, 以末 可以撲淨, 如鶻能擊禽鳥也; 一曰引戲; 一曰末泥; 一曰孤. This is copied almost verbatim in Tao, *Nancun Chuogenglu*, 306.

92. In the Song dynasty, scholar Zhou Mi's catalog of official variety plays held in the southern capital city of Hangzhou, as well as in Tao's *Chuogenglu*, includes listings of performances such as the name *cuan* at the end. The titles for these *cuan* performances are, for example, "A *Cuan* on Discussing the Hundred Fruits" 講百果爨, "A *Cuan* on Discussing the Hundred Flowers" 講百花爨, "A *Cuan* on Jumping Out of the Bag" 跳布袋爨, and "A *Cuan* on the Four Treasures of the Scholar's Studio" 文房四寶爨. Many modern scholars, following Tao and beginning with Wang Guowei, believe the *cuan* to be another term for a *yuanben* comedy performance—a sung and danced piece

that may have included some magic. See Wang, SYXQK, 72. Huang Tianji 黃天驥, "*Cuannong* bianxi" 爨弄辨析, in *Zhongguo gudai xiqu yu gudai wenxue lunwenji*, ed. Huang Tianji (Beijing: Zhonghua shuju, 2001), 45–61. For an explanation of "*Wuhua* Cuan nong," see Zeng Yongyi, "Lunshuo '*wuhua cuan nong*'" 論說 五花爨弄,in *Lunshuo xiqu* 論說戲曲 (Taibei: Liangjing chubanshe, 1997), 199–238; Tao, *Chuogenglu*, 306.

93. The foreword to the *Green Bower Collection* includes the following information: "There are female and male *zaju* comedies. The *dan* texts are played by women, this is called dissemble in the female type, while the *mo* texts are played by men and designated as *moni*." 「雜劇」則 有旦，末. 旦本女人為之，名妝旦色；末本男子為之，名末泥. Xia, *Qinglou ji*, LZJC, 2:7.

94. But not all scholars are of the same opinion. Ren Bantang believes there were real roles; see Bantang, *Tang xinong*, 777–778. Yu Weimin believes these early five types became the roles of later drama—for example, the *wai* or extra evolves from the one who gives orders (*yinxi*); see Yu, "Nanxi *Zhang Xie zhuangyuan* kaolun," 136.

95. The Ming prince Zhu Quan 朱權 (1378–1448), in his *Formulary of Correct Sounds of the Era of Great Peace* (*Taihe zhengyin pu* 太和正音譜), has a catalog of types that appear in the farce (*yuanben*) and the *zaju*. Zhu mentions a main male (*zhengmo* 正末); second male (*fumo* 付末); a main female (*dan* 狚); a comic (*jing* 靚); and other named types, including the official (*gu* 孤), the madam (*bao* 鴇), the prostitute (*nao* 猱), and the jester (*jieji* 捷譏). He also notes that the *yinxi* (引戲) was the main female of the farce. See Zhu Quan, *Taihe zhengyin pu*, LZJC, 3:53–54. In the late-fourteenth-century novel attributed to Shi Nai'an, *The Water Margin* (also translated as *Outlaws of the Marsh* and *All Men Are Brothers*), the term *se* 色 for type (or the title of a troupe leader), believed to be the precursor of "role," is appended to the five types mentioned in the description of a palace performance. We do not know, however, at what moment in its complicated textual history this section was included. See *Shuihu zhuan, Zhonzguo zudian xiaoshuo xinkan* 9 (Taipei: Lianjing chubanshe. 1987), chap. 82, 2:1078–1079.

96. See Hu Yingling 胡應麟, "Zhuangyue weitan" 莊嶽委談, *Shaoshi shanfang bicong* 少室山房筆叢 (Taipei: Shijie shuju, 1963), 2:554–573.

97. Zhou Qi 周祈, *Mingyi Kao* 名義考 (Taipei: Xuesheng shuju, 1971), 170. It is possible that the association of strange mythical animals may have come from an already established nature of the role and the costuming of roles on stage. From the Han dynasty onward, textual sources mention the use of animal masks for certain dances and Nuo New Year exorcisms played by the Imperial Music Bureau. This may have led to the use of painted masks in the theater. But painted faces in theater also may have come simply from the necessity to show facial expression to large audiences. There is really no way to know. See Zheng Daiqiong 鄭黛瓊, *Zhongguo xiqu de jiangjiao yanjiu* 中國戲曲的淨腳研究 (Taipei: Xuehai chubanshe, 1996), 208–209.

98. Zhu Yunming, "Tuyu" 土語, *Wei Tan*, 1354–1355.

99. These roles appear also in *The Lute*, and, with the exception of the *chou* clown and the *tie* second female role, in the other two *Yongle* texts.

100. See Xu Wei, *Nanci xulu*, LZJC, 3:245. Xu notes the term *sheng* may have been used historically as master. Zeng Yongyi argues that the use of the terms *sheng* and *dan* as costumed characters existed as early as the Five Dynasties. He also notes that this term appears in some *zaju*, but this is probably under the influence of southern drama. See Zeng Yongyi, "Xiqu yanjiu de yixie xinde" 戲曲研究的一些心得, in *2002 Liang'an xiqu dazhan xueshu yantao hui lunwenji*, ed. Zeng Yongyi (Taipei: National Center for Traditional Arts, 2003), 18–20.

101. See Zeng Yongyi, *Zhongguo gudian xiju de renshe yu xinshang* 中國古典戲劇的認識與欣賞 (Taiwan: Zhengzhong shuju, 1991), 223–224.

102. See Xu Wei, *Nanci xulu*, LZJC, 3:245

103. See Xu Wei, *Nanci xulu*, LZJC, 3:245.

104. See Xu Wei, *Nanci xulu*, LZJC, 3:245–246.

105. See Xu Wei, *Nanci xulu*, LZJC, 3:246.

106. Possibly because of the association of this role with the *canjun* play. During the Kaiyuan period (713–741), Huang Fanchuo 黃旛綽 played this comedy for Emperor Xuanzong of the Tang. This is mentioned in Duan Anjie (fl. ca. 894), *Yuefu zalu*, LZJC, 1:49. The Tang emperor was fond of him. For the many anecdotes around this famous performer, see Ren, *Tang xinong*, 971–977.

107. See Xu Wei, *Nanci xulu*, LZJC, 3:245. One other theory is that this term is a contraction of the term *niuyuanzi* 紐元子. The *niuyuanzi*

was the dispersal section of a *zaju* performance in the Song dynasty. The text notes that this was an imitation of country rustics who did not often come to the city: "Actors costume themselves as old village hicks from Shandong and Hebei to provide a pretext for laughing" 多是借裝為山東河北村人以資笑. See *Ducheng jisheng*, in *Dongjing Menghualu*, 97.

108. See Zeng Yongyi, *Shuo su wenxue* 說俗文學 (Taipei: Lianjing chubanshe, 1980), 291. See also Shi Xusheng 施旭升, *Xiqu wenhua xue* 戲曲文化學 (Taipei: Xiuwei zixun chuban gongsi, 2005), 528; and Li Huimian 李惠綿, *Yuan Ming Qing xiqu banyan lun yanjiu* 元明清戲曲扮演論研究 (Taipei: Wenshizhe chubanshe, 1999), 249–292.

109. The term for roles, *juese* 腳色 (or *jiaose* 角色), is first used in this play, *Top Graduate Zhang Xie*. In earlier texts, the term *se* was also used to designate a "group" of performers or the title of a person in a group of performers. For example, *sezhang* 色長 is the leader of this particular *se* group or type. See Guanpu naideweng, *Ducheng jisheng*, in *Dongjing menghualu wai sizhong*: "The *moni se* acts as the leader, and the *yinxi se* gives orders" 末泥色主張, 引戲色分付 (96). In the same text, it is used to designate different categories of musical and performance groups, including the Comedy group (*Zaju se* 雜劇色) and the Adjutant group (*Canjun se* 參軍色) (95–96). The term we now use for role categories is *hangdang* 行當, but this is a later term.

110. And this is the case in almost every *dan* role in the ungrateful scholar play. Whether this is because of the story or the requirements of the role is impossible to know.

111. See Li Huimian, *Yuan Ming Qing xiqu banyan lun yanjiu*, 256.

112. *Guji* has been interpreted variously. See Timoteus Pokora, "The Etymology of ku-chi (or hua-chi)," in *Zeitschrift der Deutschen Morgenländischen Gesellschaft*, vol. 122 (1972), 149–172. Other terms also refer to some aspect of the comic, including ridicule or mockery (*jifeng* 譏諷), playfulness (*tiaoxi* 調戲), or derisory laughter (*chaoxiao* 嘲笑) to name but a few. For a discussion on the dearth of humor in early China, see David R. Knechtges, "Wit, Humour, and Satire in Early Chinese Literature (to A.D. 220)," *Monumenta Serica* 29 (1970–1971): 79–98. For a different point of view, see Christoph Harbsmaier who notes the different intellectual and humorous sensibilities and the subtle and gentle jesting that goes on between

Confucius and his students. Christoph Harbsmeier, "Humor in Ancient Chinese Philosophy," *Philosophy East and West* 39, no. 3 (1989): 289–310. See also Xu Weihe, "The Classical Confucian Concepts of Human Emotion and Proper Humour," in *Humour in Chinese Life and Letters: Classical and Traditional Approaches*, ed. Jocelyn V. Chey and Jessica Milner (Hong Kong: Hong Kong University Press, 2011), 49–71. And Joseph C. Sample, "Contextualizing Lin Yutang's Essay 'On Humour': Introduction and Translation," in *Humour in Chinese Life and Letters*, 169–189. Lin interprets the word *guji* 滑稽 to mean laughable. The term also appears in Sima Qian's *Biographies of Jesters*, but the jesters in this case (also called *guji*) dispense indirect remonstrance to their rulers in the form of witty and ingenious remarks.

113. As men of letters began to pay more attention to these arts, they also began to temper the cruder humor of the earlier plays. For example, in the early seventeenth century, Wang Jide (d. 1623), discussing the comic nature of plays, called for the elevation of the comic discourse of dramatic song, the elimination of doggerel verse, and the need to transform "the rusticity into elegance, so that if from the first uttered sentence people double over [with laughter], that would be excellent." 須以俗為雅, 而一語之出輒令人絕倒, 乃妙. Wang Jide, *Qulun*, LZJC, 4:135.

114. A reference to the seventh-century Tang generals Yuchi Gong 尉遲恭 and Shan Xiongxin 單雄信. Li Shimin 李世民 launched an attack on Wang Shichong 王世充. During the battle, Wang Shichong asked General Shan Xiongxin to kill Li Shimin. Yuchi Gong saw Shan's gesture, and in an attempt to save Li Shimin, kicked his horse to a full gallop toward Shan shouting, "It's my turn now," knocking Shan off the horse and killing him. Shan Xiongxin was also well known popularly as one of the great fighting heroes of the Sui and Tang dynasties.

115. In other words, he informs the audience that the robber has entered the stage; "fifty men" are not hiding in the bush. Thus, the robber, like the *jing* traveler, is boasting, which is the obvious aim.

116. For example, in scene 2 of act 2, Zhang Xie sets up the questions and the *jing* and the *mo* create the jokes around them, but Zhang Xie does not directly participate in the comic banter.

117. For definitions of farce, see Eric Bentley, *The Life of the Drama* (New York: Atheneum, 1964), 298; and Eli Rozik, *Comedy: A Critical Introduction* (Sussex, UK: Sussex Academic Press, 2011), 116–120.

118. The play was adapted and staged in 2000, 2003, and again in 2013 by the Wenzhou Yongjia kunqu troupe. The librettists were Zhang Lie 張烈 and Xie Pingan 謝平安, and the music composers were Lin Tianwen 林天文 and Huang Guangli 黃光利.

119. Yannan Zhi'an 燕南芝庵, *A Discussion on Singing* (*Changlun* 唱論), LZJC, 1:161. The *Discussion* first appears as the first volume of the first anthology we have of the *sanqu* art-songs (or nondramatic sung arias) entitled *White Snow in the Sunny Spring* (*Yuefu xinbian Yangchun Baixue* 樂府新編陽春白雪), which was compiled by the mid-Yuan scholar Yang Chaoying 楊朝英 (fl. 1324–1351) and printed around 1324.

120. Yannan Zhi'an, *Chang Lun*, LZJC, 1:161. See also Wang Xueqi 王學奇, ed., *Yuanquxuan jiaozhu* 元曲選校注 (Hebei: Hebei jiaoyu chubanshe, 1994), 38–77. Stephen H. West, "Literature from the Later Jin to the Early Ming: ca. 1230–ca. 1375," in *The Cambridge History of Chinese Literature*, ed. Kang-I Sun Chang and Stephen Owen (New York: Cambridge University Press, 2010), 621–622. The last sentence is explained generally in terms of the distinguishing characteristic of southern and northern song: thus, northern song was quick paced, with more words per line of song, whereas southern song was more meandering with fewer words per line of song. Northern composition (at least by the end of the Yuan dynasty) made use of stricter prosodic and musical norms, whereas southern tunes were less constricted in terms of tones, rhyme, and modes. This sentence also may be a reference to song phonology, and the problems southerners had enunciating northern dialects and vice versa. But according to the later Wang Jide, to "*qu*" 曲 means it has to be accompanied by string instruments, while to "*ge*" 歌 does not abide by these musical norms 律 because they were sung a cappella. See Wang Jide, *Qulü*, LZJC, 4:104.

121. Zeng Yongyi, "Wenzhou qiang xitan" 溫州腔新探, in *Xiqu benzhi yu shengqiang xintan* 戲曲本質與聲腔新探 (Taiwan: Guojia chubanshe, 2007), 96–111, esp. 96–99.

122. See Jiang Xiao's preface to *Jiugong shisan diao* 九宮十三調, in *Zhongguo gudian xiqu xuba huibian* 中國古典戲曲序跋彙編 (Shandong: Qilu shushe, 1989), 1:28–29.

123. See Xu and Niu, *Huizuan Yuan pu nanqu jiugong zhengshi* 彙纂元譜南曲九宮正始, in *Xuxiu sikuquanshu* (Shanghai: Shanghai guji, 2002), vols. 1748–1749; and Yu Weimin, *Zhongguo gudai quti wenxue*, 447–448.

124. The implication is that each of these places represents a different musical style.

125. Lu Rong 陸容 (1436–1494), *Shuyuan zaji* 菽園雜記, *juan* 10 (Beijing: Zhonghua shuju, 1985), 124–125.

126. See Zhu Yunming, "*Gequ*," in *Wei Tan*, 1353–1354. The geographic focus expands from the Bay of Hangzhou and coastal cities of Taizhou and Wenzhou to further inland, Yiyang in Jiangxi, to the west of Wenzhou, and Kunshan in Jiangsu, near Suzhou. Haiyan and Yuyao are both in the Hangzhou Bay.

127. Zhu Yunming, "*Gequ*," in *Wei Tan*, 1353–1354.

128. See Yu, *Zhongguo gudai quti wenxue*, 35. See also Qian, *Xiwen gailun*, 177–179.

129. Zhu Yunming, "Chongke *Zhongyuan yinyun* xu" 重刻 《中原音韻》 序, in *Lidai quhua huibian*, ed. Yu Weimin and Sun Rongrong, 1: 227.

130. See Xu Wei, *Nanci xulu*, LZJC, 3:241.

131. Although Xu did praise the writing of Yuan authors and conceded that northern music was superior in terms of modal organization, he lamented that contemporary northern music was essentially the remnant "barbarian" war sounds of the invading Liao 遼 (907–1125) and Jin 金 (1115–1234) dynasties, which had been adapted by northerners after the music of the song-lyric (*ci* 詞) could no longer be played. The earlier northern tradition not only had been corrupted by the Liao and Jin invaders but also had transformed the language, evidence of which was the loss of the so-called entering tone (*rushen* 入聲) in northern dialects. Xu, *Nanci xulu*, LZJC, 3:243. See also Aoki Masaru, *Nan Bei xiqu yuanliu kao* 南北戲曲源流考 (Taibei: Shangwu yinshuguan, 1965), 36.

132. See Xu Wei, *Nanci xulu*, LZJC, 3:245. The sentence "The sounds of the fallen state induce thoughts of sorrow" is from the *Liji zhengyi* 禮記正義, *Shisanjing zhushu* 十三經註疏, *juan* 37 (Beijing: Zhonghua shuju, 1980), 1527b. For a history of this term, see Leung, *Hsü Wei as Drama Critic*, 173.

133. The vocalizing style or *qiang* refers more broadly to the correct enunciation of a word from the correct part of the oral cavity with its correct accompanying tone. See Koo Siu-sun 古兆申, "Wei Liangfu: Qulü," in *Writings on the Theory of Kunqu Singing* (Hong Kong: Oxford University Press, 2006), xvi–xvii and xxxiii–xxxiv. Koo notes that different meanings of the term *qiang* as the "prolonged tone of a *zi* (word) in

speech or singing, a sung phrase, the skill of singing it and the special style and flavor it generated." Luo Di has traced the term to its earliest usages, and adds that *qiang* also was used as the structure of a tune (as in "the words are correct and the tune is genuine" 字正腔真). See Luo Di, "Sida shengqiang wen" 四大聲腔問, in *Nanda xiju luncong* 9 (Nanjing: Nanjing daxue chuban, 2013), 13–24.

134. For example, Hu Xuegang explains *qiang* as "the music that is sung according to the structure of a song" (腔則是由人唱出來的曲牌聲調), and *shenqiang* as "the music sung (vocalization style) according to drama's song structures" 戲曲按照曲牌演唱的音樂唱腔. See Hu Xuegang 胡雪岡, *Wenzhou nanxi lungao* 溫州南戲論稿 (Taibei: Guojia chubanshe, 2006), 22.

135. Shang Wei notes that *guanhua* 官話, or what we now term "Mandarin," was the shared language of traveling officials, merchants, and monks employed in the Ming and Qing eras for communication purposes. It was the language of the educated elite, but it was not standardized, and there were eight different branches of "Beijing Mandarin." See Shang Wei, "Writing and Speech: Rethinking the Issue of Vernaculars in Early Modern China," in *Rethinking East Asian Languages, Vernaculars and Literacies, 1000–1919*, ed. Benjamin Elman (Leiden: Brill, 2014), 254–301, esp. 269; and Benjamin Elman, "Introduction: Languages in East and South Asia," in *Rethinking East Asian Languages, Vernaculars and Literacies, 1000–1919*, ed. Benjamin Elman (Leiden: Brill, 2014), 1–28, esp. 19.

136. Kun music was one of the four dominant southern musical/singing styles (腔) at the time, but it was not widespread. Between 1522 and 1572, the music master Wei Liangfu 魏良輔 (ca. 1489–1566), with the help of other musicians, created a reformed Kun style known as the "watermill tunes" (*shuimo diao* 水磨調), which is considered to be the foundational music of the Kun musical tradition. Wei's main changes were wrought in the singing manner and the introduction of string instruments, traditionally associated with northern music, to the southern musical style, thus mixing the two. See Shen Chongsui 沈寵綏 (fl. 1639), *Duqu xuzhi* 度曲須知, LZJC, 5:198.

137. See Gu Qiyuan, "Xiju" 戲劇, in *Kezuo zhuiyu* 客座贅語, in *Siku quanshu cunmu congshu, juan* 9 (Jinan: Qilu Shushe, 1995), 243:343. The two capitals are Nanjing and Beijing. See also Li Huimian, "Cong

yiyunxue jiaodu lushu Wang Jide nanqu duqu lunzhi jiangou" 從音韻學角度論述王驥德南曲度曲論之建構, *Xiju yanjiu* 1 (2008): 142. For Yu Weimin and Liu Shuiyun, for example, the anecdote on Yangzi and Guan Yunshi explains why Haiyan was sung in Mandarin: because Guan and Yang carried out a reform of the local music, and because they were not locals and could not speak the local language, they used Mandarin. They also argue that this was a style in which the music was set but not the tones of the words. So while composing the songs, their sole consideration was the structure of the song; they were filling words to a tune, rather than adapting words to tones. See Yu and Liu, *Song Yuan Nanxi shi*, 139–141. In fact, nothing tells us that they did anything with local music. The tune decides the tones of the words, and not vice versa. Because the words abide by the melody and are not governed by prosodic rules, they are much freer and can be adapted to a northern style of speech.

138. See Gu Qiyuan, *Kezuo zhuiyu*, (243:343.

139. See note 10 and corresponding discussion in the text for a complete translation of this passage. Zhou Deqing, *Zhongyuan yinyun*, LZJC, 1: 173. Zhou chose the so-called rhymes of the northern central plains his model because they represented the language of the current dynasty. The play *Lechang* is included in the *Yongle Collectanea* as well as in Xu Wei's catalog of "Old Song and Yuan Plays." The play is not extant but thirty-one arias have been collected from a variety of song anthologies by Qian in *Song Yuan xiwen jiyi*, 223–228.

140. Zhu Quan, *Qionglin yayun xu* 瓊林雅韻序, *Siku quanshu cunmu congshu* 426: 784.

141. Chen Maoren 陳懋仁, *Quannan zazhi* 泉南雜志, 2 vols. in *Siku quanshu cunmu congshu* (Jinnan: Qilu chubanshe, 1996), 247:858.

142. Although the Kun style may have become the favorite dramatic form of performance, it is by no means a given that all literati theater was written to this music. For example, one point of contention is the play *Peony Pavilion* (*Mudan ting*), which was so difficult to sing that it is believed to have been composed in the Yiyang vocalizing style or a variant thereof. The first extant text we have written in a regional language is the *Lychee Mirror* (*Lijing ji* 荔鏡記), which dates from the Ming *Jiajing* reign 1521–1566. See *Ming Qing Minnan xiqu sizhong* 明清閩南戲曲四, ed. Wu Shouli 吳守禮; and Lin Zongyi 林宗毅, 3rd series

(Taibei: Ding jing tang congshu, 1978); and Wu Shouli, *Lijing ji xiwen yanjiu* 荔鏡記戲文研究 (Taiwan: Dongfang wenhua, 1970).

143. See Wang Zhenglai 王正來, *Quyuan zhuoying* 曲苑綴英 (Nanjing daxue yinwu youxian gongsi, 1962): "It makes use of the reading manner of the rhymes of the central plains (northern Chinese) but with Wu language accent" 帶有吳語口音的中州韻念法 (150). This is similar to Yuen Ren Chao's description of the Hangzhou dialect that, after having been the capital of the Southern Song dynasty, also made use of Wu phonology and Mandarin vocabulary. See Chao Yuan Ren, "Contrastive Aspects of Wu Dialects," *Language* 43, no. 1 (1967): 92–101, esp. 100. Chao notes that Hangzhou is special because it adopts Wu phonology, but it maintains Mandarin vocabulary. Braegger agrees and notes that Hangzhou did not make use of Wu dialects, but a Mandarin dialect with Wu pronunciation. See David Prager Branner, ed., *The Chinese Rime Tables: Linguistic Philosophy and Historical-Comparative Phonology* (Philadelphia: Benjamins, 2006), 17.

144. Although it does not make widespread use of local dialect, it does use some expressions repeatedly. See Guo Zuofei, "Yongle da dian xiwen sanzhong jiaozhu sanshili" 永樂大典戲文三種 校注三十例, *Dushuguan zazhi* 24, no. 12 (2005): 77–80, 96.

145. See for example act 19, in which Poorlass comes to ask the Lis for money for Zhang Xie. In this sequence, both proverbs and popular idioms are used in the dialogue with little interruption.

146. Yang Shen, *Sheng'an shihua jianzheng* 昇庵詩話俙證, *juan* 11, ed. Wang Zhongyong 王仲鏞 (Shanghai: Shanghai guji chubanshe, 1987), 387–388. The first mention in which unaccompanied song is a feature of southern music is noted by in the Song by the scholar Guo Maoqian 郭茂倩 (1041–1099) who indicated that that some song-types south of the Yangzi did not make use of musical instruments. Guo wrote: "The various tunes of the Wu songs came from the region south of the Yangzi River. With the advent of the Eastern Jin, they increased somewhat. At the outset, these songs were sung unaccompanied but have since found the support of wind and string instruments." 吳歌雜曲,並出江南.東晉以來,稍有增廣.其始皆徒歌,既而被之管弦. Guo is citing the "Music Treaty" of the *History of the Jin* (*Jinshu* 晉書). See Guo Maoqian, *Yuefu shiji* 樂府詩集, *juan* 44 (Taipei: Liren shuju, 1984), 639–640. The Wu songs are included under the section *Lyrics of Tunes*

*in the Qingshang key (Qingshang qu ci* 清商曲辭*).* See also Zeng Yongyi, *Xiqu benzhi yu qiangdiao xintan,* 97. See also Liao Ben, *Zhongguo xiqu shengqian yuanliu shi* 中國戲曲聲腔源流史 (Taipei: Guanya wenhua, 1992), 41–42.

147. It is unclear what *qiangdiao* means in this context. It possibly relates to the harmonizing nature of the modes so widespread in northern music.

148. I translate *Yin* 音 here as "songs," but I suspect it means the vocalizing style of southern song, that is the manner of singing in local language. Lu Cai, "Liushi erling" 劉史二伶, in *Yecheng kelun* 冶城客論in *Siku quanshu cunmu congshu,* 246:667. Some years later, Shen Defu 沈德符 (1578–1642) agreed that southern music traditionally did not make use of instruments: "Southern drama-song makes no use of string to mark its rhythm" 南曲不仗弦索為節奏. See Shen Defu, *Guqu zayan* 顧曲雜言, LZJC, 4:205.

149. See Ye Dejun 葉德均, "Mingdai nanxi wuda qiangdiao jiqi zhiliu" 明代南戲五大腔調及其支流, in *Xiqu xiaoshuo congkao* 戲曲小說叢考 (Beijing: Zhonghua shuju, 1979), 1–67; and Zeng Yongyi, *Xiqu benzhi yu qiangdiao xintan,* 100. Most scholars believe it was unaccompanied, but none question the style. Presumably, there would have been differences, as it is established in *Top Graduate.*

150. The different vocalizing and musical styles (*shengqiang* 聲腔) established the differences between theatrical styles (*juzhong* 劇種), but these often are used interchangeably as synonyms. In the former, however, the differences are phonological and musical, whereas in the latter, the differences are essentially structural and literary. The division and expansion is complex. For a thorough discussion, see the authoritative work of Yu Cong 余從, "Xiqu shengqian" 戲曲聲腔, "Xiqu juzhong" 戲曲劇種, and "Dui xiqu shengqiang juzhong de renshi" 對戲曲聲腔劇種的認識, in *Xiqu shengqiang juzhong yanjiu* 戲曲聲腔劇種研究 (Beijing: Shidai huawen shuju, 2016), 82–135, 136–183, and 184–205, respectively; and Lin Heyi 林鶴宜, *Wan Ming xiqu juzhong ji shengqiang yanjiu* 晚明戲曲劇種及聲腔研究 (Taipei: Xuehai chubanshe, 1994).

151. Zeng Yongyi, *Xiqu benzhi yu qiangdiao xintan,* 96–111, esp. 96–99.

152. See Ye Dejun, "Mingdai nanxi wuda qiangdiao jiqi zhiliu," 1–67, esp. 6–16; and Zeng Yongyi, *Xiqu benzhi yu qiangdiao xintan,* 96–111. For both scholars, this was the original form, and then it spread to other parts of the country.

153. Gao Ming, author of *The Lute* was from Wenzhou; the Chenghua edition of the *White Rabbit* was written by a writing association from Yongjia (永嘉書會), and the plot of *The Thorn Hairpin* occurs in the environs of Wenzhou.

154. See Yu and Liu, *Song Yuan nanxi shi*, 45–107. Yu counts 168 tunes not including codas and reprises. See also Yu Weimin, "*Zhang Xie zhuangyuan* yu zaoqi nanxi de xingshi tezheng" 張協狀元與早期南戲的形式特徵, *Xiju yishu* 4 (2003): 70–75.

155. The rhyme scheme in *Top Graduate* is similar to *The Lute* and the entering tone has largely disappeared from this play.

156. The *daqu* was a long song and dance performance with a varied structure and multiple stanzas based primarily on new Tang musical sounds from Central Asia. The *changzhuan* 唱賺 appears in the Shaoxing era (1131–1162) in the area around Hangzhou, and makes use of the tunes from one key (*gongdiao*), creating suites in the same key. The following songs are exclusive to Zhang Xie: *Fu Xiangyang* 復襄陽, *Fuzhou ge* 福州歌, *Taizhou ge* 台州歌, *Heyan kai* 賀筵開, *Jinqian zi* 金錢子, *Jinpai lang* 金牌郎, *Ma lang* 麻郎, *Linli ji* 林裡雞, *Wufang shen* 五方神, *Taizi you simen* 太子游四門, *Yin fanzi* 引番子, and *Tianzi sai hongniang* 添字塞紅娘.

157. Xu Wei, *Nanci xulu*, LZJC, 3:240.

158. See Xu Wei, *Nanci xulu*, LZJC, 4:239.

159. See Xu Wei, *Nanci xulu*, LZJC, 3:240.

160. See Zhou Deqing, *Zhongyuan yinyun*, LZJC, 1:173. Zhou's full statement reads: "After our present dynasty came together, north and south have received moral teachings (*shengjiao*). The gentry, in song and declamation, have sought the correct sounds, and the works they composed were enough to sing of the country's vigorous changes. Henceforth, the northern lyric (*Yuefu*) appeared, to completely cleanse the base customs of the southeast." 我朝混以來, 朔南暨聲教, 士大夫歌詠, 必求正聲, 凡所製作, 皆足以鳴國家氣化之盛, 自是北樂府出, 一洗東南習俗之陋. As Ye Changhai has noted, the influence of this text has been crucial all the way into the composition of local Huabu (花部) northern tunes in the Qing dynasty. See Ye Changhai, *Zhongguo xiqu xueshi* 中國戲曲學史 (Taibei: Luotuo, 1993), 81; and Zhou Yibai, *Zhongguo xiqu shi changbian*, 175. In the teaching of composition, it was crucial to keep the *natural* sounds.

161. Alan Thrasher describes the *qupai* as "a repertoire of melodic models" (3) and adds that "in their basic forms, *qupai* are essentially short structures, with melodies several or more phrases in length" that can be performed at moderate or faster tempos (4). He also notes that *qupai* is the shortest unit in Chinese music, while the extended suite of melodies organized in different ways (*taoqu* 套曲) is the longest. The *qupai* typically is identified by names and, in some regions, by their number of beats as well. See Alan R. Thrasher, "Qupai in Theory and Practice," in *Qupai in Chinese Music: Melodic Models in Form and Practice*, ed. Alan R. Thrasher (London: Routledge, 2016), 3–17. Wang Jide has noted how different languages created different music and manners of singing: "The frame of music is the song, and the color and patina is in the singing. Because the pronunciation is different everywhere, the music manner also differs." 樂之筐格在曲, 而色澤在唱. 在四方之音不同, 而為聲亦異. See Wang Jide, *Qulü*, LZJC, 4:115.

162. For a detailed account of all the different song types and their variations that appear in Zhang Xie, see Yu, *Song Yuan Nanxi kaolun xubian*, 35–65.

163. See Qian Nanyang, *Han Shangyi wencun, Liang Zhu xiju jicun* 漢上宧文存, 梁祝戲劇輯存 (Beijing: Zhonghua shuju, 2009), 160–171.

164. Xu Wei, Nanci xulu, LZJC vol. 3, 241..

## TOP GRADUATE ZHANG XIE

1. That is, a lascivious display. A character is missing from the original text. Probably *sha* 沙 after *cun* 村, making the compound *cunsha* meaning "crude."

2. The *mo* is a male role and the first one to enter and introduce the play. Here he speaks as the leader of the troupe or the one to introduce the play.

3. That is, sing songs of romance and satire.

4. The Music Bureau (Jiaofang 教坊) was the imperial office in charge of palace entertainment. It is intended to highlight the high quality of the singing of the troupe of the play.

5. The Crimson and Green was a well-known troupe of comedians active during the Southern Song in Hangzhou.

6. Literally, a *Zhugongdiao* or All Keys. The All Keys was a sung and narrated form popular in the Song dynasty. It is so called because

it changed keys with each song. The All Keys begins in the next tune *Fengshi chun* and ends in *Raochi you*.

7. Other versions include an additional "mountain 山 character." Qian excised it because it does not rhyme.

8. This is a tentative translation. In the original text, the first four characters in this sentence *houhou hehe* 齁齁谹谹 literally mean "puffing and panting." Qian emended "puffing and panting" to "barbs and brambles" (*gougou jiji* 鈎鈎棘棘), and in the second sentence, he changed "column" (*zhu* 柱) to "hanging" (*gua* 掛). This potentially could be read as: "Puff! Gasp! Puffing and without breath, the path is full of thorny columns of rattan."

9. The text reads *wo* 我, or "I." These two lines may have been intended to be spoken in the first-person voice of Zhang Xie.

10. This is a pool in the mythical Kunlun Mountains where the Queen Mother of the West lives.

11. Willow floss is a metaphor for snow.

12. The crow is traditionally an inauspicious sign, whereas the magpie is an auspicious one.

13. Literally, "roles" (*juese* 腳色).

14. The *moni* role here refers to the *mo* role introducing the play.


## ACT 2

1. This is the main male role. In the text, he is marked as *sheng* and would be recognized as such by the audience, but the text plays with time to show the audience how he assumes the role on stage.

2. It is not clear whether the *sheng* is already in character, but from context—it is narrated in the third person—this can be understood as a second introduction by the *sheng* role adopting the manner of the *mo* role introducing the play. The following is a seven-character declaimed quatrain, but this is not specified in the text. There are a number of these quatrains in this section. These would have changed the rhythm of speech.

3. The Liyuan 梨園 was the imperial theater established in the Tang by Emperor Xuanzong for his personal entertainment.

4. A reference to the story of Zhang Sengyou 張僧繇 in the tenth-century text *Lidai minghuaji* 歷代名畫記. Emperor Wudi of the Liang ordered

Zhang to paint four dragons on the walls of a Buddhist temple. Zhang painted them but left out the eyes explaining that they were so lifelike that if he painted the eyes, the dragons would fly away. When he added the eyes, the dragons flew up into the clouds and mist. The phrase *"feiyunyan"* 飛雲煙 is a description of Zhang Xie's calligraphy. See Zhang Yanyuan 張彥遠, *Lidai minghua ji* 歷代名畫記, *juan* 7 (Shanghai: Shangwu yinshuguan, 1936), 236–241.

5. The *jing* role is a comic role. In the comic routines, it is generally the partner of the *mo* and the *chou* or clown. No proper names are specified for these roles, so I give only their titles and function.

6. To pass the imperial exams. According to Chinese legend, fish that swam up the Yellow River and managed to ascend to gorges at Longmen (Dragon Gate) were said to turn into dragons. The process required stamina and determination, just like passing the examinations. Thus, the metaphor: to pass the examinations is to leap past the dragon gate.

7. This section is playing with the various meanings of the term *ai*. *Ai* (third tone) 嗳 is literally a sigh generally translated as "Alas!" which expresses dejection. It is also a quasi-homophone for the character *ai* (fourth tone) 愛 for love, thus the comment by the *mo* role: "It's a common human desire." It is also used in the compound *tan'ai* meaning to lust after someone. The *mo*'s comment is intended to emphasize satirically that lust is not the same thing as love.

8. From the Tang onward, to snap the cassia branch was a metaphor for succeeding in the imperial exams.

9. *Longhu bang* 龍虎榜, a publicly posted roll of successful imperial examinees.

10. A pond within the imperial palace by the quarters of the Secretariat or *zhongshusheng* 中書省 officials; it is also a metaphor for prime minister.

11. The idea implied in *tan* 譚 (to speak) is that the *jing* friend will now say something important and well rhymed, which is contrary to the buffoonish nature of the role. Because the *mo* friend and Zhang Xie have already composed their quatrains, it is now the *jing* friend's turn to make one up. The humor of the section that follows is based on the sound of the word *tan*, making the sound of a drum, "tam, tam," as well as the incapacity of the *jing* friend to find the correct rhyme.

12. The Tang poet Du Fu 杜甫 (712–770). Here, a pun on the meaning of *du* in the compound *duzhuan* 杜撰 is fabricated.

13. The *Treatise on Rhymes* (*Yunlüe* 韻略) was compiled by Dingdu 丁度 in the Song dynasty and was used as the standard rhyming text for the examinations.

14. Literally, *yidong* (一東, one east), *er dong* (二冬, two winter).

15. Literally, "three cash of sauce and four cash of onions." The rhymes are inverted to show the incompetence of the *jing* friend.

16. This is a reference to Zilu, the famous disciple of Confucius who possessed a courageous disposition. The reference is taken from the *Analects*, 7.11. The story goes as follows: "The Master said to Yen Yüan[,] 'Only you and I have the ability to go forward when employed and to stay out of sight when set aside.' Tzu-Lu (Zilu) said, 'If you were leading the Three Armies, whom would you take with you?' The Master said, 'I would not take with me anyone who would try to fight a tiger with his bare hands or to walk across the [Yellow] River and die in the process without regrets. If I took anyone it would have to be a man who, when faced with a task, was fearful of failure and who, while fond of making plans, was capable of successful execution.' " Confucius, *The Analects*, trans. D. C. Lau (Middlesex, UK: Penguin, 1979), 87. The implication of the passage in the *Analects* is that Zilu's careless boldness would be unsuccessful without a previous plan. Hence the comment in *Zhang Xie* must be taken ironically.

17. Literally, "gruel, like uncongealed hunger-quenching medicine." In Chinese medicine, drugs are sometimes taken in the form of soft, large, round pills, but the hunger-quenching medicine *xiaoshi yao* 消食藥 should not be congealed. The comment is on the words *yuan* 圓, which in the Wenzhou dialect means both to interpret (to describe) and a medicine pill (*wan* 丸, in modern Mandarin). When the diviner says that he cannot interpret the dream, the servant understands *yuan* "to interpret" for *yuan/wan* "to congeal," hence, the comment.

18. An abridgement of the title *xunguan* (inspector), commonly used in the north of China to designate diviners. The surname Li does not match, because the name of the diviner is Chen and not Li.

19. These two lines may also mean: "Study, don't imitate those good-for-nothings," with the caesura after the third character.

20. The first couplet is by the Tang poet Du Fu, "Respectfully presented to the Assistant Director of the Left, Senior Wei [Ji]: Twenty-two couplets." 奉贈韋左丞丈二十二韻. The next two lines are based on

*Mencius* 孟子 7a.9, *Mengzi yinde* 孟子引得, ed. Hong Ye et al. (Shanghai: Shanghai guji chubanshe, 1986). D. C. Lau translated the original passage in Mencius as follows: "In obscurity a man makes perfect his own person, but in prominence he makes perfect the whole empire as well." See *Mencius*, trans. D. C. Lau (Middlesex, UK: Penguin, 1970), 183.

21. This is a reference to a legend allegedly included in the Northern Song encyclopedia *Taiping yulan* 太平御覽 (*Imperial Digest of the Reign of Great Tranquility* [983]). I have found it in the Qing 1816 edition by Sun Xingyan 孫星衍 (1753–1818) of the *Kongzi jiyu* 孔子集語 (*Collected Sayings of Confucius*), but Sun cites Ma Su's 馬驌 (1621–1673) *Yishi* 繹史 in which Ma argues this story is "vulgar and deceitful" (*youli er miu* 尤俚而謬). See Sun Xingyan, *Kongzi jiyu, juan* 14 (Taipei: Yiwen yinshuguan, 1967), 70. In the story, Confucius is besieged in the country of Chen and asked to string a crooked pearl. Upon asking the advice of some mulberry pickers, he strings the crooked pearl through the ingenious device of tying a thread to an ant and enticing it through the hole with honey. The point of the allusion is that no matter how ingenious one may be, if the time is not ripe, one still will not succeed.

22. An allusion to a story from Tang poet Jiang Fang 蔣防, "Lu Wang diaoyu huang fu" 呂望釣魚璜賦 ("Rhapsody on Lu Wang Fishing a Jade Ornament") included in the Song dynasty literary anthology *Wenyuan yinghua* 文苑英華 (*Finest Flowers of the Preserve of Letters* [986]) about a man who simply let down his hook and caught half a jade disk. This allusion is made in opposition to the previous anecdote about Confucius. The point is that however little one tries, if the time is ripe, one will succeed. See Li Fang 李昉 et al., *Wenyuan yinghua* (Beijing: Zhonghua shuju, 1966), 1:568.

23. Although the term in the text is *fei* (非), it is translated here as "phony." Qian Nanyang argues that the character is probably an error for *fei* (菲) a variant of *fei* (飛, to fly).

24. The phrase "peach blossom waves" refers to the swelling of the waters of the Yellow River in spring. This is also the time at which the peach trees bloom and scatter their flower blossoms on the river waters. It is said that in the area around Hejin, when the Yellow River swells in spring, the currents are strong and most fish cannot swim up the river, but some brave the current and manage it. This story is used as a metaphor

418 ACT 2

for the difficulty of studying and passing the imperial exams. "To reach the path above the clouds" is to climb the road to officialdom. See *Hou Hanshu* 後漢書, *juan* 67 (Beijing: Zhonghua shuju, 1965), 2195.

25. Shao Yong 邵雍 (1011–1077), a Northern Song poet and philosopher.
26. I have been unable to locate the source of this quotation.
27. *Fumo* is an archaic term for the additional male *mo* role, an assistant. Here it is used as a secondary additional male, because the role of the *mo* is already being used as a friend of Zhang Xie. The *fumo* is probably playing a household servant, but here he is called by the role name, which is unusual.

## ACT 3

1. *Daodao ling* 叨叨令 is a northern tune inserted in a southern repertoire.

## ACT 4

1. In the comic routine of this duo (but also with the *jing* comic role), all the sentences by the *mo* (servant) role are used to cap or close the joke with a "*youdao*" 又道, meaning "it can be said that . . .," stating the obvious.
2. The Buddha is considered to be the provider for monks. Here the *mo* (servant) is the one coming to provide work for the diviner, hence the comment.
3. The diviner is probably addressing the servant.
4. The *Lei shuo* 類說, a Song compendium of popular narratives compiled by Zeng Zao 曾慥, cites a story from the *Zhiyi* 摭遺, *Wuyi guo* 烏衣國 section. The story notes that during the Tang dynasty, a certain Wang Xie's 王謝 ship ran off course and drifted to the "Kingdom of Raven Robes" (*Wuyi guo*), a mythological country inhabited by swallows.
5. A reference to a story in the *Liezi* 列子. *Liezi jishi* 列子集釋, *juan* 5 (Beijing: Zhonghua shuju, 1979), 177. The story runs as follows: "Once a woman named Erh of Han ran out of provisions while traveling East of Ch'i. She entered the capital through the Concord Gate, and traded her songs for a meal. When she left, the lingering notes curled round the beams of the gate and did not die away for three days; the by-standers thought that she was still there." A. C. Graham, trans., *The Book of Lieh-tzu: A Classic of Tao* (New York: Columbia University Press, 1990), 109.

6. There is a pun on the word *chen* 陳 for the surname of the diviner and *chen* 塵 for dust. It is said that when a voice is sharp and beautiful, as the sound rises to the roof, it can make the dust in the beams rise. Literally, the line reads: "I'll beat you till the dust, quivering, rises." The *mo* takes offense at the diviner suggesting that his friend, the *sheng*, was not human in a former life.

7. The confusion between eighteen and forty-eight is probably making fun of dialect (*shiba* 十八 and *siba* 四八).

8. Literally, "You just want to save all beings." But there is a pun in the phrase *duzhongsheng* 度眾生 (save all beings) for *duzhongsheng* 度中生 (to get through midlife). In other words, it substitutes the virtuous acts of trying to save the world for a personal concern with himself and trying to get through the later years of his life.

9. Two characters for mountain, one on top of the other, make up the word *chu* 出 ("exit").

10. From the *Yijing* 易經, in *Shisanjing zhushu* 十三經註疏, *juan* 5 (Beijing: Zhonghua shuju, 1980) 49a. A leopard change *baobian* 豹變 means a dramatic turn for the better.

11. The insult means "to pass to another life buried in straw." The *mo* (servant) is retorting in kind, as convicts were buried in straw.

12. The "Great Way" (*dadao* 大道) is a Buddhist term for enlightenment (also the Great Way of the Daoists). The implication is that all phenomena can be found in the particular and all things revert to the Great Way. In other words, truth is in front of us.

# ACT 5

1. This line follows Qian's interpretation. Literally, the line reads: "If you don't listen it will naturally go away! That means there is no depressed old lady in the house."

2. The father is being sarcastic, commenting on his wife's cutthroat business practice.

3. In the Song dynasty, the successful candidates awaited the reading of their rankings from a scroll known as the Golden List (*jinbang* 金榜).

4. Hua Tuo (ca. 140–208) was a famous physician. There is a homophonic pun on the meaning of *tuo* 駝 as hunchback and to plaster.

## ACT 6

1. Literally, *Ten Thousand Blessings* (*wanfu* 萬福), a polite form of greeting employed by women. In act 35, it will be used by Zhang Xie to identify Poorlass, who has entered the official *yamen*.

2. A word is missing from the text. Possibly it is the compound *qiangsi* 強 似 meaning "better than."

## ACT 7

1. He is going to the capital of the Northern Song, Bianliang (modern-day Kaifeng), from somewhere in north Sichuan.

## ACT 8

1. Nezha is a martial Chinese protective deity of Indian origin.

2. Literally, "I am the Cishan Guangdejun Halberd-and-Club Officer of Wuyuan county in Huizhou." Guangdejun 廣德軍 was in present-day Sichuan Province. Cishan 祠山 was the name of a deity. There was a temple to Cishan in Guagdejun during the Song dynasty.

3. A reference to the seventh-century Tang Generals Yuchi Gong 尉遲 恭 and Shan Xiongxin 單雄信. Li Shimin 李世民 launched an attack on Wang Shichong 王世充. During the battle, Wang Shichong asked his general Shan Xiongxin to kill Li Shimin. Yuchi Gong saw Shan's gesture and, in an attempt to save Li Shimin, kicked his horse to a full gallop toward Shan shouting, "It's my turn now," and knocked Shan off the horse, killing him.

4. The pun is on the words *bing* 兵 for weapon and *fa* 法 for method. Because both the roles are looking for a method with a different weapon, the *mo* traveler suggests the famous military strategist Sunzi's *Art of Warfare* or *Sunzi Bingfa*.

## ACT 9

1. These are rites, music, archery, charioteering, calligraphy, and mathematics.

2. Literally, "You are not suited to be inside his smoke and flame, you should have just lowered your head." These two lines are intended to

resonate with the robber's words: "The moth is attracted to the flame and throws its life away."

3. This is directed to the audience. In the following two lines, the god informs Zhang Xie that he is kinfolk to the mountain and a local god.

4. This is "your far-reaching ambitions."

## ACT 10

1. The list of successful examination candidates.

2. This comment is made to the audience.

3. From the *Analects* 7.22. "The Master said, even when walking in the company of two other men, I am bound to be able to learn from them. The good points of the one I copy, the bad points of the other I correct in myself." Confucius, *The Analects*, trans. D. C. Lau (Middlesex, UK: Penguin, 1979), 89.

4. Possibly a pun on the two parts of the character that make up the surname Zhang. On the left is the radical for *gong* 弓 (bow), on the right should be the character *chang* 長 long. Apparently a joke, but the meaning eludes me.

5. The term *huantou* 換頭 refers to the alternative meter used in the first line or couple of lines of a *ci* 詞. In this tune the complete meter of a stanza is 337,75,3333 and the alternative stanza is 55,665,3333, thus changing the first two lines of the *ci*.

## ACT 11

1. This is a play on words. Because Grandma Li wants to avoid saying the taboo word "short life" *duanming* 短命 (*ming*, also means "fate"), she uses a close homophone meaning "peace" [*duan*] *ning* 寧.

2. For *zuozhong* 做種 I follow Hou Baipeng's 侯百朋 interpretation. See "Xiwen zhong de Wenzhou fangyan" 戲文中的溫洲方言, *Nanxi tantaoji* 南戲探討集, vol. 5 (Wenzhou: Wenhua ju, 1987), 61–73.

3. It is not clear what this last sentence refers to, but may be a response to the fact that they are well off and Poorlass is not. Hu Xuegang changes the next sentence uttered by Grandpa Li to "me" (*wo*) so that it reads: "What shame do I have?" See Hu Xuegang, *Zhang Xie zhuangyuan jiaoshi*, 58.

4. Literally, "I have a fist in my hand." Possibly a pun on the homophone *quan* 拳 ("fist") for *quan* 權 ("power").

5. An allusion to the role's painted face.

## ACT 12

1. In the previous act, Grandma Li does not explicitly mention Poorlass as his bride and persuades Xiao'er to bring the food by telling him she will find a bride for him. Here Xiao'er insists on Poorlass and Grandpa Li also tells Poorlass that Grandma Li promised him he would marry her if he brought the goods over. It may be an inconsistency of the text.

2. Literally, *Baojia* 保甲. This was a security system organized on the basis of households. Here it is a generic reference to the village head. The headman would be the head of a group of ten families.

3. A children's primer.

4. That is, to "fish" for a wife.

5. Judging by the pattern of the tune, a word is missing from the first line. Hu Xuegang adds "rain" (*yu* 雨) based on the following line. See Hu, *Zhang Xie zhuangyuan jiaoshi*, 64.

6. Literally, "made of wood."

## ACT 13

1. Beginning of maturity of a girl.

2. Jing Prefecture was known for its jade, and it was said that mermaids produced pearls with their tears. The point is that one does not appreciate the value of something unless it is scarce.

## ACT 14

1. Tentative translation. A character is missing in this line.

2. This possibly meant that there would be no one to take care of him in the temple. But it could allude to having no one to give a dowry in her name.

3. Literally, " pair the wings." From the *Erya* 爾雅. See *Shisanjing zhushu* 十三經註疏, *juan* 7 (Beijing: Zhonghua shuju, 1980), 2615c. The *Erya* mentions a type of bird with one wing that can only fly in pairs. This later became a metaphor for lovers and marriage.

4. A type of tune, also called *bushi lu* 不是路. Popular during the Song dynasty, it was often inserted between other tunes.

5. This couplet is taken from the *Liji*. See *Liji zhengyi* 禮記正義, *Shisan-jing zhushu, juan* 9, 1303b.

6. An object shaped like two half-moons with one side flat and the other curved outward. After asking a question or making a wish, these are thrown to the floor. The wish is granted when one side falls flat and the other curved. These are commonly used in temples to this day.

7. Because the *jing* role plays both the god and Grandma Li, the role will participate twice in the feast: once as the god and once as Grandma Li.

## ACT 15

1. Literally, bride to an "imperial son-in-law." She could be a princess.

## ACT 16

1. From the *Shangshu* 尚書. See *Shangshu zhengyi* 尚書正義, *Shisanjing zhushu* 十三經註, *juan* 8 (Beijing: Zhonghua shuju, 1980), 163c.

2. Literally, "to do the duck," which can mean either a male prostitute (a gigolo) or a scoundrel. It is also used to mean a cuckold. Here it makes sense in its extended meaning as "matchmaker."

3. According to the pattern of the tune, the last line should have five characters. This one has four. I follow Qian's emendation and add the character *jiu* 久 (long). Hu adds *shou* 受 changing the meaning to "be such a hassle."

4. The comment is ironic, because nobles are well fed and warm.

5. "Pay your respects as if the gods were present" is taken from *Analects* 3.12. Confucius, *The Analects*, trans. D. C. Lau (Middlesex, UK: Penguin, 1979).

6. *Maming wang* or (*matou mingwang* 馬頭明王) is Hayagrīva, a wrathful form of Avalokitêśvara (Guanyin Bodhisattva). It is represented with an angry face: glaring eyes, and a bellowing mouth. It also has the head of a horse sculpted or painted above its head.

7. The richest food is often offered to the deities, but temple custodians have access to it. Thus deities and temple custodians are all supposed to be fat.

8. This is a *Daqu* 大曲 sequence, an ancient form of musical entertainment. Its composition can be traced to the Han dynasty. It is a musical

piece that essentially consists of three parts. It has an instrumental introduction called the *sanxu* 散序, a centerpiece generally slow and also sung called the *zhongxu* 中序, and a third part, which is faster and sung and danced to music called the *qupo* 曲破. Both the second and the third parts are subdivided into sections called *bian* 遍. By the Northern Song, the *daqu* were abridged using either the last section of the *qupo*, or picking different sections and rearranging them to suit one's purpose. See Hu Ji, "Ta-ch'ü," in *The Indiana Companion to Traditional Chinese Literature*, ed. William H. Nienhauser Jr. (Bloomington: Indiana University Press, 1986), 739–741. This song is constituted of selected sequences of the third section of the *daqu*.

9. After the imperial graduates passed the examinations and their names were announced, they were paraded through the streets. Some families with daughters of a marriageable age would offer them a whip. If the candidates accepted them, they would go to their house and dismount the horse, at which point they were offered some soup to drink. See also act 21.

10. Literally, "such language," that is, of matters of love.

11. The god has been eating the meat all along, so the meaning is ironical.

12. From the *Guanzi* 管子, "Xiaowen" 小問, in *Guanzi qingzhongpian xinquan* 管子輕重篇新詮, *juan* 51 (Beijing: Zhonghua shuju, 1979), 805. Fish in water is used as a metaphor for a loving couple.

13. A reference to a mythological bird that has only one wing, and hence can fly only with a companion. "Conjugal happiness" in Grandpa Li's song continues with the metaphor. Literally, it reads ". . . and fly together" until the end.

14. The wife and the god are played by the same role.

15. During the Tang and Song dynasties, the examination halls had two statues, one of a dragon and the other of the mythical tortoise that supports the earth.

16. A term used to describe the small feet of women.

17. That is, good or not.

# ACT 17

1. I substitute 念 for the first person pronoun *yu* 余.

2. A word game in which each player decides on a flower, and then attempts to describe its qualities and shortcomings.

3. According to Qian and Hu, this may be a scribal error and this refrain should be placed before the line "Among this year's virtuous scholars." But it follows the pattern of the tune.

## ACT 18

1. In the pattern of this tune, the last two sentences of a stanza are generally sung together. Although the stage directions are missing, the pattern should remain the same.

## ACT 19

1. Folding chairs can be brought out whenever they are needed. The *mo* is saying that they cannot rely on him.
2. The meaning is unclear, but perhaps Grandma Li is alluding to the box being full of money.
3. Literally, "I have no box like that." Again, the exchange is unclear.
4. A famous pearl that shines brightly at night.
5. Literally, Chang'an, the capital in the Tang. But he is going to Bianliang, the capital of the Northern Song where the play is set, so Chang'an is used here as a general substitute for "capital."

## ACT 20

1. Han Xin 韓信 (230–196 BC) was a capable Han general put to death by the emperor. Qu Yuan 屈原 (third century BC) was a famous poet banished from his motherland. In other words, "Although I won't kill Poorlass, I will certainly chase her away."
2. The *dan*'s exit is not indicated in the text, but she probably leaves the stage right after her last song or makes a false exit, standing still at the back of the stage.
3. This is a set of four songs initiated by Poorlass in which the beginning of each song changes.
4. In the text it is written *sheng* (*Zhang Xie*). This must be a scribal error, because the text below is sung by the *dan* (*Poorlass*) role.
5. Wang Kui 王魁 was a poor scholar who fell in love with the courtesan Gui Ying 桂英. She helped him to prepare for the examinations, but

as soon as he passed, he married a noble woman and abandoned her. Gui Ying then sent a servant to the capital to bring him a letter, but when the servant appeared in the hall, Wang became enraged and chased him out. Complaining of his lack of gratitude, Gui Ying later committed suicide. Her ghost haunted Wang Kui, causing him to die soon after.

6. Two goddesses mentioned in the *Liexian zhuan* 列仙傳 attributed to the Han figure Liu Xiang 劉向 (ca. 77–6 BC). While these two women were traveling, they came across a certain Zheng Jiaofu 鄭交甫 who did not realize they were goddesses. As soon as he saw them, he took an instant liking to them and asked for their pendants. They gave them to him, whereupon he placed them by his heart and left. After a few steps, he stopped to look at the pendants, but they were gone. When he turned to look back, both women were also gone. The pendant became a symbol for a love token between two people. But in this case, the story is used to show how compassionate was Poorlass was when she saw Zhang Xie full of blood. See Liu Xiang, *Liexian zhuan*, *Zhuzi baijia congshu* 諸子百家叢書 (Shanghai: Shanghai guji chubanshe, 1990), 8a.

7. Tentative translation. I take the expression *jiaotou jin* 腳頭緊 to perhaps be an alternative to *shoutou jin* 手頭緊 (to be stingy or tightfisted).

8. That is, the gods watch over our actions; hence, if one does wrong or lies, retribution will ensue.

## ACT 21

1. Master Feng (Feng Dao 馮道, 882–954) was an important government official during the Five Dynasties period.

2. That is, to secure a son-in-law that will carry the family name of the bride.

3. If the candidate accepts the silk whip, he arrives at the house of the bride-to-be and drinks a bowl of soup before meeting the parents-in-law.

4. This is money given to the messenger who will lead the son-in-law to the house.

5. After the exams, the candidates would be paraded through the streets. Silk whips were offered to the successful candidates of the imperial exams by noble families with marriageable daughters. If the candidate accepted the whip, he would ride to the bride's house and dismount in

front of the house. The bride's family would welcome the new son-in-law with a bowl of soup and a bowl of wine.

6. That is, paper money burned in the offering to one's ancestors or to the gods.

7. The comment is in relation to a mispronunciation Wang Deyong makes when declaiming the two lines above, which the assistant corrects. Whether the pun is in the first sentence or in the assistant's comment, the meaning of this sequence remains a puzzle.

8. This line, also unclear, concludes the exchange between Wang Deyong and his assistant.

## ACT 22

1. It is said that the cuckoo's cry sounds like the words *buru guiqu* 不如歸去 ("it would be better to return").

2. An allusion to the story of Lao Laizi 老萊子, one of the twenty-four filial sons and a paragon of filial piety from the Spring and Autumn period. When Lao Laizi was approaching seventy, he would play like a child to please his parents. On one occasion, wearing a brightly colored gown, he was bringing some sauce to his parents and tripped on the stairs of the hall. In a feigned tantrum, he threw himself to the ground and, to the delight of his aged parents, cried like a little boy.

## ACT 23

1. The Chinese honeylocust or *Gleditsia sinensis* is a species of flowering plant, the thorns of which are used in traditional Chinese medicine to cure inflammatory diseases.

2. This section is supposed to be a play on minor official titles, but the titles do not really exist. Thus, the comment by the assistant in the end, "You could hardly say . . ."

## ACT 24

1. Literally, I shall fish the giant tortoise and reach the top. The tortoise *ao* 鰲 refers to a mythical animal mentioned in the *Liezi*, "Tangwen" 湯問, which is supposed to support the earth. See *Liezi jishi*, 5:150.

The candidate who earned the first place was called the top graduate (*zhuangyuan* 狀元) and was said to have "seized the tortoise's head" (*zhan aotou* 占鰲頭). See Charles O. Hucker, *A Dictionary of Official Titles in Imperial China* (Stanford: Stanford University Press, 1985), 106–107, 536.

2. Literally, "bow-radical Zhang" *gongbianzhang* 弓邊長, which is nearly homophonous with *gongbianzhang* 恭鞭長 "to let the reins hang loose," which, according to a famous account, is what Tang general Yuchi Jingde did while kicking his horse to a full gallop and attacking Shan in an attempt to save the emperor. The alternative surname is *zhang* 章 (*li* 立 and *zao* 早) generally meaning a written composition.

3. Another pun. The near homophone *zhilu* 紙錄 refers to a paper box, or the box in which name cards were presented.

4. "Luzi" means "deer."

5. *Hua* 華 is a homophone for *hua* 畫 ("to paint"). There seems to have been a custom of painting white deer on doors, perhaps as an auspicious symbol. See also acts 27 and 48.

6. A flat platform used to place the mill, which could also be used as a bed.

7. Here it means that those who sleep on makeshift beds on the ground do not all come from the same backgrounds.

8. *Jiaonu* 角奴 in the original is probably a mistake for *jiaoji* (~妓), a type of musical performer cum courtesan, and probably corresponds with *sanji* (散妓), in the Song and Yuan, a term for popular performers.

9. Lawsuits among the wealthy were often solved through extorsion; thus, the term "to kill others" refers to blackmailing others. Because the poor had no means and could not be blackmailed, they were as good as dead, thus the term "killing oneself."

10. Literally, *wanpi*, here translated as "thick skinned," means obstinate, but the comment is based on the opposite of the intended meaning.

11. To begin a quarrel is to get angry *fanu* 發怒 and to undertake the exams means to gain fame and fortune (*faji* 發跡). The pun is on the word *fa*, and hence the student *mo*'s comment *faguo* "you've made your mark in the world."

## ACT 25

1. Also a pun on his role.
2. Decorated towers built by noble families. The daughters of noble families would stand atop the tower and see the Imperial Top Graduate, and other graduates come in.

## ACT 26

1. When the candidates were successful, they changed into green robes.
2. The text reads *wo* 我 for the first person pronoun, but it must be a scribal error.
3. To wish someone a sudden turn of things for the better.

## ACT 27

1. In fact, the exams were held every two and a half years.
2. The Cheng 程 brothers refers to the Song-dynasty thinkers Cheng Hao 程顥 (1032–1085) and Cheng Yi 程頤 (1033–1107).
3. He is known as the Black Prince by the people and the Crimson Prince at court (see act 13).
4. The Bright Garden (Langyuan) was built in the Tang dynasty in Sichuan. The Apricot Garden was in Chang'an; in the Tang dynasty, scholars that passed the exams were given a feast in this garden. But the Langyuan was also known as the immortals paradise.
5. That is, I have met with the emperor.
6. Because the phoenix has a tree to itself, it does not need to compete with common birds for a higher branch.
7. The two types of hats are a larger one called a *futou* 袱頭 hat for official occasions and visits, and a casual hat called a *xiumao* 羞帽 to wear at all other times.
8. "Zhong Kui Chases the Small Demon" was a popular play about Zhong Kui 鍾馗 who, unable to pass the military exams, took an oath to chase away evil spirits.
9. As part of his role, the clown (*chou*) also painted his mouth black.
10. The assistant is referring to Wang Deyong's insistence on Zhang Xie taking the silk whip.

11. The gowns of the new officials were called "lotus gowns" because of their green color. Lotus leaves were used for wrapping up food, but once tattered, they had no value.

12. A type of prickly water lily. It produces a fruit called gorgon fruit or foxnut.

13. The official hat of the examinees was shaped like a step, high and pointed on the back and square and flat in the front.

14. Although the python has no poison, it can wrap around an animal and suffocate it to death. The point, then, is that the top graduate is extremely imposing as soon as he has passed the exams, but once he takes up his post and leaves the capital, he becomes just one more official.

15. Because he wants to impersonate his daughter, unless the gods are near at hand to work some magic, his painted face will be obvious to all passersby.

16. That is, dressed as his daughter.

## ACT 28

1. Literally, "to be hit three times and not turn one's head." It can also be translated as "You dummy!" The *jing* is so used to telling lies that even if he is selling the booklets, he still tells the *mo* that they are sold elsewhere. Although it is not indicated in the stage instructions, perhaps the *mo* also hits the *jing* on the head.

2. This role also plays Grandpa Li.

3. The name Zhou Zikuai 周子快 is homophonous with the characters meaning "speedy boat."

4. The comment "you still haven't left" is directed to the *jing* (vendor) who is in a hurry to go. "He really knows the way" refers to the hastiness of the *chou* (Xiao'er).

5. That is, but can't tell it.

6. *Deng* 登 of *Dengkeji* 登科記, the successful examinees list, is homophonous with *deng* 燈 lamp. Because Xiao'er forgot his "lamp/success" the Customer (*mo*) suggests he can borrow a candle to light to successfully find his way instead.

7. "Examination" or *ke* is homophonous with *ke* 窠 for "den" or "borrow." A stray dog has no den; hence, the Customer's (*mo*) comment.

## ACT 30

1. Grandma comes on stage and Poorlass hears her. So she is directly answering Poorlass.

2. Grandma Li makes the sound of applying makeup "pit-pat, pit-pat"; hence, Grandpa's comment.

## ACT 32

1. Judging by the general pattern of the tune, the stage instructions are missing from the last two lines.

2. Literally, the *xixue* 膝穴 ("point"). An acupuncture point on the heel of the foot that treats illnesses of the kidneys.

3. If Zhang Xie would have stayed in the city, Shenghua would have still had a faint opportunity to arrange the marriage, but once he has been appointed to a post in the provinces, no hope remains for her.

4. Once, when Xi Shi 西施 had a stomachache, she frowned. Because she was so beautiful, other women tried to imitate her frown.

5. The green dragon was a symbol of god fortune; the white tiger of bad fortune.

6. The *mo* role, playing the assistant to Wang Deyong, utters these words reflecting on other character's actions. This becomes commonplace in later drama, but more generally, it is uttered by this role in the voice that transcends his role.

## ACT 33

1. This sentence can have a secondary meaning of "You shouldn't marry too high or too low."

2. A scholar from Chu who often shut himself in his study. He was nicknamed Mr. Behind-Closed-Doors.

3. The *jing* role played both the god and the mother.

4. The Liang Gardens were built in the Han dynasty by Prince Liang Xiao in (modern-day) Henan.

## ACT 35

1. That is, a male actor playing a female role.
2. An allusion to the role's costume. The headgear was usually decorated with pearls. Here it may be meant ironically, because the *dan* was probably dressed in simple clothes showing her station in life.
3. It was taboo to use the personal name of an official.
4. This is from Wang Tong's 王通 (584–618) work, the *Zhong shuo* 中說, a collection of notes on the works of Confucius and Mencius. Wang Tong was posthumously known as "Wenzhongzi" 文中子, as was his work.
5. Literally, "If you marry a cock, you shall fly with the cock." That is, whatever fate brings, one must follow.
6. It can also be read as "I want that guilty conscience of yours to last as long as your honor and glory."

## ACT 36

1. A popular saying. Mr. Xu was an immortal and dragons are mythical creatures that could be ridden by immortals. Both are too great to be concealed by muddy waters.
2. This refers to a legend recorded in various texts. According to the legend, Emperor Wu of the Han used phoenix spittle glue to repair a broken string, which never broke again. Hence, "phoenix glue" is used as a metaphor for strong bonds.

## ACT 37

1. That is, you did not recognize our marriage.

## ACT 38

1. Zheng Chang 張敞, also called Zhang Zhaoyin 張兆尹, was a Han dynasty official who used to paint his wife's eyebrows.

2. There is a pun on the word *feng* 風: *zhaofeng* 招風 ("notice board") and *tefeng* 忒瘋 ("too crazy").

3. That is, blood relations are difficult to know; how much more difficult it is to know strangers?

## ACT 39

1. A bitter medicine.

2. From the Song poet Su Shi 蘇軾 (1037–1101), "Shuidiao getou" 水調歌頭, Zhongqiu 中秋.

3. From *Analects* 4.16: "The Master said, 'The gentleman understands what is moral, the small man understands what is profitable.'" See *Analects*, trans. D. C. Lau, 74.

4. The *jing* role plays both the character of Grandma Li and the god.

## ACT 40

1. That is, wasting my time.

2. Literally, "Although I entered the scene of men of talent (those who snap the single branch in the Forest of Cassia), to advance my career smoothly I must avail myself of the wind that blows through the hanging screens."

3. The surname is actually missing, but later, when the *mo* calls the third porter, Li Wang 李旺, the *chou* playing the same role assents again; hence, the comment.

4. Although the stage directions do not indicate in what capacity the role is acting, it is clear from context.

5. That is, having acquired wealth and honor.

6. A word is missing. I follow Qian, who suggests the word *re* 惹 (to provoke). See Qian, *Yongle dadian xiwen sanzhong*, 176n27.

## ACT 41

1. That is, you passed the exams.

## ACT 42

1. The assistant (*mo*) is calling the servants, but the Military Affairs Commissioner who is also played by the *chou* role answers, thus the comment.

2. This role *tie* was originally playing Shenghua, the daughter of the Military Affairs Commissioner. It is possible that it was conceived as a one character role, like the main male and female roles, thus the use of the term "disguised" (*jiazhuang* 假裝).

3. "To bring up" or, literally, "to raise someone up" physically. The joke consists of telling the person to be careful with her head because it can hit the ceiling.

## ACT 44

1. The horse kicks the assistant, who manages to avoid it. In the next sentence, the assistant identifies the "horse's hoof" with a type of food.

2. In the Wenzhou dialect, *wo* 臥 ("to lie down, to rest") is generally said *dao* 倒. *Daomiao* 倒廟 ("to bed down in a temple") is generally said of beggars and vagrants who have no other place to sleep; hence, Wang Deyong's comment.

3. A dream inside the temple will tell you your fortune.

## ACT 45

1. The Commissioner makes comments about the temple while his wife replies in agreement. Because she agrees to everything, she also agrees to the impossible.

2. Strange objects were taken as auspicious omens and a sign of luck and long life.

3. A pun on homophones, but it is intended to be nonsensical. *Zui* 觜 ("the beak of a bird") rhymes with *gui* 鬼 ("ghost"); hence, the assistant's comment.

4. The Goddess of the River Luo and Chang E are both paragons of feminine beauty.

5. *Youxiang wuxiang* is a Buddhist term, which literally means having appearance and not having appearance. The Commissioner's wife is asking her husband to ignore her ashen face and ragged appearance and to pay attention to the expression of her face as a window to her soul.

6. Wang Deyong calls her daughter in jest. Poorlass sings "Taizi you simen" 太子游四門 ("The Prince Travels Throughout the World"), originally a Buddhist song relating to the departure of Sakyamuni from

his palace when he embarked on a life of renunciation. Wang Deyong takes the song title literally, meaning that because the prince is traveling alone, he will be looking for young girls.

7. Grandma Li probably jokes around with the Grandma Li, but the text has been lost.

8. Unless Poorlass has informed the Wangs of Zhang Xie's ungratefulness, no one else knows, because she has kept her encounter with Zhang Xie in the capital and his attempt to kill her a secret. The comment may be directed to the audience.

9. The *jing* is addressing the *mo*, who is here playing the assistant but who also plays Grandpa Li.

10. Throughout this section, the assistant who is played by the *mo* role, the same role played by Grandpa Li, lets the audience know that he knows what Grandma is talking about.

## ACT 47

1. Roads built of wooden planks and brackets fixed into the cliff.

## ACT 48

1. The famous Song lyricist Liu Yong 柳永 (987–1053). Liu spent much of his time in the entertainment quarters and was popular among courtesans for his *ci*-lyrics; perhaps for this reason, he had the reputation of a playboy.

2. That is, they succeeded in officialdom. Wenzhou was originally called White Deer City, so it is possible that painting deer on the doors was an auspicious sign. See Hu Xuegang, *Zhang Xie zhuangyuan jiaoshi*, 188n14.

3. When two people bow to each other, they look like grain being poured into a bag. The joke is on the word "coarseness," which also refers to coarse grain.

4. Two additional characters (*jinbai* 緊白, literally, "to speak with urgency") are inserted here. Qian leaves them as part of the sentence and Hu places them in parenthesis as stage instructions. It is not clear what they mean.

5. Chen Tuan 陳摶 was a recluse who lived on Mount Hua. Every time he went to sleep, he slept for more than a hundred days. His biography is

included in the *Song shi* 宋史, *juan* 457 (Beijing: Zhonghua shuju, 1977), 13420.

6. Zhang Xie is asking the assistant to Wang Deyong, not Wang.

## ACT 50

1. The first line is an inversion of a line based on the Tang poet Li He 李贺 (790–816): "If Heaven had feelings, Heaven would age." The second line is based on a poem by the Song poet Shi Yannian 石延年 (994–1041): "If the moon had no regrets, it would stay round."

## ACT 52

1. The assistant's (*mo*) comment is made in relation to the versatility of the *jing* role now playing Vice Commissioner Tan.
2. A reference to the role of the *jing* played by Grandma Li and her desire for mirrors.

## ACT 53

1. It is not clear what characters these roles are playing as is the case with the *jing* below. They could be the assistant and the maids of the Wang household.
2. The cap worn by the groom.
3. A comic character both in Song and Yuan drama and marionette theater.
4. That is, up the social ladder.
5. A part of the text here has been lost.
6. The text does not list the *wai* role but instead gives the name of the character the role is playing. *Fu* 夫 ("wife") is not a role category.

# INDEX

## TRANSLATIONS FROM THE ASIAN CLASSICS

*Major Plays of Chikamatsu*, tr. Donald Keene 1961

*Four Major Plays of Chikamatsu*, tr. Donald Keene. Paperback ed. only.
1961; rev. ed. 1997

*Records of the Grand Historian of China, translated from the Shih chi of
Ssu-ma Ch'ien*, tr. Burton Watson, 2 vols. 1961

*Instructions for Practical Living and Other Neo-Confucian Writings by
Wang Yang-ming*, tr. Wing-tsit Chan 1963

*Hsün Tzu: Basic Writings*, tr. Burton Watson. Paperback ed. only.
1963; rev. ed. 1996

*Chuang Tzu: Basic Writings*, tr. Burton Watson. Paperback ed. only.
1964; rev. ed. 1996

*The Mahābhārata*, tr. Chakravarthi V. Narasimhan. Also in paperback ed.
1965; rev. ed. 1997

*The Manyōshū*, Nippon Gakujutsu Shinkōkai, ed. 1965

*Su Tung-p'o: Selections from a Sung Dynasty Poet*, tr. Burton Watson.
Also in paperback ed. 1965

*Bhartrihari: Poems*, tr. Barbara Stoler Miller. Also in paperback ed. 1967

*Basic Writings of Mo Tzu, Hsün Tzu, and Han Fei Tzu*, tr. Burton Watson.
Also in separate paperback eds. 1967

*The Awakening of Faith, Attributed to Aśvaghosha*, tr. Yoshito S. Hakeda.
Also in paperback ed. 1967

*Reflections on Things at Hand: The Neo-Confucian Anthology*, comp.
Chu Hsi and Lü Tsu-ch'ien, tr. Wing-tsit Chan 1967

*The Platform Sutra of the Sixth Patriarch*, tr. Philip B. Yampolsky.
Also in paperback ed. 1967

*Essays in Idleness: The Tsurezuregusa of Kenkō*, tr. Donald Keene.
Also in paperback ed. 1967

*The Pillow Book of Sei Shōnagon*, tr. Ivan Morris, 2 vols. 1967

*Two Plays of Ancient India: The Little Clay Cart and the Minister's Seal*,
tr. J.A .B . van Buitenen 1968

*The Complete Works of Chuang Tzu*, tr. Burton Watson 1968

*The Romance of the Western Chamber (Hsi Hsiang Chi)*, tr. S.I. Hsiung.
Also in paperback ed. 1968

*The Manyōshū*, Nippon Gakujutsu Shinkōkai ed. Paperback ed. only. 1969

*Records of the Historian: Chapters from the Shih chi of Ssu-ma Ch'ien*, tr. Burton Watson. Paperback ed. only. 1969

*Cold Mountain: 100 Poems by the T'ang Poet Han-shan*, tr. Burton Watson. Also in paperback ed. 1970

*Twenty Plays of the Nō Theatre*, ed. Donald Keene. Also in paperback ed. 1970

*Chūshingura: The Treasury of Loyal Retainers*, tr. Donald Keene. Also in paperback ed. 1971; rev. ed. 1997

*The Zen Master Hakuin: Selected Writings*, tr. Philip B. Yampolsky 1971

*Chinese Rhyme-Prose: Poems in the Fu Form from the Han and Six Dynasties Periods*, tr. Burton Watson. Also in paperback ed. 1971

*Kūkai: Major Works*, tr. Yoshito S. Hakeda. Also in paperback ed. 1972

*The Old Man Who Does as He Pleases: Selections from the Poetry and Prose of Lu Yu*, tr. Burton Watson 1973

*The Lion's Roar of Queen Śrīmālā*, tr. Alex and Hideko Wayman 1974

*Courtier and Commoner in Ancient China: Selections from the History of the Former Han by Pan Ku*, tr. Burton Watson. Also in paperback ed. 1974

*Japanese Literature in Chinese*, vol. 1: *Poetry and Prose in Chinese by Japanese Writers of the Early Period*, tr. Burton Watson 1975

*Japanese Literature in Chinese*, vol. 2: *Poetry and Prose in Chinese by Japanese Writers of the Later Period*, tr. Burton Watson 1976

*Love Song of the Dark Lord: Jayadeva's Gītagovinda*, tr. Barbara Stoler Miller. Also in paperback ed. Cloth ed. includes critical text of the Sanskrit. 1977; rev. ed. 1997

*Ryōkan: Zen Monk-Poet of Japan*, tr. Burton Watson 1977

*Calming the Mind and Discerning the Real: From the Lam rim chen mo of Tsoṇ-kha-pa*, tr. Alex Wayman 1978

*The Hermit and the Love-Thief: Sanskrit Poems of Bhartrihari and Bilhaṇa*, tr. Barbara Stoler Miller 1978

*The Lute: Kao Ming's P'i-p'a chi*, tr. Jean Mulligan. Also in paperback ed. 1980

*A Chronicle of Gods and Sovereigns: Jinnō Shōtōki of Kitabatake Chikafusa*, tr. H. Paul Varley 1980

*Among the Flowers: The Hua-chien chi*, tr. Lois Fusek 1982

*Grass Hill: Poems and Prose by the Japanese Monk Gensei*,
tr. Burton Watson 1983

*Doctors, Diviners, and Magicians of Ancient China: Biographies of Fang-shih*,
tr. Kenneth J. DeWoskin. Also in paperback ed. 1983

*Theater of Memory: The Plays of Kālidāsa*, ed. Barbara Stoler Miller.
Also in paperback ed. 1984

*The Columbia Book of Chinese Poetry: From Early Times to the Thirteenth
Century*, ed. and tr. Burton Watson. Also in paperback ed. 1984

*Poems of Love and War: From the Eight Anthologies and the Ten Long Poems
of Classical Tamil*, tr. A.K . Ramanujan. Also in paperback ed. 1985

*The Bhagavad Gita: Krishna's Counsel in Time of War*,
tr. Barbara Stoler Miller 1986

*The Columbia Book of Later Chinese Poetry*, ed. and tr. Jonathan Chaves.
Also in paperback ed. 1986

*The Tso Chuan: Selections from China's Oldest Narrative History*,
tr. Burton Watson 1989

*Waiting for the Wind: Thirty-Six Poets of Japan's Late Medieval Age*,
tr. Steven Carter 1989

*Selected Writings of Nichiren*, ed. Philip B. Yampolsky 1990

*Saigyō, Poems of a Mountain Home*, tr. Burton Watson 1990

*The Book of Lieh Tzu: A Classic of the Tao*, tr. A.C. Graham.
Morningside ed. 1990

*The Tale of an Anklet: An Epic of South India—The Cilappatikāram
of Iḷaṅkō Aṭikaḷ*, tr. R. Parthasarathy 1993

*Waiting for the Dawn: A Plan for the Prince*, tr. with introduction by
Wm. Theodore de Bary 1993

*Yoshitsune and the Thousand Cherry Trees: A Masterpiece of the Eighteenth-
Century Japanese Puppet Theater*, tr., annotated, and with introduction by
Stanleigh H. Jones Jr. 1993

*The Lotus Sutra*, tr. Burton Watson. Also in paperback ed. 1993

*The Classic of Changes: A New Translation of the I Ching as Interpreted by
Wang Bi*, tr. Richard John Lynn 1994

*Beyond Spring: Tz'u Poems of the Sung Dynasty*, tr. Julie Landau 1994

*The Columbia Anthology of Traditional Chinese Literature*,
ed. Victor H. Mair 1994

*Scenes for Mandarins: The Elite Theater of the Ming*, tr. Cyril Birch 1995

*Letters of Nichiren*, ed. Philip B. Yampolsky, tr. Burton Watson et al. 1996

*Unforgotten Dreams: Poems by the Zen Monk Shōtetsu*,
tr. Steven D. Carter 1997

*The Vimalakirti Sutra*, tr. Burton Watson 1997

*Japanese and Chinese Poems to Sing: The* Wakan rōei shū,
tr. J. Thomas Rimer and Jonathan Chaves 1997

*Breeze Through Bamboo: Kanshi of Ema Saikō*, tr. Hiroaki Sato 1998

*A Tower for the Summer Heat*, by Li Yu, tr. Patrick Hanan 1998

*Traditional Japanese Theater: An Anthology of Plays*, by Karen Brazell 1998

*The Original Analects: Sayings of Confucius and His Successors (0479–0249)*,
by E. Bruce Brooks and A. Taeko Brooks 1998

*The Classic of the Way and Virtue: A New Translation of the Tao-te ching of
Laozi as Interpreted by Wang Bi*, tr. Richard John Lynn 1999

*The Four Hundred Songs of War and Wisdom: An Anthology of Poems from
Classical Tamil, The Puṟanāṉūṟu*, ed. and tr. George L. Hart
and Hank Heifetz 1999

*Original Tao:* Inward Training (Nei-yeh) *and the Foundations of Taoist
Mysticism*, by Harold D. Roth 1999

*Po Chü-i: Selected Poems*, tr. Burton Watson 2000

*Lao Tzu's* Tao Te Ching: *A Translation of the Startling New Documents
Found at Guodian*, by Robert G. Henricks 2000

*The Shorter Columbia Anthology of Traditional Chinese Literature*,
ed. Victor H. Mair 2000

*Mistress and Maid (Jiaohongji)*, by Meng Chengshun, tr. Cyril Birch 2001

*Chikamatsu: Five Late Plays*, tr. and ed. C. Andrew Gerstle 2001

*The Essential Lotus: Selections from the* Lotus Sutra,
tr. Burton Watson 2002

*Early Modern Japanese Literature: An Anthology, 1600–1900*,
ed. Haruo Shirane 2002; abridged 2008

*The Columbia Anthology of Traditional Korean Poetry*,
ed. Peter H. Lee 2002

*The Sound of the Kiss, or The Story That Must Never Be Told: Pingali Suranna's Kalapurnodayamu*, tr. Vecheru Narayana Rao and David Shulman 2003

*The Selected Poems of Du Fu*, tr. Burton Watson 2003

*Far Beyond the Field: Haiku by Japanese Women*, tr. Makoto Ueda 2003

*Just Living: Poems and Prose by the Japanese Monk Tonna*, ed. and tr. Steven D. Carter 2003

*Han Feizi: Basic Writings*, tr. Burton Watson 2003

*Mozi: Basic Writings*, tr. Burton Watson 2003

*Xunzi: Basic Writings*, tr. Burton Watson 2003

*Zhuangzi: Basic Writings*, tr. Burton Watson 2003

*The Awakening of Faith, Attributed to Aśvaghosha*, tr. Yoshito S. Hakeda, introduction by Ryūichi Abé 2005

*The Tales of the Heike*, tr. Burton Watson, ed. Haruo Shirane 2006

*Tales of Moonlight and Rain*, by Ueda Akinari, tr. with introduction by Anthony H. Chambers 2007

*Traditional Japanese Literature: An Anthology, Beginnings to 1600*, ed. Haruo Shirane 2007

*The Philosophy of Qi*, by Kaibara Ekken, tr. Mary Evelyn Tucker 2007

*The Analects of Confucius*, tr. Burton Watson 2007

*The Art of War: Sun Zi's Military Methods*, tr. Victor Mair 2007

*One Hundred Poets, One Poem Each: A Translation of the* Ogura Hyakunin Isshu, tr. Peter McMillan 2008

*Zeami: Performance Notes*, tr. Tom Hare 2008

*Zongmi on Chan*, tr. Jeffrey Lyle Broughton 2009

*Scripture of the Lotus Blossom of the Fine Dharma*, rev. ed., tr. Leon Hurvitz, preface and introduction by Stephen R. Teiser 2009

*Mencius*, tr. Irene Bloom, ed. with an introduction by Philip J. Ivanhoe 2009

*Clouds Thick, Whereabouts Unknown: Poems by Zen Monks of China*, tr. Charles Egan 2010

*The Mozi: A Complete Translation*, tr. Ian Johnston 2010

The Orphan of Zhao *and Other Yuan Plays: The Earliest Known Versions*, tr. and introduced by Stephen H. West and Wilt L. Idema 2014

*Luxuriant Gems of the* Spring and Autumn, attributed to Dong Zhongshu, ed. and tr. Sarah A. Queen and John S. Major 2016

*A Book to Burn and a Book to Keep (Hidden): Selected Writings,* by Li Zhi; ed. and tr. Rivi Handler-Spitz, Pauline Lee, and Haun Saussy 2016

*The* Shenzi Fragments: *A Philosophical Analysis and Translation,* by Eirik Lang Harris 2016

Record of Daily Knowledge *and* Collected Poems and Essays: *Selections,* by Gu Yanwu, tr. and ed. Ian Johnston 2017

*The Book of Lord Shang: Apologetics of State Power in Early China,* by Shang Yang, ed. and tr. Yuri Pines 2017; abridged ed. 2019

*The Songs of Chu: An Ancient Anthology of Works by Qu Yuan and Others,* ed. and trans. Gopal Sukhu 2017

*Ghalib: Selected Poems and Letters,* by Mirza Asadullah Khan Ghalib, tr. Frances W. Pritchett and Owen T. A. Cornwall 2017

*Quelling the Demons' Revolt: A Novel from Ming China,* attributed to Luo Guanzhong, tr. Patrick Hanan 2017

*Erotic Poems from the Sanskrit: A New Translation,* tr. R. Parthasarathy 2017

*The Book of Swindles: Selections from a Late Ming Collection,* by Zhang Yingyu, tr. Christopher G. Rea and Bruce Rusk 2017

*Monsters, Animals, and Other Worlds: A Collection of Short Medieval Japanese Tales,* ed. R. Keller Kimbrough and Haruo Shirane 2018

*Hidden and Visible Realms: Early Medieval Chinese Tales of the Supernatural and the Fantastic,* compiled by Liu Yiqing, ed. and tr. Zhenjun Zhang 2018

*A Couple of Soles: A Comic Play from Seventeenth-Century China,* by Li Yu, tr. Jing Shen and Robert E. Hegel 2019

*The Original Meaning of the* Yijing: *Commentary on the* Scripture of Change, by Zhu Xi, tr. and ed. Joseph A. Adler 2019

*Plum Shadows and Plank Bridge: Two Memoirs About Courtesans,* Mao Xiang and Yu Huai, tr. and ed. Wai-yee Li 2020

*The Diary of 1636: The Second Manchu Invasion of Korea,* Na Man'gap, tr. with introduction by George Kallander 2020